AF328549

The Soul
of Strategy

The Soul *of* Strategy

Building Customer-Centric Organizations

Bernard J. Jaworski
David E. Sprott

WILEY

Published by John Wiley & Sons, Inc., Hoboken, New Jersey.
Published simultaneously in Canada.

For general information on our other products and services or for technical support, please contact our Customer Care Department within the United States at (800) 762-2974, outside the United States at (317) 572-3993 or fax (317) 572-4002.

Wiley also publishes its books in a variety of electronic formats. Some content that appears in print may not be available in electronic formats. For more information about Wiley products, visit our website at www.wiley.com.

Library of Congress Cataloging-in-Publication Data is Available:

ISBN 9781394279937 (cloth)
ISBN 9781394279944 (ePub)
ISBN 9781394279951 (ePDF)

Cover Design: Wiley
Cover Image: © Foxy Fox/stock.adobe.com

Printed and bound by CPI Group (UK) Ltd, Croydon, CR0 4YY

C9781394279937_300925

We dedicate this book to all those whose ideas, lives, and organizations

have been impacted by Peter Drucker.

Contents

Preface

THE GENESIS OF this book is straightforward. Bernie's research is rooted in the area of marketing strategy and Dave's career focus is consumer behavior. Like Peter Drucker, both of us firmly believe that it is the customer who determines the success of the enterprise. And yet, the field of strategy has been dominated by two schools of thought—the competitive strategy school and the resource school—neither of which adequately considers the customer. The first school of thought popularized by Michael Porter puts competition and external factors at the center of strategy formulation and deployment. The basic idea is that any organization must position itself against key competitors in the context of a particular industry structure. Well-positioned organizations (i.e., differentiated, focused, or low cost) would outperform their rivals. The second school argues that competitive advantage arises from the combination of unique resources, assets, and capabilities that an organization possesses. These resources were matched against competition—are they unique, rare, and difficult to copy?

As you can see, it is very easy to describe each of the schools without reference to the customer, which is exactly what has been done. But don't get us wrong, we do believe that competition matters, but customers determine the success of the company's marketplace offerings. They are the ultimate judge of "who wins" in competitive rivalry situations. Do we believe that resources matter? Of course, but only insofar as their value is perceived and received directly or indirectly by customers. If Smith Corona typewriters were still in business today, they would have unique, rare, and difficult-to-copy assets. However, there is no customer segment in the marketplace that can sustain the business, so, it no longer exists. The same is true for Circuit City, Blackberry, and numerous other organizations that have shuttered their doors. They often had unique resources but no market.

Hence, the motivation for the book is to put the customer at the center of the enterprise. It is the *soul* of strategy—its essence, its starting point, and its arbiter of success. But what exactly does it mean to be customer-centric? The academic literature has more than 50 definitions of the concept and, quite frankly, these descriptions often offer no practical guidance (e.g., put the customer at the center of the business). Our aim is simple—to provide a clear description of why "the time is now" for us to put the customer at the center of the strategy discussion and provide concrete practical concepts and frameworks to help practitioners implement a customer-centric strategy in their organizations. As expanded upon in this book, our humble aim is to provide the straightforward, definitive guide to understand and build customer-centric organizations and a customer advantage via strategy.

Who Is This Book for?

Our book was written with three primary audiences in mind.

First and foremost, we have written this book for thoughtful practitioners who are looking for a useful, comprehensive guide to setting a customer-centered strategy—one anchored in both the real-world and the academy. We base our ideas on decades of both practical and academic insights surrounding the strategy and behavior associated with customers of organizations. At the Drucker School (where we both work), the approach to the world is often characterized as "pracademic." As such, we want the book to be for senior leaders and managers who are looking for grounded insights into customers with practical application to their daily lives.

Our second target is students. As educators, we have attempted to write a book that is valuable for various types of educational programs and executive education. We both have taught thousands of students and practitioners in various settings at numerous institutions and settings around the world. While not a textbook, this book provides a standalone source for not only setting customer-centered strategy but also a resource on the basics of strategy, customer behavior, and fundamental research methods.

Finally, this book is for new audiences who are less familiar with the ideas of Peter Drucker. One of Peter's many insights surrounds the customer, noting that the primary goal of any organization is "to create a customer." Beyond anchoring our ideas in his, a major goal of our work is to reintroduce Peter F. Drucker's ground-breaking ideas to a new generation of managers and leaders. His timeless ideas have had broad global appeal for decades and we aim to keep these ideas alive in a world that perhaps has never needed his philosophy more. A philosophy anchored in the idea that human-centricity, functioning society, and the value of broad knowledge are critical to the operation of organizations across the globe.

PART

I

The History of Strategy

WE BEGIN with Chapter 1, where we provide motivation for the book and overview of the book's structure. We trace the evolution of strategic thinking and illustrate how the field has historically defined an organization's competitive advantage. We review four dominant schools of strategy, including: the Market-Based View, Resource-Based View, Operational Excellence View, and Dynamic Capabilities View. Each of these offers a unique lens—focusing respectively on external positioning, internal resources, operational execution, and organizational adaptability. Unfortunately, the concept of the customer has remained a secondary consideration (at best)—and often treated as an input or market force rather than the central driver of strategy. We critique this situation and argue that customer needs, behaviors, and experiences should be the starting point for all strategic decision-making. We argue that customer-centric strategy is a necessary evolution in strategic thought. Drawing on thinkers like Drucker and Kotler, the chapter contends that organizations must embed the customer at the core of strategic planning, not only to remain competitive in a dynamic world but also to co-create value and sustain long-term success.

In Chapter 3, we explore the rising influence of consumers in the 21st-century economy and illustrate why it is critical for organizations to consider them when setting business strategy. We contend that there is a "consumer renaissance" underway (fueled in large part by emerging technologies of our day) and outline forces related to both the customer and the organization that are driving it. Specifically, we argue that today's customers are more informed, better connected, and empowered, with unprecedented access to data, peers, and organizations. All of which allows customers to better communicate and ultimately influence how organizations understand and satisfy their needs. On the flip side, organizations are able to do a much better job in being customer-centered as they possess greater tools and technologies to understand and meet customer needs at scale. These various influences and how to be truly customer-centered are illustrated with modern examples of companies like Spotify, H-E-B, Duolingo, and Siemens.

1

The Soul of Strategy

"It is the customer who determines what the business is. What the customer thinks he is buying, what he considers 'value,' is decisive—it determines what the business is, what it produces, and whether it will prosper."[1]

—Peter Drucker

Introduction

The purpose of this book is to develop a new approach to strategy that is based on a simple premise—it is the customer who ultimately determines the success of the enterprise. Not the competition. Not the resources that the organization possesses, however valuable, unique, and rare they may be. Certainly, organizations want to outperform competition and develop unique capabilities; however, these are second-order considerations. The primary source of competitive advantage is the organization's ability to gain unique, actionable customer insights and develop solutions that customers can't wait to buy. This ability to gain insight and develop customer solutions should not be a one-time event. Organizations that do this continuously and well can accelerate this "insight to use" process such that competitors are always following them to the future. In this way, customer-centered organizations shape the future of the industry by accelerating the speed and use of customer insight.

Amazon, IN-N-OUT, Amex Black, Singapore Airlines, and Costco are a few such companies. Organizations like St. Jude Children's Research Hospital, World Central Kitchen, Charity. Water, and Crisis Text Line follow the same principles in the nonprofit sector—in these cases the organizations are built around the people they serve. Some remove financial barriers to care, others respond to urgent needs as they happen, and all work to earn and keep deep trust with key stakeholders. All these organizations, whether for-profit or nonprofit, are also strong performers (whatever the metric) since delivering solutions to highly satisfied and loyal customers is the route to strong, sustainable, organic growth. The Father of Modern Management, Peter F. Drucker, succinctly stated this in his seminal book *The Practice of Management*, "There is only one valid definition of business purpose: to create a customer." Yet decades of thought since the 1950s relegated this simple idea into the background of strategic thinking.

In this book, we introduce a unique approach to strategy development and execution, articulating that the customer must be the soul of any strategy. Our framework is distinct compared to conventional approaches. In contrast to established models (e.g., Porter's competitive strategy, the resource-based view of the organization), we argue that the starting point and essence of strategy is to embed customers' *care-abouts* into an organization's way of working, culture, and "operating system" to ensure that customer needs are continually met or exceeded. Such a customer-centric approach, for us, is the "soul of strategy." By soul, we mean the mindset, orientation, and inspiration that the customer is the essence, touchstone, and guiding light of the organization's purpose. Assets, resources, or value chain activities of the organization are important, but these choices follow from this essence or soul. When we say the soul of the strategy, we are referring to the state of mind and commitment of every employee to create, serve, and satisfy customers.

As Drucker noted, "A business is not defined by the company's name, statutes, or articles of incorporation. It is defined by the want the customer satisfies when [s/he] buys a product or service. To satisfy the customer is the mission and purpose of every business."[2] To ensure this approach is achieved, we argue that the customer must be the center of gravity for development and execution of business strategy. Traditional and often-used approaches to developing strategy miss this critical dimension. While we won't say these models are "soulless," we do argue that few (if any) leading strategy frameworks adequately reflect the mindset of customer centricity. They are rational rather than empathetic, logical rather than inspirational, and, in the end, search for "competitive advantage rather than *customer advantage*."

Start with a Customer Focus

Most strategic frameworks focus on the organization as the unit of analysis. As noted earlier, such an approach is sensible given that strategy is developed at the organizational level and directed at outcompeting other organizations. Furthermore, the historic roots of strategy from a military perspective do not align with a customer-focused approach, given military strategy is designed to defeat an adversary. At best, the customer is a vague concept of a citizen related to that particular military. For organizational strategy, we contend that focusing on the organization is overly limited and naturally takes attention away from other factors (including customers) that are not directly relevant to an organization-based view. Indeed, we contend that traditional approaches to strategy are insufficient for companies to succeed in today's business environment where the customer determines the success of the organization, whether it be in B2B or B2C for-profits, nonprofits, the public sector, or other organizations.

> *When we say the soul of the strategy, we are referring to the mindset and commitment of every employee to create, serve, and satisfy customers.*

The separation between the organization and the customer is anchored in a rich academic tradition that has promoted vastly different views of the world. Academic fields often frame their research around macro-level structures (e.g., organizations, societies, cultures) and microlevel operators (e.g., employees of a for-profit company, members of a society). For example, in economics, such distinctions are reflected in the subfields of macroeconomics (e.g., fiscal policy, economic growth, inflation) and microeconomics (e.g., opportunity costs, elasticity, supply and demand). A similar divide can be seen in the disciplines of sociology and psychology; the former studying how societal structures (e.g., organizations, governments) work together, with the latter exploring the individual person in terms of various forms of psychological processes (e.g., attitudes, emotions, self-concept).

A similar distinction between the organization and the person is seen in the academic study of business, where strategic thinking has primarily developed. The distinction between the organizational and personal is often referred to as "strategy" and "consumer behavior," respectively. Our approach to strategy is unique in that it fits somewhere between the macro/micro, sociology/psychology, strategy/consumer behavior divides. We specifically argue that traditional strategy has relegated the customer to a secondary status and that it MUST be (re)-integrated into strategy development and execution. We are not saying that the organization should be ignored when developing strategy, but rather flip the focus to the customer from that of the organization. In brief, all strategies should start with customers and consider competition and capabilities as a means to serve them.

The Dualism of Strategy's Soul

We adopt the metaphor of the human soul, as it is apt for our view that *the customer* is the soul of strategy. Consideration of what is a soul and how it shapes human experience has been central to thought (and considerable debate) in religion and philosophy throughout the millennia. According to Merriam-Webster, the human soul is defined as "the immaterial essence, animating principle, or actuating cause of an individual life."[3] Similarly, we view the customer as the actuating cause of a company's existence—without it (per Drucker) what is the purpose of an organization to exist?

In philosophy, the concept of the soul is often contrasted against that of the body. For example, Descartes is credited with identifying the philosophic difficulties of the mind–body problem. Anchored in the concept of dualism, the soul (or the mind) is the nonphysical, while the body is made up of physical substances. There is considerable philosophical debate if these two systems interact and, if so, how.

As Westphal[4] explains:

"Consider the human body, with everything in it, including internal and external organs and parts—the stomach, nerves and brain, arms, legs, eyes, and all the rest. Even with all this equipment, especially the sensory organs, it is surprising that we can consciously perceive things in the world that are far away from us. For example, I can open my eyes in the morning and see a cup of coffee waiting for me on the bedside table. There it is, a foot away, and I am not touching it, yet somehow it is making itself manifest to me. How does it happen that I see it? How does the visual system convey to my awareness or mind the image of the cup of coffee?"

A similar dualism can be used to position business strategy. We argue that properties of the organization, such as tangible assets, managerial ability, and tacit knowledge (e.g., viewed as "resources" in the resource-based view of the organization) represent the human body. It is by these means that the organization operates and interacts with the world around it. In contrast, we view the customer as the soul (or mind) of the business, which is the "animating principle" (per Merriam-Webster) of the organization's resources.

For example, the soul of Edward Jones is "putting the client's interest first." Many organizations say they are client- or customer-centered, but what sets Edward Jones apart is their mindset, culture, and emotional commitment to their clients. The Drucker School has had the good fortune of serving Edward Jones as an executive education client for a couple of decades. There is always a part of the program where the issue of "do you really put clients first" arises during the discussion. When participants are challenged on this commitment, there is always an emotional, visceral reaction. It is beyond a polite conversation. It is such a deeply embedded "essence" that to challenge this view is to challenge the heart and soul of the enterprise. It is a non-negotiable, state of mind that carries much more weight than simply being one of four values of the organization. It is "who they are" in their DNA.

A similar statement could be made about Trader Joe's. TJ's (as their fans call it) has attained cult-like status as a local neighborhood store that carries basic items as well as unique, international products.[5] For some, Trader Joe's is on their list of tourist sites to visit. As one author noted, "They are the Disneyland of grocery stores"—appealing to all senses of the customer.[6] As noted in the *Forbes* article, "what *really* makes shopping at TJ's a boost for the brain are those who work there. Trader Joe's employees are different, and the difference they bring to their work changes the psychological experience of the store's customers. There are emotional contagions in the air at TJ's and its customers catch an infectious psychosocial buzz."[7] As one employee noted, "We do everything here, and I mean everything. When that bell rings twice (gesturing to one of the hand-pulled bronze bells near the checkout lines), we go sprinting from the front to the back of the store for customers. We do anything we need to." This "all in" commitment to the customer is the soul of TJ's strategy.

Putting Customers into Strategy

The goal of our work is simple—namely, to put the customer back into strategy. As noted at the outset, our view is a simple yet powerful idea, that the customer ultimately determines the success of a business and therefore must drive strategy. Compared to traditional views, success is not about out-maneuvering competitors through manipulation of the five forces in your industry structure. And it isn't solely about leveraging the unique resources and assets that your organization possesses. However valuable these advantages may be, we argue rather that success ultimately hinges on developing solutions that customers love to buy.

Careful observance of the marketplace finds the customer as central to business success. We heavily rely on real-world examples in this book to illustrate our principles via several successful companies. Some of these organizations are well-known—Costco, Trader Joe's, and IN-N-OUT. We also focus on lesser known organizations as we introduce concepts throughout the book.

We contend that traditional approaches to strategy are in essence backward, looking with a focus on defining products and markets and then detailing "how to win" in those markets by creating comparative advantages. In contrast, we contend that strategy must start by defining a company's mission as it relates to the benefits customers desire. Such an approach requires a deep understanding of customer needs and wants, not only today but tomorrow, as well as developing business functions and activities to deliver on those desires.

Drucker stated the challenge as follows: "Nothing may seem simpler or more obvious than to know what a company's business is. A steel mill makes steel; a railroad runs trains to carry freight and passengers; an insurance company underwrites fire risks; a bank lends money. Actually, 'What is our business' is almost always a difficult question and the right answer is usually anything but obvious."[8]

The Book Ahead

Our book is organized in four sections: Part I describes the evolution of strategic thinking—one that we believe has deprioritized (if not outright ignored or dismissed) customer centricity in favor of competitive dynamics and company capabilities.[9] We also develop the core idea that customers have reemerged in today's marketplace due to a variety of factors. Part II introduces the concept of customer centricity in three chapters. Chapter 4 provides a clear definition of customer centricity and the core customer intelligence activities of a customer-centered organization. Chapter 5 introduces a new framework to build a customer-centric strategy. Chapter 6 articulates a consumer behavior framework to enable a wholistic view of customers.

The third part of the book focuses on embedding a customer-centric mindset and approach within an organization and leveraging traditional resources of the organization. Here we focus on four key levers—each representing a distinct chapter. They are leadership; structure and systems; data and analytics; and an organizational commitment to innovate and abandon as markets evolve. While no single lever can change an organization, we argue that all four levers in concert have a force multiplier impact on the acceleration of the journey to be more customer-driven. The final part turns to purpose-led companies—those that deliver on both customer needs and enhance the functioning of society.

PART I: The History of Strategy

Chapter 2: The Evolution of Strategic Thinking. In this chapter, we provide an overall arc of business strategy thinking during the last 60 years (starting with Chandler, Christensen, Andrews, to Drucker, Porter, Hammel, Collins, Kim, Wernerfelt, Barney, and to the present day). Such approaches have been framed with a secondary focus on customers, and primary foci on externalities to the organization, the competition, and internal capabilities. While critical in many ways, we contend that many of the ideas contained in these approaches are difficult to implement in real life, especially to the same degree as described in examples celebrated by the authors. This situation is primarily due to the limited circumstances when such approaches are applicable or heavily reliant on a Eureka moment that arises from "boiling the ocean for data." These ideas, though popular and with acclaimed successes when introduced, mostly have resulted in temporary (or very limited) success. Yet, today, when organizations are setting strategy, they continue to ignore (or at least avoid serious consideration of) customer centricity.

Chapter 3: The Reemergence of the Customer. The role of the customer has significantly evolved since the industrial revolution into a world that is primarily driven by consumption. As many have observed, consumer sovereignty fundamentally drives market outcomes and economies around the globe. It is therefore critical for organizations to ground their business strategy in such a way as to understand and meet customer needs. While consumers have always been important, in this chapter we argue that there is a re-emergence of customer importance that organizations must consider when setting strategy. The situation is driven by numerous factors related to both customers themselves (e.g., the rise of individualism, access to digital communities) and that of the organization (e.g., advanced manufacturing, new models of exchange). Most of these forces are being driven by emerging digital technologies, such as AI, big data, enhanced computing, that are having profound impacts on all aspects of society. Such forces have empowered not only consumers to better express their wants and needs but for also organizations to address them as a competitive advantage.

PART II: Customer Centricity

Chapter 4: Customer Centricity. Customer-centered organizations generate intelligence from the marketplace, share that information across functions, and take go-to-market action based on the market intelligence. Taking action is certainly about designing products/services that meet the needs of the customer, but it includes three other actions. The first is the identification of "where to play" in the overall market. This choice is critical and is often a source of lasting competitive advantage. The second action is to "shape" the evolution of the marketplace. This can be accomplished by shaping the behaviors of customers (e.g., binge-watching after the advent of streaming services) or shaping the structure of the industry itself. The third action is to "abandon" select ways of working, products, services, processes, and anything the organization does that no longer fits the evolution of the market.

Chapter 5: The Customer Choice Cascade: Activating Customer Centricity. In this chapter, we introduce the five-step customer-centric choice cascade. The chapter is organized in five sections, reflecting each of the key choices. Choice one is focused on the selection of a target segment and an understanding of what the segment values. The second choice turns attention to competition. Who is our competition and how are they providing value to the key segments? We cannot compete with everyone, so, which set of competition is our priority competitors? The third choice focuses on the choice of the organization's value proposition. This balances customer segment needs, competition value propositions, and our ability to deliver unique customer value. The aim is to select a value proposition that is defendable over a period of time. This third choice also includes the identification of the organization's profit model and activity system. The fourth choice focuses on how to create value for both customers and the organization. The final choice is about the future—who are our customers in the future? How does this segment emerge? How do we allocate sufficient resources to get ready for the future?

Chapter 6: The Customer Behavior Framework. A fundamental step to creating a customer-centric strategy is to understand who the customer is, their needs and wants, and what drives the decision to buy from an organization. These core principles are reflected in two of Drucker's famous "Five Questions," when he asked, "Who is your customer?," and "What does your customer value?"[10] To provide answers to these core questions, the organization must identify its key customers—something not always simple in today's complex, tech-enabled (and often overlapping) world of B2B and B2C markets. The successful organization must enter the mindset and emotions of target customers and integrate that information into the organization's strategy. In this chapter, we explore the customer journey that is shaped by processes internal to the customer (i.e., cognition, emotion, and physiology), as well as various externalities. By understanding customers' desires, the organization can diagnose what customers want and then offer products or services that meet those needs better than that of the competition. We also outline how our customer-centric approach to business strategy is *not* the same thing as marketing strategy.

PART III: Building a Customer-Centered Organization

Chapter 7: Leadership and Customer Centricity. Leading a customer-centered company involves a combination of behaviors and resource allocation on the part of the executive team. There is ample evidence that the senior leadership team "signals" its degree of customer focus by how they allocate their time and the questions they ask of their teams. CEOs from leading organizations such as Costco spend 20–40 percent of their time "in the field" with their customers, employees, and other key stakeholders. This chapter also identifies key leadership competencies that are required for customer-centered organizations.

Chapter 8: Structure and Systems. While reward systems for developing and retaining customers are the most obvious "tool in the arsenal" of an organization, there are a broad array of systems and structures to support the organization and its members to drive a customer-centric strategy. Here we overview the four dominant structures of global organizations and discuss the challenges of being customer-driven for each of these structures. We also offer recommendations to overcome these limitations. We end the chapter with a discussion of two broad schools of thought regarding reward/recognition systems to drive a more customer-centric culture.

Chapter 9: Customer Intelligence and Insights. Organizations have the unique ability in today's market to effectively and efficiently use "customer intelligence" as a source of competitive advantage. Access to customer data has never been more plentiful with sources such as geographic information systems, in-store scanner data, social media, online shopping data, to name a few. Building insights from such data has also never been greater, given increased computing power and the tools associated with AI. Of course, data and analysis are only a portion of the system required to leverage customer intelligence; another critical dimension is to build systems that allow such data to permeate the organization. In this chapter, we explore these issues and provide organizations with details required to leverage customer data and intelligence when setting a customer-centric strategy.

Chapter 10: Innovation and Abandonment. To become more customer-driven, organizations need to innovate for tomorrow and abandon yesterday. Similar to Drucker, we view innovation to be everyone's responsibility. Often organizations limit thinking of innovation to products, services, and solutions. However, as the theory of the business fundamentally changes, so too should every part of the organization—its structure, workflow, brand, financial model, alliances, and so on. Organizational abandonment (i.e., an organization completely stopping the allocation of resources to a particular activity) is a twin concept with innovation. Unless the organization can let go of products, services, processes, or structures that are no longer viable, it cannot effectively innovate. In this chapter, we dive into the complementary processes of innovation and abandonment when building a customer-centric strategy.

Part IV: The Purpose-Led Organization

Chapter 11: The Purpose of Organizations. A final aspect of developing a customer-centric strategy is to develop a clear understanding of "what business the organization is in" (borrowing a phrase from Drucker). Examples abound of developing purpose in an organization: Disney does not define their business as entertainment, rather they define their business in terms of story-telling; Satya Nadella, Microsoft CEO, attributes the remarkable shift of Microsoft from desktop to the cloud to understanding and articulating a (revised) mission of Microsoft; and Patagonia's purpose to save the planet is one of the most notable societal-focused organizations. This chapter explores the notion of purpose-driven organizations. These organizations not only meet the needs of their customers, but they also create a win-win-win for all stakeholders in the company's ecosystem. As outlined in this chapter, crafting a purpose-led strategy can accelerate customer centricity.

2

The Evolution of Strategic Thinking*

"Results depend not on anybody within the business nor on anything within the control of the business. They depend on somebody outside. . ."[1]

—Peter Drucker

Introduction

How can organizations achieve and sustain a competitive edge in an ever-changing world? This question has been central to the study of strategic management. Over the decades, scholars and practitioners have developed frameworks to help organizations navigate their environments, build capabilities, and outperform competitors. The evolution of strategy thinking reflects a dynamic progression from early foundational ideas to contemporary frameworks that emphasize agility, resource alignment, and, increasingly, customer focus.

This chapter provides a historical and thematic overview of the major schools of thought in strategy, highlighting their unique contributions and limitations. From Alfred Chandler's pioneering work on aligning organizational structure with strategy to the emergence of customer centricity as a core strategic principle, this exploration

---

* With thanks to Ajay Patel for his contributions to this chapter.

underscores the critical interplay among internal resources, external environments, and customer needs.[2] This backdrop explains why a new paradigm centered on the customer is now essential.

The Foundations of Modern Strategy

Strategic thinking as we know it began in the mid-20th century with groundbreaking contributions from Alfred Chandler, Roland Christensen, and Kenneth Andrews. These scholars laid the groundwork for understanding how organizations align their internal capabilities and structures with external opportunities. In *Strategy and Structure*,[3] Chandler argued that "structure follows strategy." His analyses of American corporations like General Motors and DuPont revealed that organizational success depends on aligning internal structures with strategic objectives. Chandler's work also introduced the importance of economies of scale and managerial expertise as key drivers of competitive advantage.

Chandler's work went beyond structural alignment, identifying key sources of competitive advantage such as economies of scale and scope. These insights laid the groundwork for later theories on cost leadership strategies. Additionally, he highlighted the critical role of managerial expertise and operational efficiency, showing how effective resource management and leadership are essential for sustaining strategic initiatives. By integrating these ideas, Chandler revolutionized the way businesses approached strategy, offering a systematic framework for achieving competitive advantage through strategic and organizational alignment.

Concurrent with Chandler's influence on management, Roland Christensen and Kenneth Andrews at Harvard Business School revolutionized the teaching and practice of strategy through their Business Policy course, which became a cornerstone of MBA education. Their seminal works, including *Business Policy: Text and Cases*[4] and *The Concept of Corporate Strategy*[5], introduced tools like SWOT analysis.

Andrews's concept of distinctive competencies—unique internal capabilities—paved the way for theories focusing on resource-based competitive advantage. Andrews championed defining an organization's mission and leveraging its distinctive competencies—unique capabilities such as specialized knowledge or proprietary technologies. These competencies were early articulations of what would later be known as sources of competitive advantage.

Meanwhile, Christensen revolutionized strategy teaching by pioneering the case method, a now-iconic approach in business education that encouraged analytical thinking and practical problem-solving. Together, Andrews and Christensen emphasized the critical role of managerial judgment in identifying and leveraging a firm's strengths, arguing that strategic advantage arises not only from structural alignment but also from effective leadership and resource deployment.

Their work expanded on Chandler's insights into strategic alignment by focusing on the interplay between internal resources and external factors. This emphasis on aligning strengths, weaknesses, opportunities, and threats laid the groundwork for subsequent theories on strategic positioning and leveraging organization-specific resources. Through their efforts, Andrews and Christensen established a lasting framework for strategic planning and education that continues to shape how organizations approach competitive advantage today.

Competitive Advantage into Focus

Central to strategy is the concept of competitive advantage: the ability of a company to consistently outperform its rivals. Scholars after Chandler, Andrews, and Christensen focused on two key questions:

- What are the sources of competitive advantage?
- How can these sources be cultivated and sustained over time?

Much of the academic underpinning of future theories on competitive strategy is the concept of sources of competitive advantage. This concept is at the heart of competitive strategy, because it provides the foundation for why and how an organization can outperform its competitors. Without clearly identifying, cultivating, and leveraging these sources, the broader strategic question—how to achieve and sustain a competitive advantage—cannot be effectively answered.

The concept of sources of competitive advantage evolved directly from Chandler's foundational ideas and the Business Policy teachings of Andrews and Christensen through a progression of thinking about strategy's relationship to organizational capabilities, environmental opportunities, and competitive dynamics. Chandler's work provided a foundational perspective on achieving and sustaining competitive advantage by shifting the focus to the systematic alignment of resources with strategic intent. Andrews and Christensen's approach underscored the idea that competitive advantage stems from matching internal capabilities with external demands.

The foundational ideas of Chandler and Andrews evolved naturally into more specific explanations for how firms outperform competitors. Chandler's focus on economies of scale and scope laid the groundwork for cost-based competitive advantages, later formalized by Michael Porter's concept of cost leadership. Andrews' emphasis on "distinctive competence" similarly advanced strategic thinking toward differentiation, wherein firms achieve advantage by delivering unique customer value. Both scholars also stressed aligning internal capabilities with external industry conditions, influencing frameworks like Porter's Five Forces. Andrews' insights into distinctive competencies prefigured the resource-based view emphasizing valuable, rare, and inimitable resources. Additionally, their shared belief in sustainable competitive advantage through long-term capability development set the stage for later theories on dynamic capabilities and enduring strategic adaptability.

The Theory of Competitive Advantage

Sources of competitive advantage emerged as a dominant concept in strategic management during the 1970s and 1980s, driven by the work of influential thinkers such as Michael Porter, Jay Barney, Richard Rumelt, and Pankaj Ghemawat. These scholars formalized the understanding that competitive advantage arises from a combination of distinct internal and external factors, offering valuable insights into the strategic choices that drive organizational success.

One prominent theory underpinning competitive advantage is industry positioning, which Porter articulated through his Five Forces framework.[6] This approach emphasizes the significance of external factors, including industry structure, buyer power, and competition, in shaping a firm's opportunities for success. By analyzing these forces, organizations can identify optimal market positions that enhance their competitiveness and create opportunities for differentiation.

In contrast to the external focus of industry positioning, another critical perspective centers on internal resources. Scholars such as Edith Penrose,[7] Birger Wernerfelt,[8] and Jay Barney[9] argued that competitive advantage is sustained by possessing unique, valuable, rare, and hard-to-imitate resources, often referred to as "VRIN resources." From this perspective, such internal assets drive an organization's enduring success by distinguishing it from its competitors in meaningful ways.

A third significant framework highlights the importance of dynamic adaptation. David Teece[10] and Henry Mintzberg[11] advanced the notion that organizations must continuously reconfigure their capabilities to address rapidly changing environments. This perspective underscores the need for agility and the ongoing renewal of organizational resources to maintain a competitive edge in an ever-evolving marketplace.

Adding to the discourse on competitive advantage, Gary Hamel and C.K. Prahalad emphasized the role of strategic innovation.[12] Their work on core competencies demonstrated how innovation within a company's strategy could foster new sources of competitive advantage. By identifying and cultivating core competencies, organizations can differentiate themselves in the marketplace and create unique value for customers. That said, in subsequent work, Porter argued that it is not the core competency in isolation but it is the network or competencies that give rise to competitive advantage. He termed this network of competencies an "activity system."[13]

Ghemawat's contributions further enriched the understanding of competitive advantage by exploring its sustainability. In his work, particularly in *Commitment: The Dynamics of Strategy*,[14] he argued that long-term strategic commitments create barriers to imitation, safeguarding an organization's competitive edge. This perspective underscores the importance of deeply rooted and carefully designed strategies that competitors find difficult to replicate.

A more recent addition to the discussion is the "right to win," by Mainardi and Kleiner.[15] This concept captures how organizations achieve superior positioning by aligning their unique capabilities, market focus, and competitive dynamics. Companies with the "right to win" consistently outperform competitors in specific markets by integrating deep insights into market needs with tailored capabilities and organizational alignment. The phrase encapsulates the strategic choices that enable organizations to dominate their chosen markets, reflecting the culmination of insights from both internal and external perspectives.

These foundational theories and ideas collectively provided the catalyst for numerous different concepts of how organizations should formulate strategy to create advantages that result in market differentiation that can be sustained over time.[16]

The Evolution into Four Schools

The foundational theories of competitive advantage, developed during the 1970s and 1980s, laid the groundwork for much of modern strategic management. Initially, these theories sought to identify the external and internal sources that enable organizations to achieve and sustain superior performance relative to their competitors. Some scholars (e.g., Porter) emphasized external market forces, while others (e.g., Barney, Penrose) shifted the focus inward to the unique resources and capabilities of the organization. Over time, as markets became more dynamic and competitive pressures became more intense, the scope of these theories expanded. Researchers began integrating additional dimensions, such as operational execution and adaptability, to address challenges posed by increasingly volatile environments.

The result of this intellectual progression has been the development of various schools of strategy. Several approaches have been suggested by different researchers to represent categories of business strategy, and we have adapted these into four general schools of strategic thought:

- **The Market-Based View**, which focuses on external positioning within industry structures.
- **The Resource-Based View**, which highlights the role of internal resources and capabilities.

- **The Operational Excellence View**, which emphasizes the importance of operational excellence.
- **The Dynamic Capabilities View**, which underscores the need for agility and innovation in ever-changing markets.[17]

It is crucial to understand that these schools of strategic thinking are not prescriptive solutions or generic strategies for companies. Instead, they represent paradigms and frameworks that provide approaches for analyzing an orgnization's unique situation. These four schools leverage the work of "eras" of strategy noted by Ghemawat and Kiechel. Each school offers a lens through which organizations can examine their competitive landscape, internal capabilities, and operational priorities. Using these frameworks, organizations can derive tailored strategies that address their specific challenges and leverage their unique strengths. Thus, these schools serve as strategic foundations, guiding the formulation of strategy rather than dictating specific actions.

The Market-Based View

The Superior Market Positioning School, also known as the Market-Based View (MBV), emerged in the late 1970s as one of the earliest extensions of the foundational theories of competitive advantage. This school of thought emphasizes the importance of external factors in shaping a firm's success. Drawing heavily on Porter's Five Forces framework,[18] it highlights how industry conditions—such as buyer power, supplier dynamics, competitive intensity, and barriers to entry—influence a firm's ability to achieve and sustain an advantage.

Organizations that excel in market positioning leverage insights from industry analysis to identify favorable opportunities and craft strategies such as differentiation, cost leadership, or focus. An integral part of this perspective is segmenting customer bases and identifying underserved areas to create tailored value propositions that address specific needs. A notable example of this approach is the Blue Ocean Strategy,[19] which focuses on creating entirely new market spaces where competition becomes irrelevant. However, while the MBV's external orientation offers significant benefits, it is often complemented by the resource-based view (more on that next), ensuring that a company's internal resources align effectively with market opportunities.

The key approaches related to MBV include: Porter's Competitive Strategy[20] and Competitive Advantage,[21] Henderson's Growth-Share Matrix[22] and Experience Curve,[23] and Kim and Mauborgne's Blue Ocean Strategy.[24] These works collectively provide robust frameworks for analyzing external market conditions and formulating strategies that align with environmental opportunities and threats. The central focus is on achieving competitive advantage through market positioning, analyzing industry forces, and, in the case of the Blue Ocean Strategy, creating uncontested market spaces.

Despite its widespread adoption since the early 1990s, MBV is not without critique. One significant criticism is the overreliance on static models like Porter's Five Forces, which some argue fail to account for rapidly changing market dynamics and industry disruptions. Another critique focuses on neglecting internal resources. By prioritizing external analysis, it is easy to overlook the role of an organization's internal competencies in shaping its competitive advantage. For example, specific to the Blue Ocean Strategy, critics argue that while creating uncontested markets is appealing, sustaining these markets becomes challenging as competitors eventually adapt or enter the space.

The Superior Market Positioning School has been hugely impactful in strategy and provides a critical lens for understanding competitive advantage through external market analysis. Its emphasis on industry positioning, customer segmentation, and creating uncontested markets has profoundly influenced strategic management. However, its effectiveness often depends on integrating insights from internal resources and maintaining adaptability in the face of market changes.

The Resource-Based View

The Superior Talent, Physical Assets, and Competencies School, commonly referred to as the Resource-Based View (RBV), emerged in the early 1980s as a pivotal approach to strategic management.[25] The RBV emphasizes the importance of internal analysis and the development of core competencies. By understanding and leveraging the RBV framework, organizations can make informed decisions about resource allocation, investment, and diversification, ensuring long-term sustainability and competitive success.

Inspired partly by Chandler's work emphasizing internal resources, the RBV serves as a counterpoint to the externally focused MBV. The RBV argues that a firm's unique internal resources and capabilities are the primary drivers of sustainable competitive advantage. Scholars have also highlighted the importance of resources that are valuable, rare, inimitable, and non-substitutable (VRIN). These "VRIN resources" form the foundation for differentiation and create barriers to imitation by competitors.

While the RBV emphasizes internal capabilities, it also acknowledges customers' indirect yet critical role. Customer preferences and market demands shape how a firm develops and deploys its resources. This is a great example of how customers are of secondary consideration in traditional business strategy. For instance, a company's core competencies, such as technological innovation or brand reputation, are often evaluated based on their ability to generate customer value. The RBV framework is further strengthened when integrated with dynamic capabilities, enabling organizations to adapt their resources to evolving customer needs and market conditions.

Unlike prescriptive strategies, the RBV provides a structured lens for strategically assessing and leveraging unique assets to achieve sustained competitive advantage. Such an approach is natural and has garnered considerable attention, with foundational works that have shaped the RBV including: Penrose's The Theory of the Growth of the Firm,[26] Wernerfelt's Resource-Based View of the Firm,[27] Barney's seminal article "Firm Resources and Sustained Competitive Advantage,"[28] and Prahalad and Hamel's "The Core Competence of the Corporation."[29] These contributions collectively underscore the focus of RBV on leveraging unique internal resources and capabilities to achieve enduring success.

In practical terms, the RBV guides organizations in identifying and leveraging their unique internal strengths to sustain competitive advantage. The "right to win," for example, emphasizes the role of internal capabilities in sustaining competitive positioning. A well-known application of RBV is Honda's expertise in engine design, which exemplifies how core competencies drive success. The VRIN framework is central to evaluating a firm's competitive potential.

Despite its strengths, the RBV has faced criticism. One significant critique is its perceived lack of actionability, with some arguing that the framework offers insufficient guidance on acquiring or developing valuable resources. Additionally, by focusing heavily on rare and inimitable resources, the RBV may underemphasize the role of operational competencies that, while more attainable, remain crucial for success. Another critique is the RBV's tendency to neglect external factors such as market dynamics and competitive threats, leading to an overly inward-looking perspective.

A core principle of the RBV is that capabilities are often rare and difficult to imitate because they consist of unique combinations of activities, people, and tradecraft. The VRIN framework provides a systematic tool for assessing the competitive potential of resources. To qualify as valuable, resources must create value by enabling the organization to exploit opportunities or neutralize threats. Rare resources are those few organizations possess, while inimitable resources are difficult for competitors to replicate. Finally, non-substitutable resources lack strategic equivalents, ensuring their unique contribution to the organization's advantage.

However, the VRIN principle has limitations. For example, knowledge and tradecraft frequently reside in the minds of key executives, making these resources highly mobile. When executives leave an organization, they may take critical knowledge with them, as illustrated by an example (name withheld to protect the innocent) from the life sciences industry. In one instance, a group of executives departed an organization *en masse* to join a competitor, bringing insights into manufacturing, pricing, and go-to-market strategies. This transfer of knowledge significantly enhanced the competitor's market position. Even with these limitations considered, there is little doubt that this view of strategy has had an enduring impact on strategic thought, replete with serious academic attention and consideration by firms.

The Operational Excellence View

The Superior Operational Excellence School, referred to here as the Operational Excellence View (OEV), emerged in the early 1980s as a critical approach to strategic management. This approach, building on

Chandler's work, emphasizes that operational excellence is fundamental to transforming strategic plans into concrete results. The OEV School focuses on efficiently executing processes, prioritizing quality, cost control, and disciplined implementation. By employing tools such as lean manufacturing and Six Sigma, firms aim to eliminate waste, improve quality, and achieve operational efficiencies that set them apart in the market.

The OEV school highlights the importance of generating operating efficiencies and economies of scope to drive enhanced financial performance. Rather than direct customer input, feedback from operational processes and metrics typically guides process improvements and resource allocation. Execution-based strategies ensure that a firm's operational capabilities and internal efficiencies align with broader strategic objectives. The OEV School provides a framework for assessing how effectively an organization translates its strategies into operational success, helping organizations diagnose execution gaps and refine their processes.

The foundational works that define the OEV include *Deming's Out of the Crisis*,[30] which laid the groundwork for quality management practices, and Hammer and Champy's *Reengineering the Corporation*.[31] They both focus on business process re-engineering as a transformative approach to operational excellence. Womack's *The Machine That Changed the World*[32] advanced the principles of lean manufacturing, while Peters and Waterman's *In Search of Excellence*[33] underscored the importance of aligning people, processes, and structures to maximize operational success.

These contributions collectively emphasized the need for coherent operational systems that deliver consistent results. A great example of these principles of how operational alignment can simultaneously lower costs and enhance customer satisfaction can be found in lean production. Lean methodologies focus on minimizing waste while maintaining value creation and are being adopted by leading companies, including Amazon, Intel, and Caterpillar, to name a few. As articulated in the "right to win," operational excellence ensures coherence across systems and processes, enabling organizations to achieve superior market performance.

Despite its benefits, the OEV is not without its critiques. One significant criticism is its focus on efficiency at the expense of innovation and being responsive to market changes, with some arguing that an overemphasis on execution can stifle creativity and hinder long-term adaptability. Reengineering efforts and Lean methodologies have also been criticized for their potential to disrupt the workforce, causing job insecurity and reduced morale. Another critique highlights the short-term orientation of many operational excellence frameworks, which often prioritize immediate cost savings and process improvements over long-term strategic goals.

The OEV has been widely adopted by industry, particularly within manufacturing, where there is value in emphasizing operational excellence as a driver of competitive advantage. With this approach, firms achieve superior efficiency and responsiveness by aligning people, processes, and structures with strategic goals. While the OEV offers valuable insights into the role of execution in strategic success, its practical implementation requires addressing cultural resistance, balancing efficiency with adaptability, and ensuring long-term sustainability alongside immediate operational gains.

The Dynamic Capabilities View

The Superior Ability to Act Quickly and Adapt, also known as the Dynamic Capabilities View (DCV), emerged in the late 1980s as an evolution of foundational theories of strategic management. This approach emphasizes the importance of continuous adaptation and innovation in response to rapidly changing environments. Scholars such as Teece and Mintzberg pioneered this perspective, highlighting a firm's ability to sense opportunities, seize them, and reconfigure resources to maintain relevance in volatile markets. In contrast to static models of competitive advantage, the DCV provides a framework for analyzing both external environments and internal structures, ensuring that firms remain adaptable and capable of sustained relevance.

The Dynamic Capabilities View builds on and integrates with other strategic schools, including the Market-Based View and the Resource-Based View. By aligning external positioning with internal resources and ensuring effective execution, the DCV underscores the interplay between adaptability and operational efficiency. Execution-based strategies further support this adaptability by facilitating the effective implementation of changes, thereby bridging strategy and action. In volatile markets, where traditional sources of competitive advantage can erode quickly, dynamic capabilities become a critical driver of resilience and success.

Foundational works that shape the DCV include: Mintzberg's *The Rise and Fall of Strategic Planning*,[34] Teece's *Dynamic Capabilities and Strategic Management*,[35] and Hamel and Prahalad's *Competing for the Future*.[36] These thinkers collectively emphasize the importance of adaptability and resource reconfiguration to address evolving market conditions and seize emerging opportunities. By doing so, the DCV highlights the role of dynamic capabilities in fostering resilience and enabling firms to maintain competitive advantage in uncertain environments.

Implementing dynamic capabilities also presents several hurdles and challenges. Translating the abstract concept of dynamic capabilities into specific, actionable strategies remains a common difficulty for many organizations. High resource requirements for adaptability—such as investments in innovative technology, skilled talent, and continuous innovation—can strain organizational resources, especially for smaller businesses. Furthermore, constant adaptation without a clear long-term strategy can result in strategic overreach, inefficient resource allocation, and diminished focus. Cultural and structural barriers within organizations further complicate the adoption of dynamic capabilities. Many companies lack the flexible structures and adaptive cultures necessary to fully embrace the DCV, hindering their ability to respond effectively to environmental changes.

The Dynamic Capabilities View emphasizes the necessity of adaptability and continuous innovation as fundamental components of strategic success—ideas that resonate with business and academics alike. By integrating external positioning, internal resources, and effective execution, this framework offers a pathway for firms to remain resilient and competitive in volatile markets. While the DCV provides valuable insights into the importance of flexibility and responsiveness, its successful implementation requires overcoming challenges related to operationalization, resource constraints, and organizational inertia.

Four Schools and Few Customers

The delineation of strategic thinking over the last 50 years into these four schools is not a mutually exclusive or comprehensively exhaustive categorization. However, these schools represent the most important concepts introduced by scholars and widely utilized by businesses across industries. Numerous stakeholders are central to the strategy choices and decisions considered in these four traditional schools of strategy. The principal actors comprise the firm's leadership, internal organizations, competitors, suppliers, market channel partners, owners or investors, and potential regulators. (See Table 2.1 for principal stakeholders related to each school.)

Table 2.1   Schools of thought and principal stakeholders

School of thought	Principal stakeholders
Market-Based View (MBV)	Competitors, regulators, investors, market channel partners, and industry players: The MBV focuses on external forces shaping industry structure, emphasizing competition, market share, and barriers to entry. Regulators may also play a role in influencing strategic positioning.
Resource-Based View (RBV)	Internal teams, leadership, and shareholders: The RBV prioritizes the firm's internal resources and capabilities, focusing on the development and deployment of assets, talent, and competencies to sustain competitive advantage, often for shareholder returns.
Operational Excellence View (OEV)	Process owners, operational teams, and supply chain partners: Superior operational excellence depends on efficient internal operations, collaboration with supply chain partners, and process execution teams who deliver consistent and reliable outcomes.
Dynamic Capabilities View (DCV)	Leadership, strategic partners, and competitors: This approach prioritizes decision-makers and leaders capable of driving agility and adaptation alongside strategic partnerships and responses to competitive actions rather than focusing directly on customers.

The Missing Piece: The Customer

In the four schools of strategic thought, stakeholders critical to the organization's success—such as competitors, regulators, investors, employees, or partners—often take precedence, with customers treated as indirect beneficiaries of strategic outcomes rather than central participants in shaping strategy. In terms of truly understanding the soul of strategy and building such strategies, this situation must be flipped on its head by putting the customer front and center in strategy formulation.

In the traditional schools of strategy, the customer is primarily considered as an implicit factor rather than an explicit one. The Market-Based View regards customers as part of the broader market forces influencing industry profitability, focusing on positioning and value capture rather than value creation. The Resource-Based View emphasizes leveraging internal assets like talent and competencies, treating customers as recipients of these resources but not centering strategy on their needs or expectations. The Operational Excellence View prioritizes operational efficiency, reliability, and cost-effectiveness, delivering consistent value but often overlooking opportunities for differentiation or deeper customer engagement. Finally, the Dynamic Capabilities View emphasizes agility and responsiveness to environmental changes, aligning indirectly with customer needs, but focusing more on adaptation than on proactive customer-centric innovation. As illustrated in Table 2.2, the focus of these approaches to strategy is on external forces, the competition, and internal capabilities.

Across all these approaches, the customer remains an external or "second order" consideration rather than the strategic nucleus driving decision-making. While these four schools of thought provide valuable insights into achieving competitive advantage, their implicit consideration of the customer leaves significant opportunities untapped—to put it mildly. By treating customers as external forces to be managed or as indirect beneficiaries of internal resources, these approaches often overlook the potential for strategy to be grounded in creating, delivering, and sustaining superior customer value.

Table 2.2 School of thought and role of the customer

School of thought	Primary focus	Role of the customer	Implications
Superior Market Positioning (Market-Based View)	External factors like industry structure and positioning within the market.	Customers are part of industry analysis's "buyer" force, focusing on value capture. Views customers through market forces, focusing on mitigating their bargaining power. Customer segmentation is used to identify underserved areas and craft tailored value propositions.	Profit capture takes precedence over understanding or enhancing customer experiences.
Superior Talent, Physical Assets, and Competencies (Resource-Based View)	Internal resources and capabilities as drivers of sustained competitive advantage.	Customers receive the outputs of resources, but customer needs are considered indirectly as preferences and demands that can shape the development and deployment of resources. Sees customers as recipients of resource-driven outputs without centering on their value.	Resources are prioritized over customer insights, risking misalignment with customer needs.

School of thought	Primary focus	Role of the customer	Implications
Superior Operational Excellence (Operational Excellence View)	Streamlined, efficient processes and high-quality execution to deliver consistent results and operational excellence.	Customers are considered as beneficiaries of consistent, cost-effective, and reliable products or services but are not the primary focus of innovation or uniqueness. Treats customers as recipients of operational excellence, focusing on reliability, affordability, and consistency rather than deeper engagement or innovation.	Operational efficiency delivers consistent value but may lack differentiation or a strong emotional connection with customers.
Superior Ability to Act Quickly and Adapt (Dynamic Capabilities View)	Ability for firms to adapt quickly to changing environments, seize opportunities, and reconfigure resources as necessary.	Customers are implicitly central, as adaptability often aligns with meeting their changing demands, but the focus is on responsiveness rather than proactive value. Treats customers as dynamic entities whose needs must be met flexibly; however, the focus is on agility rather than creating deeply tailored solutions.	Strategic adaptability enables responsiveness but can lead to a reactive rather than proactive customer strategy.

To build a truly competitive edge in dynamic and customer-driven markets (or the customer advantage), it is essential to shift from treating the customer as a peripheral factor to placing them at the very core of strategic decision-making. This transition involves understanding and responding to customer needs and anticipating, shaping, and co-creating value with them, aligning every aspect of the business (resources, operations, adaptability, and market positioning) toward enhancing customer outcomes and experiences.

The Emergence of a Customer-Centric Approach to Strategy

Peter Drucker's assertion that "the purpose of business is to create a customer"[37] provides the philosophical foundation for customer-centric strategy. Unlike traditional approaches, this emerging fifth school places the customer at the core of strategic formulation.

Drucker believed that businesses could drive innovation and achieve sustainable success by focusing on understanding and fulfilling customer needs. Drucker emphasized that marketing and innovation are the two primary functions through which companies can effectively serve their customers, thereby converting economic resources into wealth.

In contrast, Milton Friedman[38] emphasized that a business's primary responsibility is to maximize shareholder profits, provided it operates within the bounds of law and ethical customs. This perspective, deeply embedded in traditional strategy frameworks, views profit generation as the ultimate measure of business success, inherently benefiting society through economic growth and job creation. Frameworks like Porter's Five Forces align with Friedman's premise, emphasizing industry positioning and operational efficiency as pathways to superior profitability.

The divergence between Drucker's customer-centric view and Friedman's shareholder primacy underscores a fundamental debate in business ethics and corporate governance. Drucker's approach prioritizes customer needs, seeing profit as a byproduct of delivering value and fostering loyalty. Friedman's focus on maximizing shareholder value aligns more closely with traditional competitive strategy frameworks, prioritizing market forces, industry competition, cost management, and efficiency over customer satisfaction.

The tension between these perspectives is exemplified by recent business challenges, such as the takeover battle involving Seven & i Holdings, the parent company of 7-Eleven.[39] Activist investors have pressured the company to enhance shareholder value, raising concerns about whether this focus might compromise its long-standing commitment to customer service and employee welfare. This scenario highlights the ongoing struggle to balance profit maximization with broader stakeholder interests, reflecting the debate between Drucker's and Friedman's philosophies.

The formalization of a customer-centric view of strategy began in the 1990s, spurred by the realization that delivering value tailored to customer needs was increasingly critical in competitive and dynamic markets. This shift was driven by technological advancements, changing consumer behavior, and the limitations of traditional frameworks that focused on industry structure or internal capabilities. During this time, frameworks emphasizing customer value as a primary source of competitive advantage gained traction. For example, Michael Treacy and Fred Wiersema's 1995 book, *The Discipline of Market Leaders*,[40] introduced the concept of value disciplines—operational excellence, product leadership, and customer intimacy—as pathways to competitive success.

> *To build a truly competitive edge in dynamic and customer-driven markets, it is essential to shift from treating the customer as a peripheral factor to placing them at the very core of strategic decision-making.*

Marketing thought leaders like Philip Kotler also played a pivotal role in integrating customer focus into strategy. Kotler's emphasis on understanding customer needs and delivering superior value helped bridge marketing principles with broader strategic frameworks. These developments marked a shift from competition-focused to value-focused strategies, with customer satisfaction, loyalty, and experience becoming central metrics for evaluating business success.

The emergence of customer-centric strategies also challenged traditional competitive strategy frameworks, such as Porter's Five Forces, which were criticized for emphasizing competition and industry dynamics at the expense of customer focus. This re-evaluation highlighted the importance of aligning business strategies with customer needs, laying the groundwork for modern concepts such as customer experience design and personalization.

While customer-centric thinking has often been conflated with marketing communications, there is a critical distinction between the two. Marketing communications focus on communicating value to customers and capturing market demand through tactics like branding, promotions, and pricing. In contrast, customer-centric competitive strategy leverages an understanding of customer needs to drive organization-wide priorities, product innovation, and long-term market positioning. In the 1990s, the concept of "market orientation" emerged in the marketing literature; this concept focused on an organization-wide effort for generating market intelligence, sharing this intelligence inside the organization, and then taking actions to respond to the market intelligence.[41] Market intelligence refers to customer intelligence, as well as intelligence related to other key actors in the marketplace.

Technological advancements in the late 1990s and early 2000s, such as Customer Relationship Management tools, blurred the line between traditional marketing activities and customer-centric strategy. These tools tied customer centricity to analytics, loyalty programs, and segmentation, activities traditionally managed by marketing teams. However, the distinction became more apparent as businesses like Amazon and Apple demonstrated how customer-centric strategies could influence all aspects of organizational decision-making, from product development to operational design.

In the 1990s, thought leaders like Treacy and Wiersema framed customer centricity as a broader strategic imperative. Their work emphasized competing by excelling in customer intimacy, product leadership, or operational excellence. Similarly, Pine and Gilmore's book, *The Experience Economy*,[42] elevated customer centricity by showing how unique customer experiences could redefine industries and create sustainable competitive advantages.

In today's marketplace, a strategic focus on customers is more common, with companies such as Amazon and Apple exemplifying the power of customer-centric strategies. Amazon's focus on customer obsession has shaped its marketing and logistics, technology investments, and pricing models. Apple's integration of design, technology, and ecosystem thinking has delivered unparalleled customer value, creating competitive advantages beyond effective marketing campaigns. A similar evolution is unfolding in the nonprofit sector. Historically, many organizations focused on internal goals or donor priorities, but now leading nonprofits are reorienting strategy around the people they serve. For example, Feeding America has moved to a demand-driven model fueled by local hunger data and predictive analytics,[43] Crisis Text Line meets user needs through anonymous, real-time text support while also prioritizing high-risk cases.[44] St. Jude Children's Research Hospital is a great example of customer centricity with a focus on holistic care supporting the whole family.[45]

> *The starting point of all strategy must begin with customers (what we call the customer advantage), with the consideration of firm capabilities and externalities a supporting function to serve customers and outperform the competition.*

It is time for strategic thinking and frameworks for developing strategy to catch up with what organizations already know—namely, that there is a distinct strategic advantage by focusing on customers—the soul of strategy.

How Is Customer Centricity Different from Marketing Strategy?

Some readers may be wondering if there is a difference between customer centricity and the formulation of marketing strategy. There are three major differences. First, marketing strategy is focused on products, solutions, bundles, and categories of products. In sharp contrast, customer centricity is an organization-wide approach to corporate strategy. In our view, it is a new era of corporate strategy where the customer is the starting point for all enterprise-wide decisions. Second, marketing strategy is typically developed by the marketing function, whereas a customer-centric orientation is the responsibility of the

C-suite team. Third, marketing strategy is an important part of customer centricity, but it is only one part. It is a very important part, since it is the focus on the commercial side of the organization, but it must be combined with other functions, units, and enterprise-wide activities to create a customer-centered organization.

Conclusion

The aim of this chapter was to review the eras of strategy thinking and positioning the role of customers therein. Importantly, we want to stress that all these approaches to strategy add value to the dialogue and support how organizations approach the marketplace. In other words, we are not saying that competitor or organization capabilities are unimportant; rather, we are saying that they are less important than a unique, actionable focus on customer insights and knowledge. Put simply, the starting point of all strategy must begin with customers (what we call the "customer advantage"), with the consideration of firm capabilities and externalities a supporting function to serve customers and outperform the competition.

3

Reemergence of the Customer

"Any customer can have a car painted any color that he wants so long as it's black."

—Henry Ford (1922)[1]

Introduction

While companies have been serving customers since ancient times, the current notion of a consumer emerged during the industrial revolution where societies shifted from economies that were mainly production-based (e.g., local, handmade goods) to consumption-oriented (e.g., with mass production of more varied goods).[2] Such a shift in how economies worked saw rural populations moving to urban centers to work in manufacturing facilities; emergent needs manifested for those workers to purchase products that were then being produced on a large, varied scale. No longer did people purchase vegetables from neighbors, but rather in tins produced by a manufacturer and sold via a retailer.

Since the industrial revolution, consumer spending has been a major driver of economies around the globe, and that is no less true today. For example, in Q2 of 2024 estimates are that approximately 68 percent of the U.S. economy was composed of personal

37

consumption expenditures.[3] This has steadily risen from approximately 60 percent in the 1970s until today. While heavily fueled by increased levels of household debt (at least in the United States), there is no underestimating the impact of consumer spending on economic productivity. As observed by economists ranging from Bernanke to Keynes to Schumpeter, Paul Samuelson captured the situation well, when noting that, "The consumer, so it is said, is the king . . . each is a voter who uses his money as votes to get the things done that he wants done."[4] Yet another reason why putting the consumer at the center or soul of business strategy is so compelling.

As we entered the 20th century, limitations in embryonic manufacturing processes provided few alternatives to consumers, compared to today. A situation illustrated by Ford's classic statement that a customer can have any Model-T automobile as long as it's black.[5] In today's marketplace with advanced manufacturing and a desire to individualize consumption, consumers can get many cars, trucks, and SUVs in whatever color they like; and one doesn't need to be Paris Hilton working with a company like LA's West Coast Customs to realize such a perfectly pink reality.[6]

While there is little doubt of the influence of B2C (business-to-consumer) transactions on the world economy, one should not forget that B2B (business-to-business) connections are equally impactful, as they represent consumption and purchases by organizations, governments, NGOs, nonprofits, and religious organizations. When considering both B2B and B2C transactions, it is reasonable to argue that nearly the entire world's economy is driven by exchanges in which an organization sells something to another entity, whether it be a consumer or another organization.

This chapter explores forces present in today's market that will increase the role, impact, and importance of customers within the global economy. Many of these forces are fueled by the "fourth industrial revolution," including but not limited to availability of massive amounts of widely accessible data, AI tools, and ever-increasing computing power. In many ways, we expect the impact of consumption in the early 21st century to eclipse the impact of that as we entered the industrial revolution. Together, we predict that going forward there will be a true reemergence of the customer. One could easily argue that there is a renaissance underway and that organizations better pay attention to customers as they build their core strategies and a customer advantage.

A Consumer Renaissance

Existing and emerging forces in the market, emanating from consumer- and organization-based sources, provide a dual influence on the rising importance of consumers. Driven by advances in emerging technologies, consumers are more empowered in the exchange process than ever before and can more readily connect with others, thereby ensuring that their desires, wants, and needs are front and center for organizations to respond to. On the flipside, organizations have more tools available to understand their consumers and develop products that better satisfy customer needs and wants. Together, the six drivers illustrated in Figure 3.1 and discussed in the following sections are predicted to power a consumer renaissance in the market—fueled by market-oriented companies.

Consumer Drivers

The reemergence of the customer in the 21st century has been driven by various forces emanating from individuals and groups of consumers who are more empowered than any time in history. Ever since the rise of "digital natives" (i.e., those who came of age with the internet),

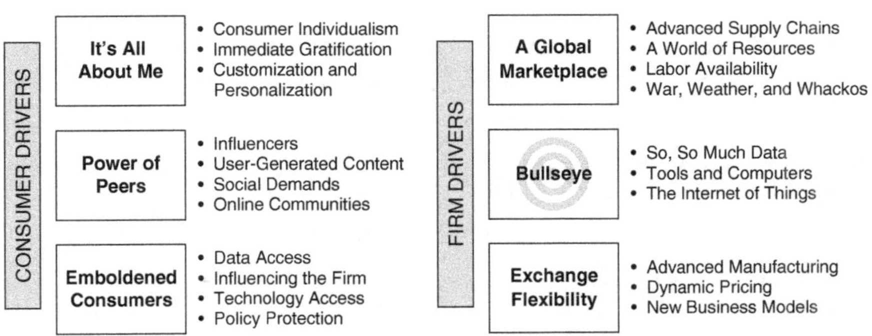

Figure 3.1   Drivers of the customer reemergence.

consumers have a range of tools literally at their fingertips (e.g., in the form of phones and smart watches) that impact, influence, and enhance consumption. Recent advances in computer processing, access to massive data (often from the cloud), and the rise of AI have further fueled consumers' influence on the market. We capture these forces in three broad domains.

It's All About Me   Consumers in today's world—particularly those in Western societies—have a belief that the person should be prioritized over the interests of the collective.[7] Such a trend has expanded in the 21st century and has influenced people in their role as consumers, where customers expect (nay demand) near immediate gratification of their wants and needs. While this may vary across different generations (e.g., Gen Z compared to Millennials), there is a shared sense in today's world that "it's all about me" as a consumer. Organizations expecting to compete in such a world must put the customer first by addressing immediate demands.

Numerous factors have affected the rise of consumer individualism, including the ability to customize products, fragmented media that allows targeted communications, and the incredible speed of delivery (e.g., consumers can get dinner from Grubhub with a simple button push).

Consumer Individualism. Mirroring trends in broader society, consumers see themselves as being central to the marketplace—an idea reflected in the euphuism that the consumer reigns supreme. Perhaps Drucker said it best, noting that, "the purpose of business is to create and keep a customer"[8]—a concept that is not lost on consumers in the 21st century. Several factors support this belief in consumers, many of which are related to organizations' efforts aimed at meeting consumer needs and wants (e.g., direct communications between the consumer and company, near human-like interactions). Examples abound of how consumers are put at the center of an organization's efforts.

Competing with the likes of Trader Joe's and Amazon, H-E-B operates more than 430 stores in Texas and Mexico and empowers its employees to create an individualized customer experience. Employees are expected to be proactive advocates of customers and allowed to make on-the-spot decisions in support. Thus, customer service is tailored to the unique circumstances or needs of each situation, creating unique interactions and providing customers a level of autonomy that is rare in most retail settings. For example, by sourcing locally through initiatives such as the "GO TEXAN" program, H-E-B highlights a community-driven approach to business and creates a more personalized experience.[9]

Immediate Gratification. Whether it be delivery of dog food to one's home for fido or a burrito to a person's office for lunch, consumers can get a plethora of items nearly immediately upon ordering in today's marketplace (often with no more than the click of a button on an app). Both technology (e.g., in the form of easy ordering systems as with Amazon) and supply chain sophistication underlie much of this disruption. Beyond the negative effects on brick-and-mortar stores (e.g., bankruptcy and closure of retail giants like Kmart and Sears), such outcomes drive the view that immediate consumer gratification is obtainable in most instances in countries like the United States. And if not, then it is easy to move on and find other opportunities—if one cannot get a ride from Lyft, then contact Uber. The immediacy is further enabled via platforms like Afterpay, a buy now, pay later service that allows consumers to make purchases immediately and pay in interest-free installments over several weeks. This model enables shoppers to afford higher-value items upfront and receive them right away—even before completing all payments.[10]

Customization and Personalization. Driven by innovations in advanced manufacturing and enabled by various emerging technologies, consumers can customize (or mass customize) products of all shapes and sizes. The ability to create a product "just for me" helps to drive the notion that we (as consumers) are at the center of the marketplace. Examples abound, ranging from custom paint on a new car to M&M candies with one's name emblazoned on them. Such customization is not only for products, but for services where consumers can enjoy anything from a private dinner at a kitchen's chef table to behind-the-scenes experiences at a concert. Spotify exemplifies this trend by tailoring music recommendations to each user. By analyzing a person's listening habits, search history, playlists, and skips, Spotify refines its suggestions to match preferences. Using natural language processing and real-time data, it even examines lyrics, reviews, and social media mentions to gauge sentiment and context of songs—a prime example of deep personalization.[11]

Power of Peers   Humans have always influenced one another—it is a fundamental aspect of the human condition. Indeed, many scholars and writers have noted that social interaction among humans has been key to supporting our success as a species.[12] Modern ideas related to social psychology help to frame many of these influences that are driven to new heights in today's uber-connected world, where sophisticated consumers influence or are influenced by other consumers. For example, Spotify Wrapped is a campaign that leverages social influence to drive engagement via various social media platforms such as Instagram and Twitter. The buzz sparked by this user-driven promotion has reinforced Spotify's reputation for tailored music experiences and digital identity expression. In this section, we explore such normative factors, including the availability and influence of social media, and the fragmentation (if not erosion) of traditional media.

Influencers. The impact of the influencer culture is omnipresent in today's market with increased usage of social media (e.g., TikTok, Snapchat, Facebook). Whether celebrities or experts or just the neighbor next door, social media influencers sway the decisions and choices of consumers by the promotion and recommendation of various products and services. Research indicates that the credibility of such sources is driven by three factors, related to the influencer's trustworthiness, expertise, and attractiveness.[13]

Influencers can significantly drive consumer purchasing behavior by building trust, providing the brand with social proof, and driving up engagement. We recently spoke with a manager at Trader Joe's who said that he often learns about new products at the company via social media influencers before he hears of them from the company. Followers often see influencers as authorities in their niche, especially when they are authentic and honest about their experience with the brand. A 2021 Nielsen study found that 71 percent of consumers trust opinions and product placements from influencers. However, businesses must be careful to align with the right influencers by carefully selecting influencers whose values align with their brand to ensure authenticity.[14]

A good example is Fiji Water's campaign aimed at building partnerships with influencers who embody a healthy, active, and entrepreneurial lifestyle—values aligned with the brand's image. A campaign with fashion designer Danielle Bernstein was designed to feel authentic. Posts were curated so that the influencer can express their personal brand while promoting Fiji Water. Water bottles were integrated seamlessly into content, an approach that helped maintain authenticity of the influencer's voice while also marketing (albeit subtly) the product.[15]

User-Generated Content. It is remarkably easy for others to share information about products and services in today's marketplace—albeit such information does not need to be factually accurate to reach and influence others. Often referred to as "user-generated content," such peer-based communications relate to experiences, evaluations, and information about organizations and what they offer in the market. Normally organic, such recommendations are perceived as credible as they come from more apparently objective sources, compared to information from the organization—the media, or other more formal sources.

Chipotle has effectively harnessed user-generated content, particularly on TikTok, by engaging in viral challenges like #ChipotleLidFlip and #GuacDance, both of which collectively garnered hundreds of millions of views. The brand's active participation in viral trends, such as adding the Fajita Quesadilla to its menu following a popular TikTok hack, showcases its ability to stay relevant and responsive to its customers.[16]

Social Demands. Much of the peer-to-peer influences of consumers on one another is grounded in theory and research on social psychology (per Allport as "the attempt to understand and explain how the thoughts, feelings, and behaviors of individuals are influenced by the actual, imagined, implied presence of other human beings").[17] Various social psychological processes exist—ranging from social influence to social identity and status.

A good example of such normative pressures is provided by "social proof" (sometimes called the bandwagon effect), where people use other people's behavior to guide their own (particularly when there is uncertainty regarding what to do). A poignant example of social proof is provided by the insanely long lines of customers at IN-N-OUT locations—the California-based burger chain and leader in the industry. Many factors can be attributed to this company's success (e.g., quality food, excellent service, its famous "secret menu"), but the lines of cars spilling into the streets at many locations cannot be underestimated. As suggested by social proof, customers driving by a busy IN-N-OUT location are likely to be influenced positively by all those waiting for a burger.[18]

Online Communities. It is easier than ever to find others who are like us, something done very often via social media platforms ranging from Facebook to Reddit. Such communities allow consumers to interact with those who share common interests, attitudes, values, and experiences—traditional market segmentation variables. While all sorts of online communities exist, many are anchored on shared consumption related activities such as travel, specific brands, food, fashion, and automobiles. The importance of such communities has become even more significant with supporting technology (e.g., logarithms that maximize automatic delivery of relevant content to consumers related to their interests) and societal trends (e.g., a more polarized society in the United States that can drive consumer action based on politics).

Duolingo—the popular language-learning app with its iconic owl mascot—has successfully used TikTok to connect with its audience through meme-inspired, chaotic content. By staying on top of trends and engaging actively with users, Duolingo has built a strong, interactive community of 15.3 million followers, fostering both brand loyalty and user interaction.[19] Online communities are also in other sectors; for example, TalkingPoints (an education technology nonprofit) uses mobile technology to connect teachers and families, particularly within underserved communities. By enabling two-way messaging in different languages, the technology helps to build trust and engagement via shared, ongoing conversations. Like Duolingo, it shows how tech can strengthen community around a common goal.

Emboldened Consumers Today's consumers have incredible power in the marketplace with organizations, and they are not afraid to exercise it. Such strength is more than perceived. It is propelled by consumer access to vast amounts of information leveraged with supporting technology (e.g., online reviews, websites, now AI-powered tools), the ability to directly or indirectly contact and influence the organization (e.g., via social media, user-generated content), and protections provided by policy. Consumers are becoming tremendously sophisticated in the ways they express their desires, search for information, shop, and choose products. To survive and thrive in today's market, organizations must be customer-centered to meet the needs of these empowered and sophisticated customers—to ignore them is to do so at the organizations' peril.

Data Access. Consumers, particularly in developed economies, have never had more access to data related to consumption than today. Fueled by personal technologies, consumers have nearly infinite data available to them ranging from company-provided product information to third-party online comparison tools of products and services. As detailed further in Chapter 4, information is critical for consumer decision-making as it reduces uncertainty, allows easier comparisons, and can shape customer preferences.

Organizations can also play a role in providing customers with data access; Caterpillar is an example of a company that uses data in such a way. Utilizing data from its 500,000 connected assets, Caterpillar can provide all sorts of customer solutions related to its products (e.g., maintenance needs, service requirements, efficiency improvements). The company's VisionLink subscription service provides real-time insights for fleet management, enabling businesses to optimize equipment usage and resource allocation. Through this data-driven decision-making, Caterpillar empowers customers to improve productivity and enhance operational planning.[20]

In the nonprofit arena, Crisis Text Line exemplifies how live data can transform mental health services. The organization offers around the clock, free support through text messaging—a technology that connects people in crisis with trained volunteer counselors. Crisis Text

Line uses machine learning to scan each incoming message for high-risk language (e.g., terms like suicide or self-harm) and provides those texters with help first. The nonprofit's system analyzes millions of anonymized conversations to improve customer service (e.g., how counselors are trained, trend identification).[21] This is a great example showing how nonprofits and their customers can benefit from the use real-time data.

Influencing the Organization. Customers can now more readily and directly connect with companies. Whether it be via chatbots, messaging apps, or the ability to post user-generated content online, organizations and consumers are more readily connected than in prior years. Such access to organizations allows consumers to more directly influence them either individually or collectively. Recent illustrations of this are commonplace around customer reactions to DEI efforts of organizations. For example, when Budweiser provided a customized beer to a trans influencer, customers expressed an extreme negative reaction (including Kid Rock with a machine gun) and the company responded. Organizations face a tough situation attempting to address such issues—Kid Rock reconciled with Bud to the chagrin of many who celebrated his initial reaction.[22]

Technology Access. Consumers have ready access to many and varied forms of technologies; a situation not restricted to advanced economies but also prevalent in emerging economies. Indeed, the ability to purchase such technology is within reach to many consumers—whether it be via a cell phone or connected devices such as Alexa from Amazon (often referred to as Internet of Things). With the current advances in AI and technology supporting such smart systems and assuming basic internet access, there is likely to be an exponential impact of technology used by consumers.

In the world of B2B, Salesforce, a cloud-based software company, leverages AI-driven predictive analytics to enhance decision-making for its users. The Einstein Prediction Builder allows its clients to create custom AI models without needing coding expertise, predict product demand, and anticipate customer behavior. Salesforce also focuses on ensuring data accuracy by using tools for segmentation, duplicate detection, and consistency checks. These AI-powered insights allow customers to optimize operations, improve customer service, and make more informed strategic decisions.[23]

Policy Protection. While it varies across countries, consumers are often provided power in the form of protections embedded in public policy—with such protections ebbing and flowing alongside changes to politicians who win the elections. Such consumer protection emerged during the industrial revolution, where consumers no longer had direct access to the producers of items they consumed (e.g., as impactfully outlined in Upton Sinclair's *The Jungle*).[24] Unfortunately, in many countries, consumers lack simple protections (e.g., in the United States there are few policies related to the internet and social media, yet alone AI).

One area of focus relates to data security and privacy; a recent example is the European Union's law called the General Data Protection Regulation (GDPR). Established in 2018, the regulation sets standards for how organizations collect, store, and process data of European consumers. Such regulations impact how organizations do business. While Microsoft ensures compliance with GDPR, the company faces ongoing challenges. For instance, LinkedIn, a Microsoft subsidiary, was fined €310 million in October 2024 by the Irish Data Protection Commission for processing personal data without a proper legal basis for targeted ads—a fine underscoring the complexities of policy compliance.[25]

Organization Factors

Organizations are better able than ever to meet the needs and wants of consumers. Various factors now provide organizations with the ability to address the collective (and individual) needs of their customers. We represent these forces in three broad areas. These factors include a truly global marketplace whereby organizations can sell and source their wares. With the advent of "big data" (reflecting the three Vs of data, including volume, velocity, and variety),[26] massive computing power, and new tools provided by AI, organizations have an ability to target customers better than before. Finally, there are more options available to organizations providing new approaches to address consumer needs.

A Global Marketplace   The capability to source products from across the globe has provided organizations with the ability to provide an incredible range of products and services to customers—at a level unavailable to prior generations. Such a process impacts the entire production system, from natural resource extraction to consumption and disposition. With this tool at their disposal, organizations can tap into a range of human and natural resources from emerging and developed countries around the globe. Of course, the downsides of such a global marketplace can be seen when external factors disrupt the expansive and sophisticated system; something illustrated clearly by the impacts of COVID-19 in nearly every country.

Advanced Supply Chains. Elaborate, sophisticated, and advanced supply chains are at the core of what allows organizations to expand globally. These supply chains are highly interconnected, span multiple countries, and pull together production, transport, and distribution. Supply chains have advanced recently due to emerging technologies, JIT (just-in-time) inventory systems, and enhanced project management of organizations.

Zara, a leader in the fast fashion industry, is an example of a company with an advanced supply chain that is universally recognized for its speed and responsiveness. To meet market demand, Zara can introduce new designs in as little as two weeks—a situation facilitated by its efficient supply chain, real-time inventory management, and data analysis. To further these efforts, Zara's parent company, Inditex, recently acquired Spain's largest logistics center in Zaragoza to enhance its distribution capabilities and streamline its ability to respond to customer demands.[27]

A World of Resources. Today's organizations can tap into the world's natural resources and processed goods to produce products and supporting materials used in services. (At least until the recent trade row between the United States and various U.S. trading partners.) Recent advances in material science have transformed how organizations offer products in the market (e.g., as related to composites, nanomaterials, and polymers). Going forward, AI will dramatically increase additional breakthroughs and have impact in a wide range of industries. Such advances have direct impact on the lives of consumers in many product verticals, ranging from agricultural products to manufactured goods.

A great example of such supply chains is provided by Parker Aerospace, a leading provider of aerospace systems and components. The firm sources materials from literally across the globe, including titanium-matrix composites, to produce lightweight, high-performance parts for the aerospace industry. Such materials enable the creation of more efficient and durable aircraft components, which help Parker's customers reduce weight while maintaining strength and performance. Further efficiencies are provided by AI technologies and the firm's heavy investments in research and development.

Labor Availability. Organizations tapping into workers have shifted from developed to emerging economies in the last 30–40 years, a trend that continues today. Various factors underlie this shift in where work is done, including globalization, the rise of China, India, and emerging economies, and technology, to name a few. We recently spoke to the president of a small, U.S.-based firm who is regularly sourcing workers in the Philippines and Africa. The right balance between local and foreign labor markets is not without debate or concern, as the shift to emerging economies has been criticized for poor working conditions, weak worker protections, negative impact on the environment, and "stealing" jobs in developed countries. Indeed, with the rise of truly global brands, organizations are right to be concerned about how labor is sourced and used to produce their goods.

Returning to Zara, this company has faced scrutiny over its labor practices, especially regarding outsourced production to countries with lower labor costs. While the company maintains a significant portion of its manufacturing in Spain, about a quarter of its production takes place in Asia and Africa. Labor concerns have haunted the organization since reports surfaced in 2011 about conditions in its São Paulo factories. Such allegations highlight the ethical challenges that come with outsourcing in the fast-fashion industry, particularly regarding the treatment of workers. Such controversies raise questions about how global brands address competing needs to meet immediate customer demand while ensuring fair working conditions throughout their supply chains.[28]

War, Weather, and Wild-Cards. There is no doubt that the global marketplace can be impacted by externalities, such as wars (e.g., war in Ukraine and Gaza), natural events (e.g., wildfires in the western

United States), and governmental actions or what we call wild cards. (such as the rash of tariffs being launched by the second Trump presidency). Disruption of a global consumer order can easily be seen all around us, such as advertisements in 2025 informing consumers to buy that new car before the tariffs begin.

A clear example of how geopolitical conflict can reshape global business operations occurred when McDonald's, Starbucks, and Apple stopped operations in Russia following the invasion of Ukraine. This move not only disrupted their brand presence in the Russian market but also had ripple effects on their global strategies. However, it also resonated with consumers in the United States, where these actions were viewed largely as positive. Based on this decision (at least at the time), it appears consumers value companies that take a stand on ethical and social responsibility issues. Of course, the political context facing organizations in 2025 is entirely different and it is reasonable to question whether such a Russian withdrawal today would be received the same.[29]

Bullseye Central concepts in marketing are segmentation and target marketing—two key issues underlying an organization's ability to meet the needs, wants, and desires of customers. Segmentation is the notion that markets can be divided into groups based on commonalities (e.g., behavior, values, lifestyle), while target marketing is the tool by which organizations select specific segments to offer goods and services. We discuss this issue in more detail in Chapter 6. The organization's ability to tackle these marketing strategies has increased considerably with access to more data, tools to analyze it, and growing numbers of media channels. These factors allow organizations to "hit the bullseye" in terms of meeting the needs of its customers, thereby creating a true customer advantage.

So, So Much Data. Organizations currently are flush with massive amounts of data (all three Vs) available to make decisions about how to serve their customers. As detailed more fully in later chapters, central to a customer-centric strategy is understanding your customers' needs, wants, and desires, using such shared information to make strategy and refine decision-making. It is not only the amount of data that should be noted, but also the speed and variety of its availability to organizations. Advances in cloud computing have forever changed the fundamental nature of how data is used by organizations.

With such data advances, firms and organizations are racing to develop new processes, relationships, and means to leverage such assets. In Europe, B2B markets are exploring how to share data between different firms and across the supply chain. An example is Catena X, which is a blockchain network working to enhance the auto supply chain in a collaborative fashion. The goal of the project is to promote transparency, efficiency, and sustainability of data across manufacturers, suppliers, and other stakeholders.

Tools and Computers. The ability to get the most from big data has increased drastically in recent years due to tremendous increases in computing power (Moore's law is alive and well) and readily available digital tools such as machine learning. No longer is it an era when only large Fortune 500 type companies (that can have their own mainframes) leverage such tools—indeed, such computer-based resources are available to nearly any sized organization. This situation is only likely to accelerate in the near future with even greater advances in computing power driven by quantum computers.

Both small and medium-sized enterprises can now leverage powerful tools to enhance their operations and remain competitive to better address customer needs and wants. One example of this democratization of technology is Swoop, a U.K.-based fintech founded by Andrea Reynolds. Swoop uses open banking and artificial intelligence (AI) to connect small businesses with lenders, helping them access much-needed funding. This use of AI and cloud-based systems illustrates how even smaller organizations can now utilize cutting-edge tools to streamline their operations.[30]

The Internet of Things (IoT). Internet and Bluetooth technologies have enabled the interconnections of "things" in consumers' lives that allow organizations greater understanding of their needs and ability to serve them. This spans from controlling functions within your home at a distance (e.g., as provided by Nest or similar products) to suggesting meals in your fridge based on ingredients contained therein (e.g., offered by select Samsung refrigerators). With increased automation, AI, and better connectivity, IoT will likely be further integrated into daily life and expand to broader systems (e.g., healthcare systems, smart cities).

A great example is provided by Samsung's SmartThings platform that has seen explosive growth in tech-savvy South Korea with more than 20 million domestic users. Such rapid adoption signals a major shift in consumer behavior, as AI-powered appliances become integral to everyday life. The platform has been used on various products including vacuums and washer-dryers. The platform provides customers with various features, ranging from diagnosing malfunctions to monitoring pet status. These features have driven an 80 percent increase in usage. Samsung is further expanding its SmartThings ecosystem with the upcoming launch of "AI Home."[31]

> *Central to a customer-centric strategy is understanding your customers' needs, wants, and desires, using such shared information to make strategy and refine decision-making.*

Exchange Flexibility   Central to nearly any for-profit, not-for-profit, or NGO is the idea of "an exchange." The father of modern marketing thought, Phil Kotler, was one of the first to frame marketing as an exchange process between a purchaser and a buyer. Key to this is the transfer of products, services, and even ideas between a buyer and seller with both parties receiving benefits. Traditional B2B and B2C exchange relationships—at least since the industrial revolution—are often between a customer (the buyer) and the organization providing the product (the seller). Due to advances in manufacturing and technology, new approaches to exchange are evident in the marketplace, thereby providing organizations with flexibility to better and more fully meet the needs, wants, and desires of their customers.

Advanced Manufacturing. Innovations in manufacturing now allow organizations to provide unique offerings that satisfy their customers' exact wants and needs. No longer are customers required to select from a limited set of product options (a black Model T from Ford); rather, they can personalize or customize all sorts of products and services provided by organizations. As noted previously in this chapter, satisfying the individual needs of consumers is now something organizations can do and should consider doing as part of their overall business strategy—advanced manufacturing allows organizations to do so. Advanced manufacturing has other benefits to organizations as well, including increased efficiency, reduced costs, improved quality, and the ability to respond quickly to changes in the market.

Industrial automation giant Siemens is a prime example of a company leveraging advanced manufacturing to gain a competitive edge. The company integrates additive manufacturing (aka 3D printing) across its operations from product development to maintenance and service. Siemens has reduced product development time by up to 25 percent, particularly through improved prototyping, allowing new products to reach the market and customers' hands faster. Rather than maintaining large inventories of spare parts, Siemens relies on digital 3D models, enabling on-demand production and eliminating the need for costly retooling. Not achievable through traditional methods, advanced manufacturing has strengthened Simens' ability to respond to customer needs while improving operational efficiency and enhancing innovation.[32]

Dynamic Pricing. New personalized pricing models are being used by firms (e.g., in e-commerce, airlines) to adjust prices in a real-time manner based on demand, competitors, and various market forces. Such approaches can help organizations maximize profits and are likely to be adopted more widely in the future as organizations have greater access to big data, computing power, and AI tools (such as machine learning). Recent concerns raised by consumers and politicians regarding the ethics and transparency of such pricing models need to be considered.

Airbnb's pricing system relies on machine learning algorithms to continuously refine pricing based on data input and host feedback. The company's Smart Pricing tool analyzes considerable amounts of data (e.g., local demand, seasonal trends, property history, pricing of similar properties) to determine optimal pricing. AI helps ensure that pricing remains attractive without undervaluing the property. While this approach enhances revenue for hosts and maintains competitive pricing for guests, there are concerns about data privacy regarding use of host data to train its algorithms. Such reactions to AI-driven pricing highlight the balance that companies must strike among maximizing profitability, serving customers, and maintaining consumer trust.[33]

New Business Models. Organizations are now providing consumers with a range of different approaches for accessing products, features, and services. For example, firms operating in the "gig economy" (e.g., Uber, Lyft) provide services to customers via temporary workers, often enabled via mobile technology. This is different from the "sharing economy," where consumers share the consumption of a service or product in collective fashion. Producers of products also are benefiting from new business models (e.g., purchasing cell phones via service providers, accessing movies via streaming services). In the automotive industry, companies ranging from BMW to Tesla allow consumers to purchase "features-on-demand" (often desirable and exciting) on their existing cars. Broadly framed as software-as-a-service, systems like BMW's ConnectedDrive allow consumers to unlock new features on an automobile with a simple app and fee.

Conclusion

Over the past 30 years the world has increasingly shifted to enable suppliers to offer highly customized and personalized real-time experiences and products. The power has completely shifted to the customer—their needs, wants, and desires. As a result, competitive advantage is not about out-maneuvering the competition—it is about obtaining deep, unique customer insights that can be gained, used, and deployed on a continual basis. These are the lasting sources of competitive advantage, or what we call the "customer advantage."

The Nature of Customer Centricity

THE INTENT OF Part II of the book is to present the "core logic" of a customer-centric approach to strategy. In Chapter 4, we begin with a description and definition of customer centricity. While this may seem very basic—the reality is that there are many different definitions of the concept—it makes it difficult for practitioners to implement the ideas in practice. So, we begin with a crisp, clear definition of the term. We also take time to describe each key term in the definition—again, our aim is clarity and specificity. As a side note, while our focus is on practice, the definition also meets the psychometric criteria that academic audiences will appreciate (e.g., various types of concept validity).

We next describe the flow of intelligence that is at the heart of being customer-driven—gathering customer insights, sharing and reaching conclusions about the insights, and using the insights to drive organization-wide decisions (e.g., new product introductions, choice of segments to target, and abandoning activities that no longer add customer value). Given the importance of customer intelligence, we provide an even deeper treatment later in the book. Importantly, we introduce the concept of "table stakes" insights and "unique, differentiated" insights in this chapter. Customer advantage is built on novel insights that the organization continually collects and uses to shape the evolution of their industry.

In Chapter 5, we present our view of strategy formulation taken from the point of view of the customer. We term this strategy process "the customer choice cascade." It is a five-step process where organizations must make five key choices regarding their customers. Steps 1 and 2 are where to play choices while steps 3, 4, and 5 are how to win choices. Step 1 begins with the selection of the target segment and an articulation of what that segment values. The second step examines competition—who are they, what is their value proposition, and what is their activity system to deliver that value. So, competition enters the picture—at the second step—not the first step in the process. The third step entails a shift from "where to play" to "how to win" choices. Here we focus on the organization's value proposition, its activity system, and its profit model. In Step 4, we introduce the concept of mutual value. Any customer-centric approach must provide value to both the customer and the organization. It is not about providing outstanding customer value while losing money, nor making money without consideration of the customer (albeit some companies do). Customer-centric organizations are able to generate above average profits because loyal customers love to do business with the organization. Finally, in Step 5, we introduce the idea of managing in two time periods. Organizations must balance competing in the present while allocating sufficient resources to the future.

In Chapter 6, we "dive deep" into customer insights. Certainly, we can think of customer preferences for our products versus competition, but this is really the tip of the iceberg of customer insight. To construct a 360-degree view of the customer, we introduce a customer behavior framework that is rooted in decades of research on consumer behavior and framed around the customer journey. The aim here is to provide practitioners with a roadmap to understand the various facets of customer behavior, thoughts, and emotions that can be used to gain customer advantage in the market. Think of this chapter as a "checklist" of things you need to know about your customer to make the key choices in the customer choice cascade.

4

Customer Centricity

"What the producer or supplier thinks the most important feature of a product to be—may well be relatively unimportant to the customer."

—Peter Drucker

Introduction

Since the term customer centricity was introduced in the 1970s, there have been more than 3,000 journal articles and more than 100,000 popular press articles on the concept. Indeed, while the term was introduced in 1978,[1] the notion of building a business around the customer can be traced to Drucker, who noted in 1954 that "it is the customer who determines what the business is. What the customer thinks he is buying, what he considers 'value,' is decisive—it determines what the business is, what it produces, and whether it will prosper" (p. 37).[2]

Fast-forward to today, and it is difficult to find an organization that does not strive to be customer oriented. Indeed, many Fortune 500 companies now have customer centricity as part of their corporate values. One of Merck's core values is to put patients first. They note, "We are all accountable for delivering high-quality products and services. We aspire to improve the health and wellness of people and animals worldwide and to expand access to our medicines and vaccines. All of our actions must be measured against our responsibility to those who use or need our products."[3] USAA, the financial services firm built to serve the military, has a credo of "putting the member first," which reflects their dedication to providing exceptional service and financial products tailored to the unique needs of their military market.[4] Intel's first company value is "customer first." This customer first philosophy is comprised of three activities. "We listen, learn, and anticipate our customers' needs. We deliver to our customer commitments with simplicity, clarity, and speed. We nurture partnerships and foster growing ecosystems."[5]

The rationale is that customer centricity is the most straightforward and reliable route to sustainable economic performance. Researchers and thinkers have made the case that customer centricity drives profitability, margins, market share, and competitive advantage.[6] Furthermore, it has been argued that customer centricity increases customer satisfaction, loyalty, and referability.[7] Finally, organizations that are customer-centered also have more engaged and enabled employees.[8]

Despite this body of work, there is little consensus on what exactly is customer centricity.[9] For example, some authors argue the starting point is the choice of particular segment; others contend that segmentation is now irrelevant and that customer centricity is about one-to-one relationships; and still others hold that the organization should focus on segmentation and on one-to-one relationships, by focusing these resources within a segment. To take another example, some authors contend that the key to being customer-centric is the creation of value for customers, whereas others assert it is mutual value creation for customers and the organization. More recently, authors have claimed that all stakeholders in a given ecosystem must benefit.

Given this lack of clarity, we begin the chapter by providing a clear definition of customer centricity. This is followed by an overview of the three-phase market intelligence process that enables an organization to be customer-centric. We conclude with some general observations about the journey to be more customer-driven.

Definition of Customer Centricity

Customer centricity is an organization-wide effort to serve target segments by making evidence-based, market choices that create mutual value.

We have learned over time how important vocabulary is within organizations. While this is certainly true of global firms where English is a second language for many employees, it is important for every organization. Take the concept of "value"—if we talk to folks in finance, they think in terms of shareholder value, whereas if we talk to salespeople, they think of customer value. Our intent in this section is to discuss each element of the preceding definition so there is no ambiguity in the meaning of customer centricity—each of these dimensions is a choice that organizations need to consciously make when being customer-centered.

The Target Segment

Firms either implicitly or explicitly serve target segments. For Amazon or Alibaba, there are multiple segments reflecting both their B2B (e.g., Amazon web services) or B2C focus. Within B2C, Amazon has a variety of ways to classify its target customers (e.g., Prime vs. non-Prime). The choice of target segment is not as straightforward as some authors argue. For example, there has been a debate regarding whether to include future customers, noncustomers, and the "right" choice of segments. Some argue that there is one right choice of segment—those customers who provide highest lifetime customer value. While we explore this issue in more detail in Chapter 5, it is important to stress at this point that organizations need to prioritize and select key segments. While there are exceptions to the rule, the vast majority of successful organizations have focused on a segment or a small number of segments to constitute their core business. They do not serve the entire market—and they make it clear to everyone in the organization the segments that they do not serve. We refer to these groups as "spillover segments" to reflect the fact that some sales come from nontarget customers, but are not the focus of the organization.

Organization-Wide Effort

Customer centricity is an organization-wide activity. It is not restricted to the marketing function or even the commercial function. As Drucker noted, "Marketing is the distinguishing, the unique function of the business. It is not a specialized activity. It encompasses the entire business seen from the point of view of its final result, that is, the point of view of the customer. Concern and responsibility for marketing must permeate all areas of the enterprise" (p. 39).[10] The notion here is that every primary function of the value chain and every support function (e.g., IT, human resources, accounting) must be able to justify its choices, actions, and resource allocation based on the customer. This approach stands in stark contrast to other approaches to strategy, where the focus is often on the support function first. Justification can be direct (e.g., how billing is done from accounting) or indirect (e.g., IT supports billing software to enable timely, accurate billing).

Evidence-Based Decisions

Decisions are based on the voice of the marketplace, not management judgment or intuition. We had the opportunity to work with a cosmetics client several years ago. The target segment was young girls in the United States who were just starting to use cosmetics—in particular colorful nail polish and other "fun products" within the cosmetics line. The client believed that the solution to their organic growth challenge was either celebrity affiliation or social media. These seemed like reasonable hypotheses to test. In the course of our field research, we discovered something very different. If these young girls did not sample the company brand at the point of purchase display in the store, they bought the company brand 11 percent of the time; if they sampled the company brand, they bought it 76 percent of the time. The result was market-facing choices that related to trial of the brand—taking the cosmetics out of blister packs, making them easy to try on, with mirrors to "see the look," and prices that made sense for teen girls. Importantly, this quantitative evidence was critical for the decision—since conventional wisdom would have suggested a different route (e.g., allocate a significant portion of the marketing budget to social media). In some cases, the evidence can be qualitative; it all depends on the "burden of proof" that is necessary to facilitate decision-making. The role of market intelligence is the focus of Chapter 9, where we dig deeper into how organizations develop market-based insights.

Keep in mind that the evidence can also drive internal choices, not just market-facing ones. Since customer centricity is an organization-wide activity, all functions need to understand how to allocate time and resources to the voice of the marketplace. Looking again at teen girls' cosmetics, we can imagine a number of internal choices (e.g., do we organize our product teams by segments, such as the teen girl segment?) that follow from this customer insight. If the teen segment is a priority segment, how do we allocate more resources to this segment and decrease resources in less important segments? Our message is that every function needs to see this evidence and ask, "what can we do to support this customer insight?"

Market Choices

When authors identify decisions that are "customer-based," they often focus their attention on the organization's offerings and associated value propositions. This makes perfect sense since the aim is to offer products at a price point that is seen by target customers as better than the next best alternative. This product choice is one key element of the overall marketing mix choice (e.g., the organization also needs to communicate the value proposition of this product to the chosen segment). However, there are three other choices that reflect a customer-centered organization. The second choice is related to segment prioritization. The reason you collect customer insight is not just about the marketing mix; it also includes the selection of priority segments. The third choice is related to shaping the market—not just accepting customer behavior as a given, but leading the customer into new behavior/choice patterns (e.g., Netflix and Amazon Prime driving binge-watching of streaming programs). A final choice is related to abandonment of markets, products, and value chain activities that no longer reflect the evolution of market needs. We provide a deeper treatment of these four choices later in this chapter.

Create Mutual Value

The aim of a customer-centered organization is to create value for the enterprise and outperform competition. The reason companies want to deeply know about customer needs, preferences, and desires is to "capture value" for the organization. The more customer-oriented they are, the more money they can make and the more they can stay ahead of competition. Customer-centered organizations make a lot of money because customers "can't wait" to buy and use their products. Think Costco and Trader Joe's as two customer-centered firms that drive significant firm value. Obviously, there is an interplay here—the higher the customer value, the higher the firm value. The more companies can leverage unique customer insights to drive the four choices, the happier the customers and the happier the shareholders.

In summary, customer-centered organizations are driven by the unique, novel insights that can be deployed to create both customer and organization value. Often this is an exercise driven by marketplace "pilots" and "experiments." Organizations do not have to go all in on the four choices related to being customer centric; they can run selective pilots to test the efficacy of a key decision.

Three Core Activities

Now that we have established a definition of the customer-centered organization—one that uses customer evidence to make key market-facing choices to create value for both the organization and customers—we need to articulate the flow of intelligence that is necessary to support these market facing decisions. We will describe the flow of intelligence in three phases. In the first phase, the organization generates market intelligence from outside the organization's boundaries, and brings it into the organization. Once the intelligence is collected, the second phase involves "making sense" of intelligence and reaching conclusions. Per the definition, this is an enterprise-wide activity. It is not relegated to the commercial function. Finally, this intelligence is used to make four key choices. We explicate this three phase process in the following sections and explore more fully in Chapter 9.[11]

Phase 1: Market Intelligence Generation

The essence of market intelligence is going deep with customers to get beyond the obvious insights that companies can deploy to outperform competition. As we have learned over the past couple of decades, it is also important to understand the context of the consumer and how it impacts their attitudes, beliefs, and decisions.[12] The result is that customer research often needs to include insights related to competition, distribution channels, substitute products, and evolution of core technologies. This broader market intelligence enables the organization to gain a broader understanding of the evolution of the market. While books have been written on this topic, we want to make a few key points specifically related to customer centricity.

Table Stakes versus Unique Insights   Over the years we have seen hundreds of market research reports that have been conducted by well-meaning, talented executives. These reports have been rigorously designed, the sampling was precise, and the findings were valid. The catch however is that the vast majority of reports produce findings that create the following reaction, "Yes, this confirms our expectations," or "Great, we already know this." Does price matter to the market? Yes, apparently it does. Do customers want their product delivered in time? Yes, apparently they do. Do they want a full refund if they return their product? It seems so. In effect, the majority of research that we have seen "confirms" what is already well-known. Not enough research is exploratory—to learn new things about customers that others do not know. Indeed, the best of this research provides compelling, rigorous evidence that challenges the status quo, surprises the executives, and forces debate.

The Essence of Unique Insights   When judging unique insights, companies should apply three lenses to the intelligence. First, and key to acceptance, is that the research findings must be defendable on scientific merit. When findings emerge that challenge the status quo, the first reaction is surprise, and the second is "that cannot be true." Indeed, something must be wrong with your research methods. As we know, people anchor their beliefs and it is hard to challenge beliefs that are strongly held. Thus, the research must be airtight—a topic we dig into further in Chapter 9.

Second, the insights must be differentiated. While it can never be known with certainty, there must be a view that the firm uniquely knows this particular customer insight. In our cosmetics example above, there was no guarantee that others did not know the overwhelming evidence about the role that trial played in brand choice. That said, when the firm launched its campaign—with the best "trial-friendly" displays in the industry—sales rose significantly, and it became one of the top five "cool" brands for teens.

Third, the findings must be deployable in the field. That is, it must be easy for the firm to act on the findings. Again, for the teen cosmetics brand, the changes that were made were easy to implement. The brand was priced near $11, which was the average spend for teen girls and the colors were fun and lively. Furthermore, at the point-of-purchase display the teen girls were shown photos of various complexions and how the color can match different skin type. The product design choices were very clear. Also, it was very clear what products to abandon—such as cosmetics that required more knowledge to apply, were too costly, or designed for a more mature skin type.[13]

Time Horizon   In general, there is a bias toward the collection of market intelligence that has immediate application to today's marketplace. This makes sense for a variety of reasons: (1) the pressure on the organization to produce results in a quarterly timeframe, (2) the ability to secure funding for research where companies can assess the return on investment in a short time horizon, (3) the average length of time within a particular role is often around three years, so companies want to impact results "now," and (4) it is much more challenging to design research focused on future customer needs as compared to present where products and their competitor sets are quite clear.

However, per Drucker's viewpoint that 20 percent of executive time needs to be spent on the future, we advocate for more balanced research funding that combines the present and the future. To the extent that the organization can paint a picture of the future—how it will evolve, key players who will influence the transition, and how customer behavior will change—the organization is better able to allocate resources well in advance of events unfolding. Too often, we see organizations conduct scenario planning exercises that enable executives to avoid the responsibility of predicting or creating the future. The future can unfold in many different ways—let's wait and see what the future brings. This is in sharp contrast to the Drucker view, which advocates that the best way to predict the future is to create it.

Noncustomers   There are two types of noncustomers—those who are part of the target segment, but do not buy from the organization and those who are not part of the target market. Depending on the situation facing the organization, either or both of these audiences may be the appropriate source of customer insight. It is perhaps more obvious to focus on target customers who are not buying or buying from the competition. This group needs to be examined on a regular basis. If competitors have a significant share of wallet, the company needs to focus on comparative research to see why customers are making this choice versus the focal company. The less intuitive group are those who do not buy from the focal organization or the competitors, but nonetheless have an expressed need that is similar to others in the target market. This is where the "openness" to hear and understand is so critical. Are customers doing it themselves? Doing without? Waiting for a better time to purchase? Or simply finding another route to meet the particular need?

Research Methods   While covered in more detail in Chapter 9, we wanted to make a few comments that are central to the generation of customer insight. First, there is a proliferation of research techniques that have emerged for both mobile and online customer behavior. These include web analytics, social media listening, A/B testing, customer reviews, and others—many of these methods are easily accessible with the help of AI agents who can write code for you. This does not mean that the classic qualitative and quantitative techniques are no longer relevant: they are highly relevant depending on the research question. Interviews are a wonderful tool to ask "why" questions related to a range of consumer behavior decisions. Observation methods are of great use when customers are not able to articulate their specific actions and behaviors in a retail context.

> *While there are exceptions to the rule, the vast majority of successful organizations have focused on a segment or a small number of segments to constituent their core business.*

Newer web analytics techniques—such as data scraping and data mining—enable companies to get big data insights to go deep and broad with a range of consumers. Our key timeless point is that the research method needs to fit the particular "knowledge gap" that exists within the organization.

For any research approach, there is a burden of proof question. The burden of proof is related to the size of the potential opportunity and the risk profile of the organization. The key here is to establish the burden of proof very early in the design of the research project. There are two examples that represent ends of the burden of proof continuum. The first was a global energy services firm that competed in a highly contested market for vary large, multimillion dollar contracts. Here we mapped more than 900 buying situations and uncovered a unique insight that enabled the firm to generate tens of millions of incremental revenue. For this firm, a large body of quantitative evidence was needed to change the fundamental direction of its go-to-market strategy for the executive team to be convinced, and only a large sample would do it. For a medical device firm launching a slight modification in its product line, the approach was to interview a small number of surgeons and supplement this data with more in-depth conversations with field sales reps. This combination led to an alternative marketing strategy. Indeed, we posited the evidence as a "working hypothesis" that would be confirmed once the marketing strategy was launched. As such, the burden of proof for the evidence was quite modest.

Finally, for all projects, companies need to meet the decision-making unit "where they are" in their journey. Some teams simply want the evidence since they have limited knowledge of the customers in the market, while others need to resolve a debate with the firm regarding the right course of action. The key here is that companies need to understand the "decision needs" of the particular group who is accountable for the go-to-market decisions.

Phase 2: Sharing and Reaching Conclusions

Once the evidence-generation stage is complete, it then needs to be shared with other stakeholders inside the organization. This results in a series of conversations with all key stakeholders to solicit their view on the results. These sessions could be termed "joint sense making" of the marketplace. The key is having a diverse set of stakeholders (e.g., R&D, operations, finance, marketing) provide their perspective on the findings. What additional data can each group share to provide deeper insight into the consumer behavior? At the end of this sharing, discussion, and debate process, the group should summarize the key observations concerning the research. These observations need to be an organization-wide perspective and not focus on one functional area of the organization (e.g., product design).

This organization-wide lens is often difficult to achieve, since there are forces at work in any organization that get in the way of an enterprise view. First, most organizations have siloed functions, geographies, and franchises and, as a result, do not communicate on a regular basis. Second, functional areas may have a vested interest in a particular outcome that favors their function. Third, organizations always operate under uncertainty and with imperfect consumer insight. As a result, companies can always find limitations regarding the consumer research. That stated, the clash of opinions, debate, and even "devil's advocate views" are all important parts of the sense-making process and should be encouraged and reinforced.

If the idea is to generate defendable, differentiated, and deployable insights, the list is not likely to be long. And that is actually good news. Think back on the girls' cosmetics story—it was one key insight that drove the entire go-to-market strategy. Our experience is that organizations often try to collect "a lot" of data, have many conclusions, and draw recommendations. The result is a diffusion of opinions and a spreading of resources to multiple initiatives. Look for "big insights" and drive resource allocation around those insights.

In summary, the second phase of the intelligence flow is to make sense of the intelligence and reach conclusions—ideally on just a few critical consumer behavior insights. That stated, at this point, the organization has not acted. All that has happened is general agreement on the findings from the lens of the entire enterprise. In the next section, we explore four actions that can be taken based on customer insight.

Phase 3: Using Intelligence to Make Four Choices

Lots of organizations collect and share customer insight—and then surprisingly do not use most of it. There are a variety of reasons why this is the case. For example, it is not unusual for an organization to have regular reports on such measures as NPS or customer satisfaction where they are not tied to decision-making. A similar issue applies to regular secondary market research reports on industry trends, competitive trends, and customer dynamics. They are all interesting and informative, but the ties to decisions are indirect at best. In this section, we describe four choices that customer-centered companies need to make using the market intelligence evidence gathered in Phase 2.

Choice 1: The Design of the Marketing Mix (the 4Ps)   There are four marketing mix choices that result from customer insight. Everyone tends to identify the obvious choice—design of new products and services. However, the other three marketing mix choices— choice of channels, marketing communication routes and content, and pricing. These are all tied to the customer insight. Let's discuss each in turn.

Customer insight is most often used to design new products or modify existing offerings. This is not just the product itself, but it relates to the services, intelligence that can be exchanged between organizations and consumers, nature of the relationship, and the transaction itself. The aim here is to provide the building blocks for the right value proposition for the whole offering. There is a tendency for organizations to go deep on "features and functions" of the offering and spend less time on the "outcomes" or "benefits" that customers are hoping to realize. Indeed, the value curves proposed in the Blue Ocean approach often include a mix of features, services, benefits, and outcomes.[14] Certainly, this is one way to look for differences in offerings that could be desired by a particular target segment. However, during the product design phase, we recommend that companies focus first on benefits, since they are less historically dependent than product features. So, begin with a benefit comparison and then move on to features.

In the final analysis of product or service design, the key is to look for customer insights that enable companies to "significantly" improve a key benefit that matters most to its target audience—or ideally introduce a new benefit to the marketplace. The introduction of Wi-Fi service by airlines is an example of a new benefit.

Customer insight should also be used to make the choice or modification of routes to market. The challenge today has been termed omni-channel, since market routes have increased exponentially. Companies need to examine channel choice from the perspective of the customer rather than the company. Many organizations would love customers to buy directly from their company website; however, Amazon's dominance of the marketplace has forced many firms to offer their products through Amazon. The reason is simple. Customers strongly prefer the easy access, reliable service, and overnight delivery offered through Prime. Again, our key point is that the target customer preferences should determine the choice of channel.

Customer insights are also used to design and shape market communications. The nature of the communications is, of course, strongly linked to the value proposition. For Safelite Autoglass, the core value proposition is that they will come to you—at a time and place that works for you—to replace cracked or broken glass. They accomplish this through 5,000 mobile repair "shops." Customer communication readily extends to the nonprofit space, where donors and beneficiaries can both be seen as "customers." One organization, charity: water, responded to the insight that donors care about transparency and made the decision that 100% of public donations go to projects (overhead is funded separately). They provide "proof of impact" by communicating GPS coordinates and photos showing completed water projects.[15]

Finally, the pricing decision also requires customer insight. Customer willingness to pay is a function of the organization's offering relative to the next best alternative. It is the customer who determines what is the next best alternative and how well the organization's offering stacks up against competition. For Uber, surge pricing reflects a simple demand–supply issue. In these situations, Uber algorithms provide a surge pricing offer to potential customers. Customers then have the option to purchase or decline the surge offer. The customer may also check Lyft or Alto pricing, consider driving themselves, or even delay the trip.

Choice 2: Selection and Sequencing of Segments   The second choice is the "where to play" choice. In many ways, this is a more important choice than design of the product itself. Our experience in many B2B markets is that segmentation is often a "check the box" exercise. That is, customers are classified into some form of large, medium, and small accounts. And some B2B firms further classify the customers into industry verticals (e.g., government, automotive, education markets). This is highly problematic since it means that competitors then compete on offerings within those segments. However smart organizations realize that segmentation is a source of competitive advantage. If they can see and classify markets differently—due to unique customer insight—they have a longer runway to gain competitive advantage.

IKEA, TI calculators, Emirates Airline, and NVIDIA all began with a relentless focus on a single segment that competitors either did not see or simply ignored. The ability to spot a segment that is underserved or not served and design an offering specifically to that segment can create a lasting source of competitive advantage. Back in the late 1970s, no calculator manufacturer targeted middle or high school students. Everyone was focused on the corporate market. Indeed, it was seen as almost ludicrous that the secondary school market would be viable. Fast-forward to today, almost every U.S. high school student owns a TI graphing calculator. While specific numbers are hard to come by, the graphic calculator market has been estimated to be $1B and TI has been estimated to have 80 percent of the market share with very high margins.

The ability to spot a segment that is underserved and not served and design an offering specifically to that segment can create a lasting source of competitive advantage.

The lesson we have learned is not to accept the industry wisdom on segmentation. Doing so means companies are forced to compete head-to-head on offerings. Customer-driven organizations use customer insight to "see the market" differently and therefore they attack the market in unique ways.

Southwest saw a market for short haul travel; Amex Black saw a market for invitation-only, bespoke services for a high net-worth segment; Zip cars saw a market for short term, hourly car rentals; and many other firms have taken this route.

A second lesson is to focus on a single segment at the start of a journey. It may feel like it is risky just to select one segment. However, a riskier strategy is to spread resources across several segments. This rarely works in practice. The rationale is that the organization is spreading resources across several opportunities—all of which may be legitimate—so they should be funded. However, targeting multiple segments often slows down time to market, enables competition to attack weaker segments, and deprioritizes the most important segments. Our view is that organizations need a foothold in the marketplace to prove the concept. Often this means starting with a segment that strongly desires your product and is willing to take some risk. Think of the early users of Waymo, the driverless car services.

A third lesson is to plan a sequential roll out of segments. Some authors have argued that the key to customer centricity is to focus on a segment of consumers who have the highest lifetime value of customers. Certainly, this is one strategy. However, there are many other options that an organization can pursue. For example, an organization may decide to focus on a segment in which it can easily test a new product concept or a segment that creates the best references for future work in the category. Or it may focus on a segment where competition is nonexistent or weak. Our key point is that choice of segment needs to fit the strategy of the organization and the industry context in which the organization operates.

Choice 3: Shaping Markets   This third choice uses the market and customer insight to shape markets. Figure 4.1 shows a simple 2 × 2 diagram that identifies both "market-driven" and "shaping markets" strategies. The basic idea is that one axis is the structure of an industry (take industry structure as a given or try to change market structure) and the second axis is the behavior of stakeholders within the industry (accept all behavior of actors as a given or try to change one or more actor behaviors).

The bottom-left quadrant (accept the structure as a given and accept the behavior of actors as a given) is a customer-centered

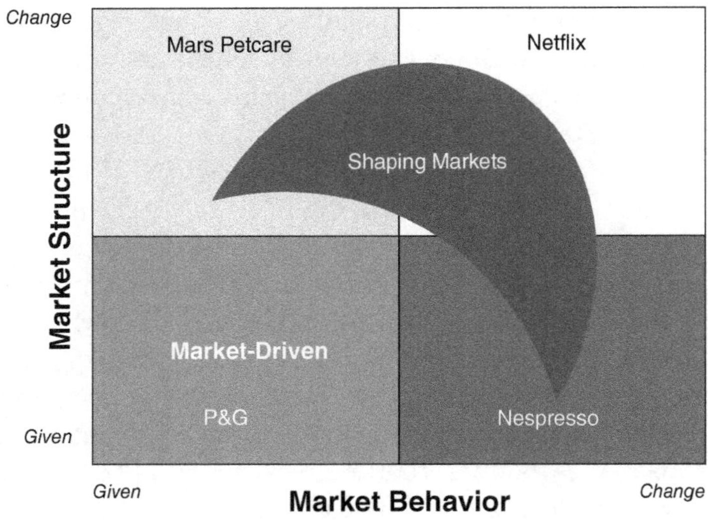

Figure 4.1 Shaping markets.

organization that takes the existing conditions of the marketplace "as is" and competes with those constraints. This represents the "baseline" state of an organization simply attempting to compete against known competitors with existing customer preferences and behaviors. A good example is any consumer packaged goods companies competing for supermarket shelf space. Or Cisco competing with Huawei in the routers and switches market. These are typically well-contested markets with a clear known competitor, and the consumers have stabilized their buying criteria.

The other three quadrants are shaping strategies since they alter the structure and/or behavior of key players. In the upper-left quadrant, we observe an organization that first focuses on changing the industry structure, often with the notion that subsequent behavior of players will change. Any roll-up strategy in an industry is fundamentally a "change the industry" structure play. This could also be a player who wants to offer "the full product line" within an industry. So they acquire various product lines to complete the portfolio.

Within the bottom-right quadrant, the aim is typically to "lead the consumers" into a new set of behavior(s) that change the basis of competition. A good example here is Resmed, which embedded a chip inside of their sleep apnea equipment to allow patients to obtain sleep scores and diagnostics information each morning (e.g., how many apnea episodes, how long did you wear the mask, any technology issues). Physicians also have access to the scores—so, they could have more evidence-based conversations with patients. Distributors saw their labor costs drop by 50 percent—they could do much more remote servicing of equipment. Finally, payers could now observe compliance data and reimburse accordingly.

In the top-right quadrant, both the structure and behaviors of players is shaped. Netflix changed the players in the industry and the behavior of customers (e.g., binge-viewing, reliance on recommendations). Every industry has examples of this shaping behavior. Banking apps (e.g., mobile bill pay, mobile check deposits), payment apps (e.g., Venmo), and navigation apps (e.g., Waze) have all focused on new customer behaviors through technology-enabled services. All electric automobile manufacturers have shaped industry structure (e.g., no gas stations) and the behavior of consumers (e.g., charge the vehicle).

Choice 4: Systematic Abandonment The final choice using the customer and market insight is to abandon products, services, brands, work activities, channels, and other actions that no longer are valued by the marketplace. Our observation is that most organizations do not think of this activity in any systematic way. Firms have organized and structured systems for innovation, but not for abandonment. However, customer insight should be used to inform what products, services, and activities should be discontinued. Firms are often forced to do this by external forces, such as the conversion to designing and selling electric cars by traditional car manufacturers. Since this concept is so important, we elaborate on abandonment in Chapter 10.

As Drucker noted in 1954, "The first step in a growth policy is not to decide where and how to grow. It is to decide what to abandon. In order to grow, a business must have a systematic policy to get rid of the outgrown, the obsolete, the unproductive."[16]

Summary—The Big Idea

It is the speed and effectiveness of the *cycle* of getting intelligence, reaching conclusions, and taking action that is the source of competitive advantage for a customer-centered organization. It is not a one-time event—it is a continuous process, like H&M and Zara do. Firms that can excel in this activity can continually stay ahead of the market and shape not only customer behavior, but competitor behavior as well.

Conclusion

The foundation of customer centricity is evidence-based decisions that are based on the needs, demands, and wants of the organization's target segment(s). Employees need to see the "line of sight" that decisions are not based on management judgement or intuition, but on a rigorous, fact-based understanding of the marketplace and, in particular, the organization's customers. We also introduced a three-phase approach—generate, share, and use customer intelligence. In many situations, organizations collect customer intelligence but do not share nor use it. Organizations need to excel in all three phases to be customer-driven. Finally, it is not a one-time event—the big idea is that organizations need to speed up the cycle of intelligence so that they lead—and not follow—the evolution of their industry.

5

The Customer Choice Cascade: Activating Customer Centricity

"The only thing one can do is to make the future. Through innovation, one can shape markets and their demands."

—Peter Drucker

Introduction

In this chapter, we turn our attention to the process of customer-centric strategy formulation, which we frame as a *choice cascade*. One of the most well-known strategy cascades was developed by Roger Martin during his time at Monitor Group. He used this process to develop strategy in a number of organizations and Monitor deployed the cascade in hundreds of client engagements across the world. The best documentation of this strategy cascade can be found in the co-authored book titled *Playing to Win* with A.G. Lafley, which describes the use of the strategy cascade. In this "Playing to Win" cascade, strategy is developed by making five key choices that are centered on two core themes—where to play and how to win.[1]

While Bernie was at Monitor Group, he deployed the cascade in several successful client engagements. In this chapter, we modify this classic work to put the client at the center of the entire process. We still use the "where to play" and "how to win" language—as it is a simple, powerful, parsimonious way to explain the decisions that an organization makes regarding its market choices. However, we adapt the model in three specific ways to focus on customer centricity:

- First, we start the process with a deep dive into two key customer questions—what do customers value and how does the customer value vary by segments?
- Second, we add a choice related to mutual value creation. The aim here is to point out that in the design of customer-centric strategy, companies need to make sure that both the company and customer win. It is not enough for the organization to drive financial performance; customers must feel that they received sufficient value, and they are very satisfied with the transaction. As a result, they will continue to do business with the organization.
- Third, our last choice in the cascade is future-oriented. It is not enough to compete successfully in the present—organizations need to balance investments in both the present and the future.

As a result of these changes, we introduced a revised five-step choice cascade. The chapter is organized in five sections—reflecting each of the key choices (see Figure 5.1). As shown in Figure 5.1, the first two choices are related to the "where the play" choices and the next three choices are related to "how to win" choices.

The first choice is focused on the selection of a target segment and an understanding of what the segment values. The second choice turns attention to competition. Who is your competition and how are they providing value to the key segments? You cannot compete with everyone, so which set of competition is your priority competitors? The third choice focuses on the choice of the organization's value proposition. This balances customer segment needs, competitor value propositions, and your ability to deliver unique customer value. The aim is to select a value proposition that is defendable over a period of time. The fourth choice is to identify both the profit model of the organization and the type of value that will be delivered to key customers. What do you want the customer to believe and feel about your

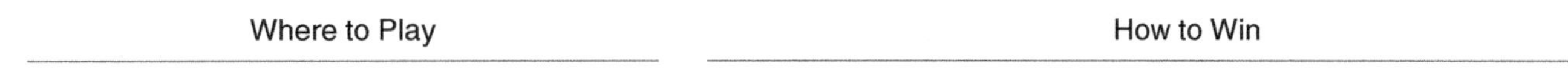
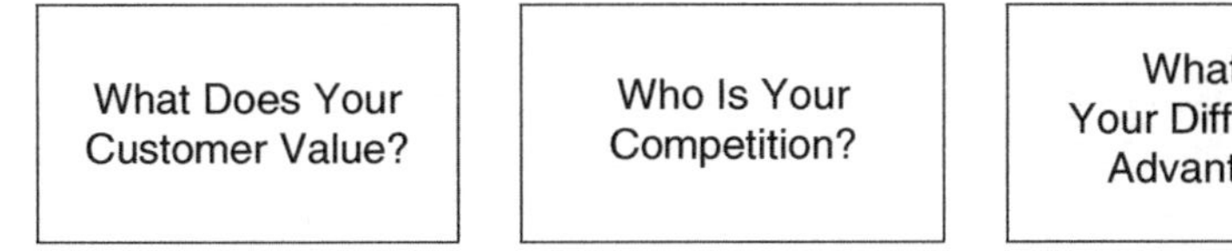

Figure 5.1   Customer centricity choice cascade.

offering? What value did you create for them? The final choice is about the future—who are your customers in the future? How does this segment emerge? How do you allocate sufficient resources to get ready for the future?

Customer Centricity Choice Cascade

Sound strategy is based on choice. Choice enables an organization to focus resources in particular areas where it can gain a sustainable competitive advantage. One of the fundamental flaws in strategy development is to allocate resources across a range of customer segments, customer benefits, and capabilities. The more an organization can focus resources allocation, the greater the likelihood of success.

The customer choice cascade is a five-step process to develop a customer-centric strategy. The cascade is an integrated set of choices that build on one another to create a strategy. Each choice informs the boundary conditions for the next stage. So, for example, if a financial services organization decides to focus on high-net-worth individuals, the type of value propositions it develops and the capabilities that it builds need to "fit" this segment. This is what we mean by integrated set of choices. (This is reflected in the feedback loops in Figure 5.2.)

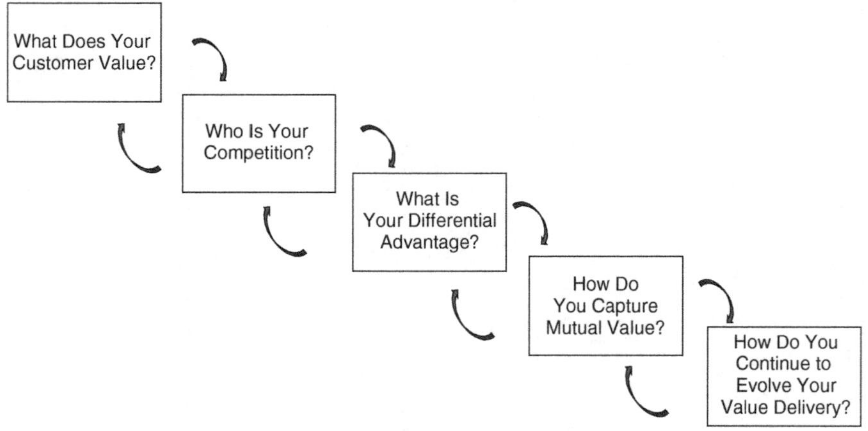

Figure 5.2   Customer centricity choice cascade: feedback loops and inter-relationships.

Often during the process of answering these five questions, companies need to assess and test whether these choices fit together. It has been our experience that companies need to constantly challenge how well the choices reinforce each other. Teams should not be polite at this stage. It is often the clash of opinions that produces the best strategy outcome. Indeed, Michael Porter argues that it is not about a single capability or core competency; rather, the key to strategy is how well the capabilities fit and reinforce one another.[2] We address each choice in turn.[3]

Choice 1: What Does Your Customer Value?

This is the most important step in the process, since it sets up all the other choices to follow. There are two significant decisions at this stage. The first is a decision on the segment and the second is to articulate the specific benefits and experience that is desired by the targeted segment. Most readers are familiar with the basics of segmentation; as such, we focus this discussion on two areas: (1) the rationale for segments and (2) segment choice. We do not discuss the various segmentation approaches (e.g., demographic, benefit-based) since those can be readily found in other sources.[4]

Segmentation Rationale   Market segmentation is the process of dividing the overall market into subgroups of customers who share similar buying behavior and consumption and, as such, will respond in a similar way to a particular marketing mix or program. The goal of segmentation, therefore, is to group customers so that an organization can most efficiently and effectively reach them with a unique marketing mix.

We dissect each of these keywords in more detail since there are subtle nuances in this definition. Consider the automobile rental market. By overall market, we are referring to all customers who are considered potential customers for automobile rental. Importantly, the overall market can be defined broadly (e.g., all customers who have transportation needs regardless of type of transport—walking, public transportation, automotive) or narrowly (only those who actively note that they are rental customers).

Second is the phrase "share similar buyer behavior and consumption." Potential customers can be divided in many different ways (e.g., price-sensitive, convenience, car preference). What matters, however, is whether their buyer behavior—motivations, attitudes, and consumption—is similar. Third, they must respond in a similar way to a particular marketing program (e.g., pricing of a BMW EV, location of the retail establishment, type of media used). Thus, for example, business customers are both similar in buyer behavior and respond the same way to a particular marketing mix (e.g., less price-sensitive, prefer airport location, appreciate range of BMW vehicles, value the frequent user programs).

Recently, it has been argued that segmentation is no longer relevant to marketing.[5] That is, in an era where customers can customize their consumption experience and suppliers can mass-customize offerings, every customer can be treated as a segment of one. While compelling in certain markets, the problem with this viewpoint is that there are both demand-side and supply-side reasons for continuing to practice segmentation. On the demand-side, consumers benefit from being classified as a "target segment" since they will be served in a more efficient and effective way by the organization, as compared to being served as a single consumer. For example, American Airlines provides different services to its executive platinum customers than its gold customers, given their yearly spend on airline travel. This designation makes it very clear the benefits to the executive platinum segment. IKEA, for example, provides its "housing bundle" to new apartment dwellers—including items for living rooms, kitchens, baths, and bedroom. And, as a result of this bundling, the new apartment dweller could receive price discounts for this volume purchase.[6] Hence, customers benefit by being classified as a target segment.

Equally, if not more important, the economics of serving "groups of customers with similar buyer behavior" works much better for the organization as compared to serving every customer uniquely. IKEA's ability to design a marketing program for the new apartment dweller segment is significantly less costly than designing a unique program for each individual customer. Recall in Chapter 2 that both the resource view of the firm and the operational excellence view of strategy are about the designs of operations and resources that are unique and efficient. Both strategy schools emphasize a segment focus. In sum, segmenting and then targeting customers works well for the organization (if done properly, they make more money) and for the customers (they receive the right product/products at a lower cost).

Balancing Multiple Criteria to Select Target Markets Organizations need to carefully consider a few criteria in making this critical choice. In this section, we describe the five most important considerations in the prioritization of segments to target.

Financial Considerations The most important factor is the financial viability of the target segment. Within the segment, what is the unconstrained upside and feasible untapped opportunity? Growth potential? Cost to serve? Organizations often focus on the "lifetime value" of the target segment.[7] Here, they need to factor in the price customers are willing to pay. Thus, a segment may appear to be very promising given the revenue potential, but the cost to serve the segment is prohibitive. For example, Hertz has selected business travelers as their most important segment. Business travelers are less price-sensitive and will pay for various service features (e.g., curb-side drop off). Even though business travelers are willing to pay more, Hertz must structure its operations and pricing strategy to enable them to grow profitably.

Competitive Implications and Reactions Does a focus on the segment improve your overall competitive position? Where will competitor reaction be strongest? Weakest? As you might expect, going head-to-head with similar offerings is very challenging (e.g., Avis vs. Hertz, Hilton vs. Sheraton, BMW vs. Audi). In the best of all worlds, companies should select target segments where competition is either nonexistent or very weak. Often this is difficult to do. Interestingly, Enterprise, as a first mover in the local market, was able to move quickly to establish itself as a provider of local car rental services. For a period of time, they were the only national player who served this market. Yes, there were local car rental agencies and "loaner vehicles" from autobody shops, but they did not have the national brand and advertising reach. Eventually, Hertz developed Hertz Local.

Industry Structure Implications   Does the segment present an opportunity to influence industry structure, giving you a favorable and sustainable competitive position? Enterprise was able to work closely with local repair shops to build a preferred network of membership that constrained Hertz as a second mover. Thus, Enterprise was able to partner with other players in the industry value chain much earlier— and, hence, had their pick of preferred partners. In this way, they were able to shape the industry structure in a way that favored their offering. Zipcar and other auto rental firms that rent hourly are also market disruptors. Recall our discussion of shaping markets in Chapter 4, where we introduced a 2×2 framework to shape markets. One of the axis was to change the industry structure. This is an example of segment choice that sets the context for an organization to shape a market.

Capabilities Implications   Does pursuing the segment allow you to develop or enhance capabilities, which will pay significant dividends beyond this specific opportunity? How well does it fit with your current and potential capabilities? Companies often target the segment that has the most revenue potential, but the problem is that this must be balanced with the organization's assets, resources, and capabilities to serve that segment. The key issue is to match the organization's ability to service customers relative to their needs and wants. Take Sunshine car rental near Los Angeles Airport. Certainly, they want the same target customers as Hertz. However, with no advertising, no shuttle bus, a limited selection of cars, and a location that is hard to find, it is difficult to imagine how they can be competitive. This is an extreme situation, but the basic idea is the same. A company must realistically evaluate its capabilities to serve a segment from the perspective of the target customer.

Step on the Path   Will successful pursuit of the opportunity open the door to additional opportunities? Is a potential sequence clear? Are there "spillover" benefits to other segments? Selecting the first segment to target in a product launch is a bit like a chess game. Given the first move, how likely is the competition to respond? What then is your next move? Oftentimes companies will run a war gaming exercise to consider how to target segments and establish a preferred sequencing of target market entry. Importantly, establishing credibility in certain segments enables a company to "earn the right" to target additional segments. For example, the German automotive market is a very finicky and difficult-to-serve segment. They have exacting standards and quality control. A company that is a long-time auto parts supplier to BMW, Mercedes-Benz, and Audi, all else equal would have an easier time gaining access to other geographic markets.

In sum, after balancing all of these criteria, an organization must make a decision to focus on segments where it can win versus against the competition. This is a balancing act if thinking deeply about segment needs, the strategy of competition, and the organization's unique resources in the segment. Once this decision is made, the organization need to turn its attention to a more comprehensive mapping of what their target customer values.

What Does Your Target Segment Value?   After the selection of the target segment, the organization must immerse itself in the life of the customer by collecting market intelligence. This certainly could involve co-creation activities with customers. Indeed, the ability to experiment, test, and pilot "concepts" with customers enables the organization to learn what works and what doesn't. In the next chapter, we introduce a customer behavior framework. It is at this stage in the customer choice cascade that companies apply customer insights to understanding the needs and wants of key target markets.

Illustrative Case Study: Resmed   In this chapter, we illustrate the customer centricity choice cascade with a company that we know deeply and one that is a great illustration of the decisions required to become customer centered. The example case study (which we will illustrate with each of the choices) involves the company Resmed. Resmed's target segment is patients who suffer from sleep apnea, insomnia, or respiratory insufficiency. Their key product platform that addresses sleep apnea is a continuous positive airway pressure (or CPAP) device that forms a pneumatic splint in the upper airway enabling natural breathing and (importantly!) natural sleep during the night. The prevention of *apnea* (i.e., sleep suffocation) episodes is critical to avoid hypoxia and poor sleep quality. Regarding choice 1, their target customers value a small, quiet, comfortable, connected, intelligent, and easy-to-use system that gives them the gift of breath and the gift of sleep. With its cloud-connectivity and intelligent algorithms, their patient-customers value "real-time" sleep scores from an app called myAir when they awaken each morning. Their physician-customers and provider-customers value the lower cost of care provision and better outcomes that come from the digital engagement of their hardware and software solutions imbedded into their clinical care pathway.

Choice 2: Who Is Your Competition?

Once you have identified the most important benefits that customers value most in choice 1, these benefits must be mapped against the key competitor's ability to deliver the value. This second choice forces companies to be "market-oriented"—focused not just on customers but also competitors. History has shown that companies can be very customer focused and still be outmaneuvered by the competition (e.g., Circuit City and Best Buy).[8] This is a two-stage process. First, you need to identify your competition. Next, you need to evaluate how they provide value to your target customers.

Who Are Your Competitors?   This seemingly straightforward question is actually quite complex—and has been studied by business school academics for decades. Fortunately, George Day and colleagues have provided a very straightforward approach to identifying a potential competitive set.[9] The two approaches—top-down and bottom-up— are complementary and often used in tandem to understand the market structure and competitive set one is facing. The top-down approach uses supply-side factors such as raw materials, production systems, and scale economies to identify competition. Frequently this approach uses SIC codes to classify competitor firms. For Ruffles potato chips, as an example, the competitive set would be packaged goods manufacturers that produce similar snack foods. Put concretely, these chips would be found in the same supermarket shelf location as Ruffles. These would include Lays and Cape Cod chips.

The bottom-up approach, in contrast, uses judgmental or behavioral data from customers. This data can be used to identify market boundaries to reveal fine-grained market structures. The best-known approaches are behavioral methods based on cross-elasticities and brand switching data. Judgment data may also be used; namely, perceptions of brands versus other brands. Finally, Day and his colleagues also have used "substitution in use" to understand the acceptability of products for various usage situations—to understand the competitive market structure. So, for example, companies can ask customers questions like: "Which appetizers/snacks do you serve when (1) you are home alone, (2) you are having a party with friends, (3) you invite your in-laws over for the Super Bowl?"

Consider for example, a very open-ended question on consumption of beverages: "What beverages do you consume for breakfast or when you go to parties with friends?" In some situations, you may be making a choice within a product category (e.g., tomato or orange juice) where in other situations you may be across product categories (e.g., Coca-Cola or Budweiser at a party). The competitive set can even be broader when you look at these substitution patterns—for example, if you have discretionary income on Friday night, the choices might be to go to a movie, go to a party, stay at home, or go to a restaurant. Here the competitors for your dollar are quite broad.

In sum, the key point of this discussion is to make a choice of where to focus resources and attention. For example, consider Costco. Costco could focus their attention on Walmart and Target, since these three companies are the largest discount retailers in the United State. At the same time, Costco also faces competition from national warehouse clubs like Sam's and BJ's and regional players like Smart and Final. Amazon also offers similar products and has convenient delivery options. Since Costco also has a significant online presence, Amazon provides a number of challenges—particularly as related to same day delivery.

How Does the Competition Provide Value?   Once you identify your two or three most important target competitors, you then need to craft a plan to "outcompete" with them for the same customers. Here you need to do a deep dive into two areas. The first is to understand the customer value proposition. Since we provide a detailed description of the construction of a customer value proposition in choice 3, we simply want to highlight here that you also need to articulate the competition's value proposition to the *same* customers. In particular, you should be specifically concerned with the key benefits these value propositions deliver to these customers and the "activity system" they deploy to deliver those benefits.[10]

The second area of focus should be on the resources, assets, activities, and operations that an organization uses to meet customer needs. While there are many tools to analyze competition we prefer to use the Porter activity systems approach.[11] Figure 5.3 shows such an activity system for Costco. The key to any healthy activity system is that some parts of the system are unique. Ideally, all capabilities are unique, but that is a rare situation. Second, for each capability there needs to be direct line of sight to the customer benefits that they provide.[12] So, for example, the limited product selection of Costco provides exceptionally competitive price points. Third, it is not about any one capability—it is the system of capabilities. Here, we leverage Porter's thinking that it is not about one "core" competency. Rather, building linkages, synergies, and consistency in the activity system is the source of competitive advantage.

For Costco, let's now consider the five capabilities that provide a source of competitive advantage. Considering first, supply chain management, they have developed strong supplier relationships to negotiate favorable deals. They have also optimized the flow of goods from suppliers to the warehouse and stores. They have implemented state-of-the-art inventory management systems to minimize holding costs. Second, they have enormous economies of scale. Their large-scale operations and bulk purchasing power allow them to negotiate lower prices with suppliers. Third, they are operationally efficient and operate their large-format warehouses with a limited product selection. Costco has implemented standardized operating procedures, point-of-sale systems, and inventory management software. They have completed their in-store efficiencies with online e-commerce capabilities. Fourth, they have limited SKUs. This has enabled them to focus on high-volume, high-margin items. Finally, their membership model generates recurring revenue. When was the last time you saw a Costco advertisement? Costco's promotional activities are another efficiency with the firm relying more on word-of-mouth marketing and customer

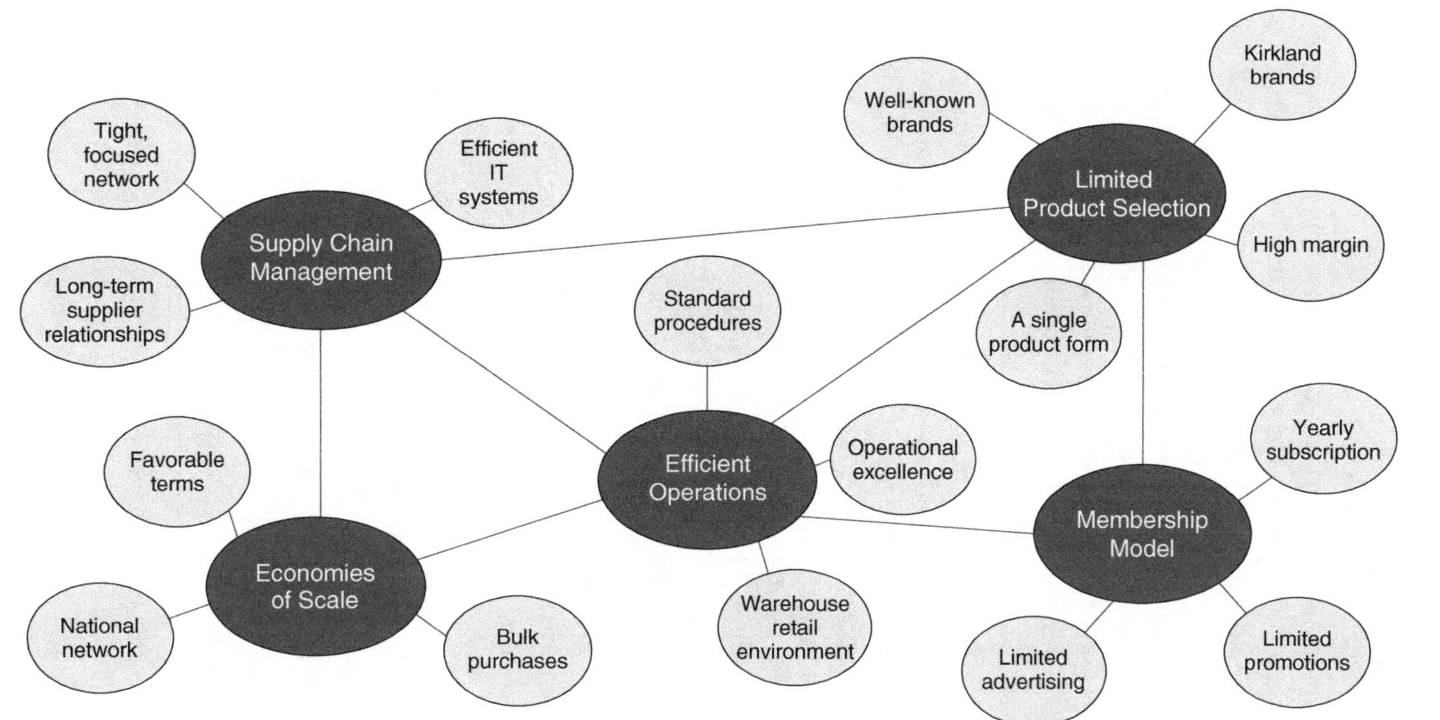

Figure 5.3   Costco activity system.

loyalty programs. Hence, they focus on building strong customer relationships through value and convenience.

The aim in articulating the competitor value proposition and activity system is to understand their competitive advantage at a point in time and predict the likely moves that the competition will make in the future. This requires that companies also attempt to identify their goals for the future. If they can identify their goals, their capabilities, and value proposition, they can have a strong working hypothesis about likely moves in the future. In our next choice, we turn our attention to the organization's value proposition and its profit model.

Illustrative Case Study: Resmed   Returning to the case study example, Resmed's key competitors are traditional players like Philips Respronics. Most notably, this is a true head-to-head competitor, with a similar value proposition. However, Respronics has had several product recall challenges with the FDA, so they have lost significant market share. The key for Resmed's is to continually innovate—to push forward and shape the market. Resmed is currently tracking 1.6 million people with GLP-1 prescriptions (Ozempic, Zepbound, etc) and these patients when also being diagnosed with sleep apnea receive a prescription for CPAP. They are 11% more likely to start CPAP versus patients without a GLP-1 prescription. In other words, GLP-1s will provide demand generation for Resmed. By bringing in more new patients and, as it it turns out, more motivated patients into the funnel for Resmed. Resmed tracked these patients at 1-year and 2-years post CPAP prescription and they also show higher adherence and resupply rates than patients without a GLP-1 prescription.

Choice 3: What Is Your Differentiation Advantage?

By this stage, you'll have a very deep—and ideally unique—understanding of your target customer and what they value. You'll also know the value proposition of competition, their activity/capability system, and their likely moves in the future. You can now articulate your customer value proposition *relative* to competition.

Keep in mind that the key source of competitive advantage is the uniqueness of your understanding versus competition. If you have the same knowledge as your competitors, it is difficult to gain competitive advantage. We often use the phrase "differentiated insight provides differentiated offerings." What do you know—that others don't know—that you can activate in the marketplace to your advantage?

In this section, we turn our attention to four decisions: (1) the construction of the value proposition, (2) a consideration of factors that make the value proposition more or less sustainable, (3) the articulation of the capability system (with reference to competition), and (4) the underlying profit model (i.e., how do you make money?).

Constructing a Value Proposition A value proposition specifies four choices: (1) the target segment, (2) the most important benefits that you want to establish in the minds of target customers, (3) the competitive set that you are attempting to outperform in the marketplace, and (4) the reasons that the target customers believe that you can deliver the benefits better than the specified competition. This section reviews each of these four parts in more detail (see Figure 5.4 for an IN-N-OUT Burger illustration of these ideas).

Target Segment

   o Young men, 18–25 with incomes less than 70,000*
- **Core IN-N-OUT Benefit(s)**
   o Taste (i.e., "quality you can taste")
- **UNLIKE. . .**
   o Five Guys
- **Reasons to Believe**
   o Fresh, never frozen ingredients
   o Narrow product range (vs. hot dogs, grilled cheese)
   o Drive through (vs. sit-down only)
   o Company-owned, tightly controlled 200 stores in core western states (vs. almost 800 franchised stores, nation-wide)
   o A cult-like fan base with an off-menu language system
   o A simple communications theme—"quality you can taste"

***Note: *They have* intensely loyal customers at all ages. However, this segment has been noted as one of the core target segments.**

Figure 5.4   IN-N-OUT Burger value proposition.

Target Segment   Since we covered segmentation and target market section earlier in the chapter, there is no need to review these concepts here. That stated, the key point to stress is that target market selection is based on all the careful analysis we noted previously. Frequently, it takes months to conduct the research to "find" an underserved, new segment or "classify the market differently." So, while the principle of target market selection is simple, the work needed to support the analysis is often time-consuming and complex.

As noted earlier, one of the most important sources of competitive advantage is segmentation. If an organization is able to understand and classify segments differently—because they know company market so well—it is a more sustainable source of advantage than even a differentiated value proposition. For IN-N-OUT Burger, there is no evidence that they have found a unique segment or have targeted segments differently than other fast-food burger restaurants. Thus, young adults and families with small children tend to be the focal segments. That said, IN-N-OUT is unique in that their focus has largely been Southern California and the Western States.

Another example relates to the nonprofit, World Central Kitchen, founded by Chef José Andrés, that responds to disasters by delivering fresh, locally sourced, and (importantly) culturally appropriate meals to communities impacted by a disaster. Instead of distributing "generic relief," the organization adjusts food content to meet the needs of different beneficiaries during crisis. As Andrés explains, "We don't just dump free food into a disaster zone: we source and hire locally wherever we can, to jump-start economic recovery through food."[13] Such a culturally responsive approach to segmentation is clear differentiation for the kitchen in the humanitarian space.

In Figure 5.4, we focus the value proposition on 18–25-year-old men with incomes less than $70,000.[14]

Customer Benefits   A benefit solves a particular customer problem or improves their life in some way. Benefits tend not to be historically dependent and can last for years if not decades. Features, on the other hand, tend to change often depending on the product category. Thus, we strongly recommend that companies develop a value proposition at the benefit-level—not at the feature-level.

Turning to IN-N-OUT Burger, there are seven key benefits. The first is convenience. Convenience in this context relates to accessibility and speed of service (either at the counter or at the drive-through). Fast-food restaurants tend to be more affordable than traditional sit-down restaurants and IN-N-OUT Burger is no different. Consistency is the level of reliability of the dining experience. Can the consumer expect the same service, food, and environment each time they visit? Taste is the consumer assessment of the quality of the meal—burgers, fries, and milk shakes. The breadth of menu relates to the range of menu items, from burgers, salads, chicken, soups, and other items. Customization is the ability to modify the standard menu items to fit individual tastes. The last benefit is unique to "cult-like" brands who nurture an emotional fan base that supports the brand experience. There is a business school case study on Real Madrid where the general manager notes that it is easier to change spouses or political parties than it is to change one's commitment to a football club.[15] It is similar for the IN-N-OUT Burger segment—they are deeply loyal and committed to the brand. This fan base is a customer benefit, since they are able to share their IN-N-OUT experience directly or on social media with other fans.

Relative to Competition　Once a company has identified the top benefits that customers value most, they must be compared to competition. IN-N-OUT may claim they have the best taste, but do customers believe that they have the best taste relative to the competition? Since all choice is "relative to an alternative"—you must carefully analyze if your offering is truly outperforming competition in the eyes of customers and on the benefits that matter most to them. Here the right approach is to ask IN-N-OUT customers who the competition is. There may be some surprises here, since IN-N-OUT customers are so loyal to the burger chain, their fast-food competitor may be a different product category such as Mexican food.

Reasons to Believe　It is often the case that organizations (1) target the same customers and (2) "propose" to offer the same benefits. Both IN-N-OUT and Five Guys target "fast-food consumers" with the proposition that they offer the "best taste." So, who do target customers believe? The answer is that customers believe those organizations

(1) whose product features are superior to competition *and/or* (2) whose activity system—capabilities, resources, assets, or skills set—are better equipped to deliver the value proposition benefits.

Let's consider first the feature set. Earlier we noted that benefits are different than features. Features provide one of the "reasons to believe" that your benefits are better than competition. For IN-N-OUT Burger, there are several features that support the "best taste position." These include never frozen ingredients, a very limited range of burgers, fries, and shakes (vs. hot dogs, grilled cheese, and so on), and the ability to order in the restaurant or drive-through. Indeed, to be clear, every benefit has a set of features that support the benefit—we have simply isolated features that are distinctive.

A second way to support the idea that you can beat competition on particular benefits is through the leveraging of your capabilities, assets, or skills. However, it is not simply enough for the capabilities to provide a particular benefit. These capabilities—or reasons to believe—must be better than the competition. Lots of airlines can say they have reliable, frequent departures, but which competitors have the best activity system to deliver this benefit? IN-N-OUT Burger has some very distinctive elements of its activity system— most notably, the tightly controlled, family ownership versus a

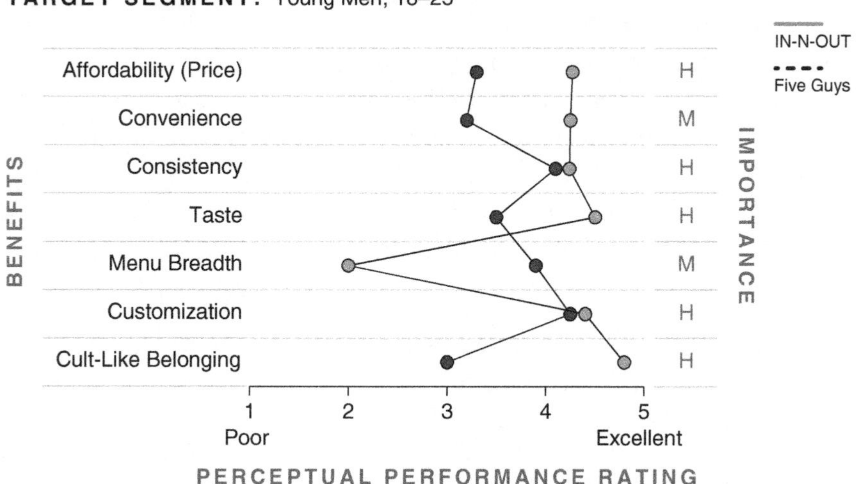

Figure 5.5   Benefit comparison map of IN-N-OUT versus Five Guys.

typical franchise model of Five Guys. The laser-focused, narrow menu selection and highly trained and loyal employees are also unique to IN-N-OUT.

Figure 5.5 shows a benefit comparison of IN-N-OUT to Five Guys. This chart represents target customer perceptions of a product versus competitor offerings. There are several key aspects of this "snakeplot." First, focus on customer benefits, not product features. Second, it is not about an objective assessment of each benefit. It is the target market's *perception* of the benefit versus competition. A fast-food restaurant may believe it has the best tasting burgers, but it is the target market who decides. Third, it is not just about perceptions, it is also about importance weights. So, on the far right of the chart, you can see "high, medium, and low" importance weights. The notion here is each benefit is evaluated by the target market with respect to its importance in making the buying decision. So, a given company may have the "best prices" for burgers, but if that does not matter to the target market, then it is largely irrelevant.

With this in mind, the snakeplot reveals that IN-N-OUT Burger is perceived by their target market as better than Five Guys on pricing, taste, convenience, and the cult-like brand experience. All four of these benefits have been weighted as "high" in importance to this segment. So, the question is which benefit should the company select to build value proposition? We have a few suggestions here. First, you should focus on one or two benefits. Otherwise, the message becomes diluted. Second, you have to consider importance weights. Focus attention on the benefits that are most important to the target segment. Third, you must select a benefit that you can accelerate and manage over a period of several years. Value propositions need to last years, not months. Fourth, roll the rock downhill, not uphill. Take what your consumers believe to be true for you and run with it. In the end, IN-N-OUT Burger decided that taste was their most important benefit, so the value proposition is Figure 5.5 illustrates their choice.

How Sustainable Is Your Value Proposition? Assuming the company is successful in attaining a unique position in the mind of its target customers, what are the key threats to sustaining the position?

This section notes four main challenges in sustaining a position in the market.

- *Evolving customer tastes.* Even though a company is able to secure a favorable position in the minds of target customers at one point in history, customer tastes and preferences constantly evolve. While it is easy to observe fashion fads and trends, we see evolving tastes in conventional B2B business. The past several years have seen a significant trend to solutions and, in particular, digitally enhanced solutions.
- *Changing competitive dynamics.* Moves by existing and new competitors can also shift the nature of the position. Over the past few years, Amazon has made aggressive moves into the healthcare space, with online and physical locations for Amazon "One medical, pay-per-visit." It has also made a bet on a one-day Amazon pharmacy delivery service. Both of these moves have the potential to shake up healthcare and pharmacy-based providers such as CVS.
- *Unique company capabilities erode.* Recall the discussion of "reasons to believe." These reasons to believe were based either on feature superiority or on the unique assets/resources of the organization. Companies must continually advance their capability set, given changes in customer needs and demands. Costco has invested very heavily in e-commerce capabilities, and, as a result, increased their e-commerce business by 40 percent in the 2024 calendar year.[16]
- *Ecosystem partners evolution.* Increasingly we are seeing the evolution of organization strategy to be "ecosystem" plays—they involve many different partnerships to deliver their value proposition. Habitat for Humanity takes such a systemic approach to create value through its "sweat equity" model, where future homeowners participate in building their own homes alongside volunteers and the organization. As one homeowner described it: "I'm actually building my own house. Putting my own heart, working with my own hands, the sweat, blood, everything into it."[17] Another example can be found in the highly competitive coffee capsule market where a number of partnerships have emerged, such as between Nespresso and Starbucks that has leveraged the Nestle retail channel. That stated, these partnerships often change with new players entering (e.g., Dunkin pods) and

existing players exiting. Companies need to articulate the industry evolution in order to place the right bets on the stakeholder of the future—not of the past.

What Is Your Activity System?   We have covered the activity system concept in choice two, so we do not need to discuss it here. However, our key message is that if you were going to craft the IN-N-OUT Burger activity system, you need to be forward-thinking. That is, to articulate the activity system that is in play today and to map out the activity system you need to compete in the future.

What Is Your Profit Model?   The final decision in choice 3 relates to the articulation of the organization's profit model. Simply put, the profit model answers the question: "How does the organization make money with its value proposition?" The answer to this question should be a very "naming" of the profit model and the articulation of the three to four key success factors for this profit model. Several authors, such as Adrian Slywotsky, have identified general "profit models" and the underlying economics of those profit models.[18] Here, we describe two profit models—but there are numerous options.

- **Industry standard profit model.** Within the technology sector, organizations often attempt to be the "standard" offering in a particular market. The term standard is often based on technology standards (e.g., "Bluetooth" is a particular standard) that are established by standards boards. The idea is to have the biggest market share of brands that are competing to be the standard. The key success factors for this industry standard profit model include (1) rapidly accelerating of market share to become the standard, (2) locking in customers so the perceived cost of switching to a new product is exceptionally high, and (3) holding positions on the right standards boards, so that regulatory policy can be managed.
- **Pyramid profit model.** A pyramid profit model is based on the logic that an organization needs to establish a core offering (the base of the pyramid) that will enable it to "earn disproportionate profit" on other products that build on the scale base of the

initial product. Consider the basic American Express card. Certainly, profit is attained in the core segment of American Express users. However, even more profit margin is attained for customers who carry the Platinum card or the Black card (which requires a $5,000/year membership fee).

Case Illustration: Resmed   We noted the Resmed value proposition earlier—it is a solution that addresses the sleep apnea condition while simultaneously providing real-time data to all players in the healthcare ecosystem, including their target patients. Resmed has an activity system that rests on several key capabilities—quality of ventilation equipment (i.e., reliable, quiet, small), lightweight, comfortable, and easy-to-wear masks, digital monitoring for sleep apnea, and "connectedness" of this digital data to all key stakeholders in the healthcare ecosystem. This activity system is superior to Respronics and provides value to all key stakeholder groups. Their profit model can be described as one based on loyalty and compliance. If patients experience the benefits of the treatment, they will stay loyal and comply with the treatment regimen. This is a win-win for all ecosystem players.

Choice 4: How Do You Create Mutual Value?

While the aim of a customer-centric strategy is to increase customer satisfaction, advocacy, and loyalty to the organization, the organization must also benefit from this effort. The previous section introduced the concept of organization profit models as one concrete way that the organization benefits. Our key message is that it must be a win-win for both parties; otherwise, the relationship will not last.

Consider the circumstance where the customer benefits, but the organization does not. There are two situations where we have seen this occur. First is when organizations over-deliver to their largest or "best" customers. In the world of professional service organizations, there are situations where the largest customers are not the most profitable customers. The reason is that the organization often "over-delivers" to these clients. Scope creep of project work, imprecise pricing, adding senior partners to the project team—these can all drive up the cost of service and impact margins. A second situation is when a startup company "gives away" all of the created value to the customer. The thinking behind this strategy is that in the short run, they lose money, but over the long run the large customer base can be monetized. This works sometimes (e.g., Amazon), but often it does not work.

At the same time, we have also observed situations where the organization benefits at the expense of the customer. A classic situation is when an airline charges for flight changes. This is an example of a situation where the customer is penalized for very questionable reasons. Indeed, it is often their best customers—the heavy business traveler—who pay these fees. From our perspective, this is an example of bad profit. It is also notable that when some airlines charge and others, such as Southwest, do not, the customer frustration is even higher.

While these two stakeholders must both benefit from the exchange, we are observing more complex buying situations where there is an ecosystem of players involved in the exchange. Again, it is the same principle—all players must win for the relationships to endure. Again consider Resmed, the dominant player in the sleep apnea market. After launching their AirSense 10 offering several years ago, the organization carefully considered the benefits of all stakeholders. The patient woke up each morning with a sleep score that reported key indicators of their sleep, such as the amount of time that they correctly used the ventilator mask, the number of apnea episodes, and the overall performance of the equipment. Physicians were able to discuss the sleep scores with the patients, the distributors were able to reduce their costs by up to 50 percent since they did less in-person customer service, and the insurance companies were able to track compliance with the therapy. In short, it was a win-win-win-win.

In sum, mutual value is the careful consideration of the design of exchange so that both the company and the target segment win. The central tenet is that relationships endure when both parties feel that the "give/get" assessment is equally balanced. If one party believes they are putting more into the exchange then they are getting out, they will end the relationship.

Illustrative Case Study: Resmed In our case study example, all stakeholders win. Resmed is highly profitable. Customers have an excellent experience that solves their sleep apnea condition. Insurance companies can see compliance data. Physicians get best information on use. Distributors reduce labor costs.

Choice 5: How Do You Continue to Evolve Your Value Delivery and Capture?

One of Drucker's key strategy principles is the need for organizations to balance continuity and change. His observation was that organizations do not spend enough time thinking through the business of the future. Indeed, Clayton Christensen's work on the innovator's dilemma is a classic story of how very successful incumbent players often have difficulty getting to the future because the legacy business is constantly pulling them to compete "the same way." Thus, they are overcommitted to continuity and do not allocate resources to adapt and change.[19]

Nespresso's recent challenges in "missing" the youth market is an example of how focusing on current customers often is the wrong approach to migrate to the future. Nespresso's core customers are 45 to 65 years old and value in-home coffee consumption as part of their regular routine.[20] In sharp contrast, the 20–30-year-old segment has shifted their caffeine experience to largely out-of-home coffee shops or on-the-go consumption. Furthermore, their caffeine beverage is often a "milk"-based drink (e.g., latte, Frappuccino) or a canned beverage (e.g., Monster drinks)—a situation that does not serve Nespresso's core competencies in high-quality, at-home making of traditional coffee drinks.

Drucker's message is that 20 percent of the senior executives' time—and a budget that remains stable even in difficult times—are key levers to help get to the future. Indeed, he often uses the phrase "abandon the past in favor of the future" (a topic we dig into in Chapter 10). That said, we recognize that the vast majority of organizations allocate most of their time to running the business and "hitting" quarterly targets. Drucker's solution is to allocate a separate unit to figure out the future set of customers. Indeed, he further notes that this activity should be carried out by the "next generation of leaders" rather than the current C-suite. His argument is that it is the next generation of leaders who will be running the business of the future—so, let them establish the go-forward strategy.

While it is impossible to predict the future, we can make a few observations for organizations that are looking to identify your customers of the future.

- **First, be curious, open-minded, and interested in how customers are evolving in your market.** Customers constantly evolve—the market is never static. Thus, the challenge is not to be locked into the mental model of how, why, and where customers buy. Here the search for anomalies, outliers, or seemingly irrational behaviors that represent "early indicators" is an approach we advocate.

- **Second, constantly test the strongly held assumptions that "everyone believes" to be true about your customers.** Let's return to the burger example. It is interesting to note that Five Guys does not have a drive-through, and it is often in urban locations that require walking to the restaurant or finding parking nearby. There are no parking lots. The core assumption of Burger King and McDonalds is that parking and drive-through windows are desired by fast-food customers. However, Five Guys challenges that underlying logic.

- **Third, constantly ask a modified version of Drucker's key question, "if we were going to start the business all over again today, who are the most attractive customers to target?"** The thinking behind this question is to be "unconstrained" by your current customers, activity system, and profit model. This would be an interesting question for Nespresso, or any capsule-based, single-serving coffee maker. Would Nespresso target 45–65-year-olds, or would they target the 18–30-year-old consumer? And, if they did, what type of coffee experience would they offer?

- **Fourth, look for the future that is already here, but unevenly distributed.** More than 20 years ago, Netflix saw the steep growth rate of streaming users. This was back when these users were less than 1 percent of the market. Netflix knew it was simply a matter of time when streaming would overtake DVDs.[21]

Illustrative Case Study: Resmed   Returning to the case study example, the key challenge for Resmed moving forward will be from new-to-market competitors such as Zepbound. As of this book's publication date, Resmed is on record as noting that they believe this is good news for the market and that the combination of drugs and their equipment may be the best solution for a segment of the market. Importantly, the questions noted in the next section should guide Resmed thinking about actions to take as this competitive dynamic unfolds (see Figure 5.6 for an integrated summary).

How Can Your Organization Adapt?

Even if an organization is fortunate to identify and understand the customers of the future, it does not guarantee the company will be able to migrate the business to meet these needs. The most important message we can deliver is that this will not happen without considerable time, effort, and resources. Organizations simply do not get lucky and migrate the future. The following list describes five best practices that enable the organization to transition to the future:

- **First, create the vision of the future and its associated business case.** You have to articulate what the world will look like in five to seven years, what your organization needs to do to be successful in that environment, and craft the business case for change. We term the articulation of the future a "point of view." A point of view isolates the five to six most important trends shaping the future of the industry. This is a prerequisite for the vision. These trends need to be precise, choiceful, and evidence based. Anyone can articulate 100 trends—the key is to isolate the five to six most important ones. Next, the C-team needs to create the vision of what the organization will look like in five to seven years. What does the customer value? What capabilities need to be built? Where will value be created for the organization and its customers? Finally, the organization needs to see at least a ball-park revenue model for the organization. In short, the economics need to be clear to everyone why this vision is the right one for the organization.
- **Second, make this visible and communicate how the future customer will be learning, buying, and using your future offerings.** The employees need to buy into the idea that their target consumer will be changing, and if they continue on the same path they will lose to competition. The key for the C-level team

What Does the Customer Value?	Who Is the Competition?	What Is the Differential Advantage?	How Do You Capture Mutual Value?	How Do You Continue to Evolve Value Delivery?
Who are the customers? *What do they value?*	*Who are the competitors?* *What is their value proposition?* *What is their activity system to provide value?*	*What is the value proposition?* *How sustainable is the advantage?* *What is the activity system to provide the value?* *What is the profit model?*	*How do customers and the firm benefit?* *How do you create win-win-win for all stakeholders in the ecosystem?*	*How do you find the "customers of the future?"* *How does the firm adapt to fit this evolving customer value?*
Patients with mild to severe sleep apnea. Patients value quiet ventilators, easy-to-wear masks, and accurate monitoring of breathing to enable them to overcome their sleep apnea condition.	Traditional players like Respronics. Respronics offers similar value proposition. Activity system similar—but not as high quality on several competencies Newer, nontraditional weight loss drugs that also address sleep apnea condition (i.e., Zepbound).	Resmed has similar value proposition to Respronics—but continually innovates with digital technology. Hence, it has gained market share and has a stronger activity system—particularly in software. Zepbound passed FDA test in Dec 2024. Different activity system. Profit model based on customer loyalty and compliance to use.	All stakeholders win. Resmed is highly profitable. Customers have excellent experience that solves sleep apnea condition. Insurance firms can see compliance data. Physicians get best information on use. Distributors reduce labor costs.	The key challenge for Resmed will likely be the new competition from weight loss drugs like Zepbound. Do they partner with Zepbound—rather than compete directly? This will be key challenge over next few years for Resmed.

Figure 5.6   Customer centricity choice cascade with Resmed case study.

is to articulate their viewpoint on what the target consumer of the future will care about, experience, and consume. One starting point to craft this customer of the future viewpoint is to carefully consider implications for your organization based on the framework described in Chapter 4.

- **Third, allocate resources to this future initiative.** The future does not happen randomly. The organization first must allocate sustained resources—budget, people, and time. There must be incentives set up to encourage the team to test, explore, and pilot offerings that represent the future.

- **Fourth, put some of your best talent on this initiative.** One specific resource that signals the organization's commitment to the future is talent. If employees can observe that some of the best talent in the organization is working on future initiatives, it reinforces the key communication message that this is a significant strategic investment.

Mutual value is the careful consideration of the design of exchange so that both the organization and the target segment win. The central tenet is that relationships endure when both parties feel that the give/get assessment is equally balanced. If one party believes they are putting more into the exchange then they are getting out, they will end the relationship.

- **Fifth, provide a different set of performance metrics that focus on "successful" pilots and short-term wins.** This is a pivot game not a "get it right" the first-time game. The organization needs different metrics about profit, experimentation, and learning. Are the iterations of the offering receiving more positive feedback as the organization continues to pilot? What are the right tests to run to "prove the concept"—both from the customer's and organization's perspective?

Conclusion

The aim of this chapter was to introduce the customer choice cascade. These five choices form the basis of a customer-focused strategy. As noted at several points, these choices need to be integrated and "fit together" into a coherent story. Our experience is that the process is iterative—often going back-and-forth between the five steps. That is typical since each choice needs to be aligned. In the end, the strategy must be clear, concise, and easy to tell. It must be "tested" with employees—to see if it passes these three criteria. In the end, the strategy will be valuable only if the employees "get it" and know how their role supports the strategy.

6

Customer Behavior Framework

"Consumers, by definition, include us all."

—John F. Kennedy (1962)[1]

Introduction

In March of 1962, President John F. Kennedy spoke to Congress about the increasing need for the government to intervene and protect consumers from unsafe products, inadequate information, and misleading practices. He began his remarks with the quote opening this chapter—namely, that we are all consumers. Think about your own household consumption and that of your friends and family (whether it be a trip to the mall or delivery of a box from Amazon); it is easy to see why we are a consumption-based economy. These experiences that each of us can identify with illustrate why corporate strategy should be anchored in the customer and not the actions of competitive companies.

Ever since the dawn of the industrial revolution, the customer has had an indelible impact on our world, not only in terms of the economy (as detailed earlier), but in so many other ways. Take, for example, the amount of waste created by end-user consumption. According to the EPA, most municipal solid waste in the United States is driven by individual consumers. As of 2018, it is estimated that approximately five pounds of waste is created daily per person in the United States alone. While progress has been made in terms of recycling, energy recovery, and composting, most of our trash still goes into municipal solid waste streams for disposal.[2] Such a situation is not surprising, given that each of the 8+ billion inhabitants on Earth consumes various foods, products, and services on a daily basis.

Of course, there is more to the buying process than the consumer or end-user. There are many organizations and people that facilitate an exchange between producers (or service providers) and consumers of a product or service—such entities are often referred to as customers. Thus, academics in the field typically view the consumer as the end-user, while the customer is considered the person who buys the product or service. In many instances these are the same person (e.g., a person can be a customer of Costco's roasted chickens and also a consumer who eats the food), but in other instances they differ (e.g., a nonprofit customer who buys the same chicken and serves it to homeless clients).

In this chapter, we explore both customers and consumers in terms of why they do what they do—processes that are critical for organizations to set a customer-centric strategy. We frame this chapter (as seen in Figure 6.1) as how customers experience a journey with an organization, along with considering internal factors of customers; environmental, social, and cultural influences; and how ultimately customers behave.

A Rich Tradition, Absent of Strategy

The study of consumers has had a long and rich history since the industrial revolution. As captured by James's observation regarding the role of products in how we view ourselves, academics and scholars have often considered why customers behave as they do.[3] The importance of the consumer did not escape the attention of turn-of-the-century businesses that considered customer insights when developing strategy. For example, N. W. Ayer and Son in 1879 conducted one of the earliest documented cases of marketing research to set business strategy. The company (which shuttered its doors in 2002) used the telegraph to create a "crude but formal" market study of grain production for its client, the Nichols-Shepard Company.[4]

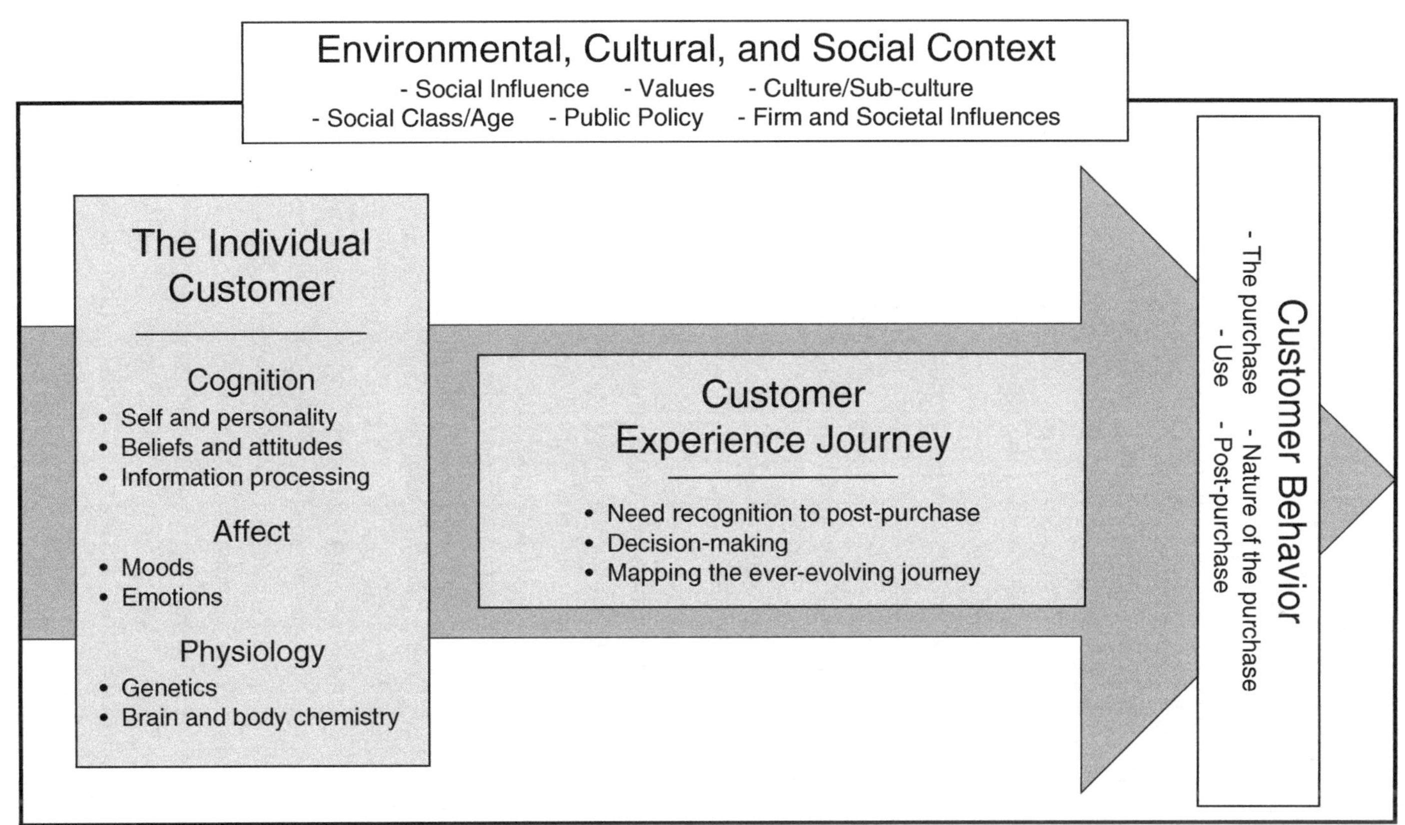

Figure 6.1 The customer experience journey.

Over the last approximately 75 years, research by academics and practitioners has offered deep insights into how consumers feel, think, and behave. As anyone who has attended a business school in the last seven decades can attest, there is nothing better than a good theory for many PhD-qualified faculty members. It may come as a surprise to some, but this has not always been the case.

In the early 20th century, business schools were much more practically oriented, including teaching skills such as typing and stenography. Business schools were catapulted into being an academic pursuit after the publication of two scathing reports from Ford and Carnegie institutions regarding the state of business education in the mid-20th century.[5] The impact of this change toward an academic view of business was also felt in the field of consumer behavior, where much of the content in this chapter is derived. As noted by the review provided by Malter et al., the field embraced "theories and methodologies from psychology, sociology, anthropology, and statistics, there was an increased emphasis on understanding the thoughts, desires, and experiences of individual consumers."[6]

The leading journal in the area is the *Journal of Consumer Research* (JCR), and it clearly reflects the ground from which the field sprung—but one not including strategy. JCR is overseen by a policy board composed of directors from various academic organizations ranging from the International Communications Association to the Society for Personality and Social Psychology.[7] The organizations representing the historic roots of the field—namely those aimed (primarily) at understanding how a single customer thinks, feels, and behaves—reflect how the field came about. One of the organizations noticeably absent is the American Management Association, which is often the academic lead for issues related to strategy. It should be of no surprise that basic concepts of strategy are not actively nor often deeply considered within the field of consumer behavior.

As we noted earlier in this book, the micro side of consumer behavior and the macro aspects of business strategy are unique, siloed academic entities that often do not meet. There is little doubt that they are treated as separate domains—macro versus micro, firm versus person. Our approach in this book is fairly unique in that it bridges this divide by putting the focus of strategy on the customer. While traditional strategy has too often sidelined the customer, we begin with them. Such a framework as we have created therefore requires an understanding of how consumers think, feel, and decide—all of which is critical to creating a customer advantage and a customer-centered organization.

The Individual Customer

Various factors influence how customers go about making choices within the marketplace regarding products and services. In some instances, people adopt a rational, cognitive perspective that allows them to make decisions in a more calculated, thoughtful way. For example, a customer might adopt such an approach when deciding on a large purchase, such as a home. Information typically found on Zillow or Realtor.com (e.g., home features, square footage, zoning details) is provided to support such decision-making.

At other times customers may use emotion to make a decision. Much of the recent well-publicized reactions to brands making political decisions (e.g., Costco's support of DEI) are anchored as much in emotion as cognition. It seems safe to presume that Kid Rock's shooting of Bud Light with a machine gun is one such example. Decisions also can be driven by physiological aspects of the customer, related to the five senses but also other physical functioning of the human body (e.g., neuro chemicals, DNA). A recent trend in brewing, for example, is the tendency for firms to offer non-alcoholic beers due to mounting evidence of health concerns related to consuming alcohol. The marketplace has had mixed reactions as customers view such products as a compromise in terms of taste, thereby slowing adoption.[8]

The fascinating array of decisions and behaviors that customers take on a daily basis has driven considerable interest by academics. Indeed, much of the academic research published in the field's leading journals often deals with individual differences between customers that affect anything from recognizing a need to the disposal of a product after it has been consumed. The field has adopted a shared view that the basic internal processes are related to the cognitive, emotional, and physical aspects of being a customer.

Such a tri-partite view of the consumer was first introduced by John Howard in 1963 in his marketing textbook and built from ideas of Plato. In *The Republic*, Plato argues that the soul includes the rational, spirited, and appetitive (framed as cognitive, affective, and conative by Howard). Plato argues that harmony in the soul is generated when reason dominates emotions and desires, thereby resulting in virtue and balance. This view of the customer, where rational decision-making governs choice, has been a dominant view of consumers since the 1960s.[9]

Cognition

Customer behavior is often framed as being driven via information processing, and the metaphor of a computer, with input, storage, processing, and retrieval of information. This view of customers has dominated how the field considers the way people select products and services at least since Howard's groundbreaking textbook. His consumer decision-making process has remained a staple in the field in terms of what is taught in business schools and researched in journals.

While newer approaches to how customers decide have been introduced to the field (more on that throughout this chapter), the idea that consumers make cognitive and thoughtful decisions when making choices is a useful approach to decision-making—particularly where decisions are complex and important. Companies can help shape behavior in such contexts by providing decision aids to customers that help make effortful and difficult decisions easier than doing so alone. In today's world dominated by technology, data, and AI, there are a number of tools available to help improve customer decision-making framed around cognition.

Take, for example, Google News's use of AI to provide a more nuanced and balanced news consumption experience in an attempt to combat misinformation, highlight diverse perspectives, and provide context to complex news stories.[10] Cognitive decision-making is supported with their "Full Coverage" feature, which allows users to compare multiple information sources on the same topic, encouraging a more comprehensive understanding. Further, Google is investing in AI tools to analyze source credibility and fact-check information, supporting informed decisions amid the overwhelming flow of digital news.[11]

A cognitive-based approach to understanding consumers relates to a variety of psychological principles including but not limited to exposure, attention and perception, knowledge and understanding, memory and retrieval. Each of these concepts has garnered considerable research attention and (most importantly for the reader) has demonstrable real-world implications in terms of how consumers think and behave. Countless examples can be generated around these core issues; take, for example, memory and its role in retrieval of options in a decision. A customer thinking about lunch options generates a small set of restaurants nearby work (often called the choice set) from which the decision is made. This choice set can be influenced by various factors. While advertising might influence awareness of options, it's often the customer's memories of past meals, a *New York Times* food review they read last month, or recommendations from coworkers that can equally determine which restaurants make it into their choice set for lunch.

Emotion and Affect

Of course, we are not computers; rather, we are feeling entities where emotion, affect, and mood all influence how we behave in situations. Research has shown that emotion and affect influence how customers react to advertising, make decisions, and build brand relationships, to name only a few customer processes. Indeed, it is for this reason that many organizations use emotion within marketing communications to "cut through the clutter" of saturated social media and capture the hearts of customers.

A much-studied area is that of affect (both positive and negative) and its impact on how customers respond to firm-related activities. A classic idea is what researchers call "attitude toward the ad" whereby affective responses to the advertising appeal itself (and separate from content contained in the ad) influence the customer.[12] In today's technologically enabled marketspace, we see similar effects with influencers in modern social media.

Recently, Tatcha, a beauty brand, collaborated with Claire Marshall, a beauty and lifestyle influencer who also possessed expertise as an avid player of Nintendo's *Animal Crossing: New Horizons*. The game allows players to create and customize their own virtual island.

Marshall leveraged her deep understanding of the game to design and build "Tatchaland," a branded in-game island reflecting her aesthetic and values. This partnership allowed Marshall to create an immersive, emotionally resonant experience within the game, offering players a "sense of sanctuary and escape" (particularly during the pandemic). Such an authentic integration of the brand into the gaming environment, through a trusted influencer, fostered positive emotional responses and significantly boosted Tatcha's product launch.[13]

The ability for organizations to shape customer emotions is wide ranging. There is quite a bit of research on how consumers react to products with human features (e.g., an anthropomorphized car face). A recent paper shows that products with face-like features that are happy (compared to showing surprise or anger) result in greater customer attention and exploration of products. Such a study may sound academically fanciful, but the reality is that many products (ranging from cars to washing machines) can be designed to reflect a human with simple design changes (e.g., a different arrangement of buttons on a clothes dryer).[14]

Physiology

The physical dimensions of the human body have also been shown to affect a variety of different behaviors, mental processes, and emotions of people in various settings. For example, the concept of embodied cognition, where physical aspects of the human body influence how people think, could easily be applied within a customer context. For example, handing someone a warm drink can result in the person perceiving others in the setting to be more trustworthy and friendly.[15]

The human body is made up of various systems and chemicals that can easily influence how we behave in a particular setting and often influenced by organizations. An obvious way to do this is through the human senses (touch, taste, feel, smell, hear), which are often referred to as forms of sensory memory. For example, a large body of research indicates scents can have a significant impact on how consumers interact with and make decisions in a retail setting. Such olfactory cues (whether diffused in a store or emanating from products) have been shown to impact customer shopping behavior when aligned with the product being sold.[16]

Beyond the five senses, there are plenty of other physiological factors that can influence how people behave in customer settings. Processes related to aging, sleep, nutrition, brain activity and neurochemicals, and DNA are some of the many factors that have been shown to impact customers. One of the faculty members at our university, Paul Zak, has studied the effects of oxytocin on various human behaviors. In a customer context, he and his team have shown that oxytocin can make people more susceptible to advertising. In one study, the researchers had people smell oxytocin, or a placebo, and then asked them to view an ad. Those in the presence of oxytocin were more likely to donate money to the advertised organization than those in the placebo condition.[17] While conducted in a scientifically rigorous manner, this type of research has shown that brain chemicals can easily affect people in very meaningful ways when applied in the right manner.

Customers Within Context

Customers often find themselves within a variety of environmental and contextual situations that can impact how they behave, think, and feel. As noted earlier in this chapter, customer behavior was viewed in the first half of the 20th century in a rational, cognitive manner—the way that Plato defined the soul. While economists may appreciate such an argument, intellectuals in the 1950s began to debate assumptions underlying a rational view of "economic man." For example, Sid Levy (in his classic "Symbols for Sale" article) in the *Harvard Business Review* made the case that customers are interested in products for not only the function they perform but also how other people and society perceive them. He contends that firms must understand the societal significance of a product to truly understand the customer. Any of us who survived high school will recall the attention paid by classmates to our shoes or clothing choices.

Understanding the macro context in which a product or service is consumed can be incredibly important for an organization, particularly for companies that wish to shape customer behavior in terms of the product. Take a cultural example from the luxury industry where companies work to balance customer needs with maintaining a product's cultural meaning. Ferrari has recently raised concerns about customization of their products by customers that they consider as out-landish and brand inconsistent. While leaning into such customer practices can be a profit booster, Ferrari's leadership went so far as to issue a cease-and-desist order to a social media influencer who painted his Ferrari with a garish internet meme. While Levy would not be shocked by the behaviors of Ferrari customers, in this instance Ferrari executives are questioning exactly what sort of symbols they really do have for sale.[18] Suffice it to say it is critical for organizations to consider the contextual dimensions in which a product or service is perceived in broader society.[19]

Various contextual factors are likely to influence or be used to influence how customers behave within particular contexts. Indeed, most of the external factors often considered by businesses when setting strategy (e.g., regulatory, environmental, legal, technological, cultural, or political dimensions) are prime candidates to consider for shaping customer behavior. In this section, we explore three general areas that are worthy of consideration by organizations deploying a customer-centric strategy.

Social Influence

Psychology has long appreciated how others can influence the actions of a person. Represented by the field of social psychology (defined as "the attempt to understand and explain how the thoughts, feelings, and behaviors of individuals are influenced by the actual, imagined, implied presence of other human beings," Allport, 1954), customers are often influenced by others (other customers, employees, etc.) in various settings.[20] The core ideas introduced and expanded upon by the field include a range of processes: the role of the self-concept, social influence techniques, conformity, dissonance, and others related to how people interact.[21]

Given that much of this work was established in the mid-20th century, it is reasonable to view social psychological ideas as "oldies but goodies." Take for example one of the most classic concepts, Festinger's cognitive dissonance theory.[22] Probably learned in a college psychology course, the theory remains relevant today, having implications for any company wanting to shape post-purchase customer behavior. The basic idea is that if a customer is deciding between two choices, dissonance (discomfort) will be generated related to the product not chosen. For example, consider a person who is deciding between the Ford Mustang and Chevy Camaro and choses the Camaro. The customer may still like Mustang and wonder "what if" they made a different decision. A firm's employees can shape such behavior by providing the right type of post-purchase decision support, such as what is called the "blissful ignorance effect"—the preference of customers for ambiguous information about the choice.[23] Such information could also be provided via social media.

In the 21st century, the influence of other people has not waned; indeed one can readily argue that it has massively increased due to the influence and presence of various social media platforms. Influencers, user-generated content, online communities, and the "Power of Peers" (as noted earlier in this book) are all driving factors for customers in modern society. Consider the collaboration between Duracell and Ariana Madix (a well-known influencer from the reality television show "Vanderpump Rules") a "Power On" campaign. Duracell recognized the value of connecting with people on a personal level, by leveraging Madix's established audience, recent media attention, and relatable persona to drive brand awareness and demonstrate how Duracell batteries "power on" through everyday life.[24]

In contrast to celebrity influencers, other forms of normative influence emerge from observing peer behavior in action. A good example of such normative pressures is social proof (as discussed in Chapter 3), where people use other people's behavior to guide their own. The nonprofit DonorsChoose builds on this core concept by publicly displaying who's donating to which of its projects, which in turn encourages others to support the campaigns. Such peer visibility is designed to shape donor behavior.

Organizations and Society

Organizations can readily shape customer behavior by leveraging macro-level trends in society and reminding customers of such issues when attempting to shape their behavior. Take the case of home electrical generators that have become increasingly popular since the COVID-19 pandemic[25] and further fueled by various forms of societal uncertainty, ranging from environmental emergencies to political unrest. An organization selling such products can easily influence decision-making by reminding customers of the environmental situation in which they live. Both of this book's authors live in Southern California; an advertisement featuring imagery of wildfires, earthquakes, and mudslides can easily influence even the savviest of customers (us) to consider installing a generator at home. As one homeowner explained on Reddit, "It was worth it to me. 27KW $14,000 turnkey installation including 500-gallon propane tank. Haven't had to use it ever since, but it's there if I need it." This sentiment captures how the value proposition has shifted from immediate utility to preparedness and peace of mind.[26]

There are various societal issues that can impact how customers think, feel, and behave, and ultimately influence needs and wants. One area of important consideration is societal norms as they can shape the actions, beliefs, and expectations of customers.[27] Such norms are socially constructed and vary across time and context. They also help to support order in society by making it clear what behaviors are acceptable and unacceptable. This is well illustrated via norms associated with products considered "sinful" in the United States.

For example, societal norms related to the consumption of cigarettes have dramatically shifted in the 20th century, going from being what many would consider normative (in our childhoods) to being a societal pariah (the new norm for our kids). An opposite pattern of shifting norms can be seen in the growth and popularity of medicinal and recreational marijuana. In a relatively short period, we have moved from a shared negative view of the product (aka the "reefer madness" perspective) to marijuana being viewed as acceptable by the majority of U.S. citizens (and now legal in 41 states in one form or another). Numerous business opportunities have emerged as the product has gained acceptance, including new types of retail outlets to cannabis being an ingredient in all sorts of products.

As just illustrated, societal trends can easily shift and have dramatic influence on consumers. At times, it is difficult for a company to act in a manner that helps the organization, rather than hurts it. Perhaps nothing better illustrates this than the drifting sands of DEI (particularly in the United States since the 2024 presidential elections). Returning to an earlier example, two large U.S. retailers have taken markedly different approaches to the DEI issue, resulting in remarkably different customer responses.

Costco has demonstrated a commitment to diversity, equity, and inclusion through its programs and initiatives. Their approach has generally been well-received, although the company faces ongoing challenges and scrutiny regarding its DEI efforts, as evidenced by recent proxy battles challenging its programs.[28] Conversely, Target faced significant backlash and a period of customer boycotts following controversies surrounding their Pride Month merchandise displays in 2025, resulting in a period of decreased sales and negative media attention.[29]

The takeaway here is that organizations must monitor and understand changing trends within society to meet their customer needs, wants, and desires (a topic we return to later when focusing on customer intelligence). Opportunities clearly arise for organizations that move early into new areas and peril potentially awaits those that ignore or misinterpret such trends. The good news we have is that monitoring such societal trends has become much easier with the advent of technology (e.g., AI that can scrape, collect, and analyze data that is generated via social media).

Public Policy

Various entities (e.g., NGOs, nonprofits, government) aim to watch over the rights and safety of consumers; many times this is done by influencing and directing organizations in terms of how they interact with customers. Public policy, one form of such influence, reflects laws, regulations, decisions, and actions enacted by government organizations. Typically, such policy is aimed at addressing various societal issues with clear objectives in mind.[30] For example, the NLEA (Nutrition Labeling and Education Act) became law in 1990 and has influenced how food nutrition information has been presented in the United States ever since.

The importance of public policy within the realm of consumers emerged from the industrial revolution and the rise of a production economy. For example, the issue of food safety first came to prominence from the detailed (and sometimes disgusting) description of

Chicago meat production in Sinclair's *The Jungle* (1906). No matter your political views on the right amount of government regulation within society, such regulation undoubtedly impacts customers and that of companies aiming to meet their needs and wants. Returning to the NLEA example, researchers in our field have shown that this regulation also affected companies, whose responses to the act impacted (both positively and negatively) their customers.[31]

The importance and influence of public policy remain significant in the 21st century. Emerging challenges related to climate change, social inequalities, political polarization, AI, and the fourth industrial revolution all spur on regulators to new policies (at least hopefully so). Further, there is a push and pull in terms of policy regulation that comes from issues arising within society. Our message here is that organizations setting customer-based strategies need to take such public policy shifts into account when satisfying their customers. This can be complicated (and expensive!) at times when what the customer wants is not what regulators will allow. A great recent example is red food dye—lovers of Nerds, candy corn, and Hot Tamales be forewarned. While many of us enjoy these brightly colored candies, some specific dyes like red dye #3 have faced increased scrutiny and restrictions due to potential health concerns, creating a challenge for candy manufacturers seeking to meet consumer preferences while adhering to evolving regulations.[32]

An area ripe for potential regulation today relates to customers' online activities. With the emergence of a truly AI-enabled world, it is likely that pressures for regulation will only increase going forward—but will policymakers respond? This situation is similar to what we saw in terms of consumer protections emerging in the early 20th century when society wrestled with a range of not-seen-before consumption issues. Unfortunately, it is unclear where such policy will head. On one side, consumer advocacy groups in the United States argue for additional regulations on unfettered access to social and digital media (and the organizations that profit from them). For example, in the United States, regulation (e.g., Section 230 of the Communications Decency Act of 1996) has been argued to be woefully inadequate in protecting basic rights and safety of U.S. consumers, particularly vulnerable populations. In contrast, many for-profit firms are happy with Section 230 and prefer fewer regulations on such digital activities of customers. How the government responds to such different views is complicated (particularly with the emergence of AI) and part of the unpredictable political process of many societies. Our message here is that the ebb and flow of such policy is key for organizations to monitor when building customer-centric strategies.

How Customers Behave

Organizations do not always consider enough the actual behavior of their customers. It is easy to fall into the trap of focusing on factors that predict or influence customer behavior (e.g., attitudes, SEO metrics, willingness to sample a product), rather than the behavior itself. Several reasons explain why this is the case, but we believe that the most prevalent reason is the relative ease of measuring things other than how customers behave. While this may be the case, we argue that any outcome should ideally be assessed in terms of actual behavior of the customer. Focusing on this outcome is well exemplified by the Organic Growth Playbook framework, which is anchored on the core premise that it is easiest to shape markets by understanding how customers act regarding products and services. Behavior is often treated in a categorical manner (e.g., purchase = 1, not purchase = 0). But the reality is that how customers purchase and use products can be quite nuanced and complex. If one considers a product's life after purchase (through disposal), then the complexity of customer actions expands dramatically. Recent themes of "reduce, reuse, and recycle" within the circular economy further complicate issues related to how customers behave. All of which, we argue, should be considered when creating a strategic customer advantage.

The Purchase

The purchase of a product or service by a customer may be a simple act with relatively little complexity, such as when a single customer purchases something for personal use (whether it be a head of lettuce or a new car). However, the reality is that purchasing a good or service can be considerably more complex, a situation that is likely driven by purchase goals. Often there are times that someone may make a purchase for another, such as when looking for a gift for a family member or other loved one. As illustrated by O'Henry's *Gift of the Magi*, gift exchange can be particularly complicated due to social and psychological factors influencing how societies exchange gifts (including the power of reciprocity).[33]

Further, new business models have emerged to support the developed world's convenience culture by others making purchases for end-consumers, such as Grubhub for restaurant food and Instacart for groceries in the United States. B2B firms also make purchases for other than end-consumer reasons, such as when a manufacturer sources ingredients with exacting formulations required for the production of a product to be sold to end-consumers. We have spoken to firms recently that have struggled sourcing ingredients with the 2025 trade war between the United States and other countries. Purchasing agents working for large entities such as state or federal governments can also face complex purchase settings with detailed policies to ensure appropriate procurement. In each of these situations, it is critical for the organization to understand the decision processes and customer journey that make up how the ultimate purchase occurs. We return to this idea later in this chapter.

As we noted in earlier chapters, Drucker said that the core focus of any business is to "create and keep a customer."[34] Implied in his quote is that keeping existing customers is equally as important as acquiring new ones. Research supports Drucker's view by finding that the cost of obtaining a new customer is considerably higher than retaining a customer.[35] The Ritz-Carlton exemplifies Drucker's principle through exceptional customer retention efforts. This luxury hospitality leader sets the standard for personalized service by empowering employees with a $2,000 discretionary fund and maintaining detailed guest-preference databases.[36] These practices create memorable experiences that foster loyalty, demonstrating the value of retention over acquisition. There is considerable research on this critical marketing topic. A classic study on customer retention and acquisition identified that these efforts have an impact on an organization's innovation. The paper reported that organizations that consistently implement a single engagement strategy (acquisition or retention) result in amplified effects on innovation performance. In contrast, a balanced approach can result in negative impacts of innovation outcomes due to resource misalignment.[37]

Firms can introduce support mechanisms to facilitate the purchase of their goods and services. In the retail space, such means range from providing convenient ways to pick up purchased items from the store (via BOPIS, Buy Online, Pick Up In-Store) to the provision of retail-issued credit cards. Such approaches not only make for easy purchase and acquisition but also can enhance customer loyalty. These efforts are clearly working—as of 2023, U.S. consumers held $126.9 billion of debt on retail-issued credit cards.[38]

Other means by which to enhance and shape the purchases of goods and services include robots, self-service checkouts, online decision support systems, and simplified funding mechanisms, to name a few. Amazon Fresh has used technology like smart carts and automated checkout to streamline purchasing for its customers. However, their "Just Walk Out" systems, which rely on cameras and sensors to automatically detect purchased items, have faced challenges, as seen by Amazon's shift to smart shopping carts. This shift highlights potential reliability issues with these advanced systems.[39]

Use

Once obtained via purchase, customers will use products and services that they have purchased from organizations for some specified period of time. While it may seem safe to assume that customers will use products as expected, our experience is that sometimes this is not the case. For example, manufacturers of the Q-tip product explicitly state that it is not to be used for cleaning one's ears, yet many consumers do so. A dramatic example of product misuse is the viral Tide Pod Challenge, where people (mainly teens) bite into or eat the product and post online videos challenging others to do the same. P&G (makers of Tide Pods) did an excellent job in responding to this including communication efforts and product changes.[40] The value of considering such extreme examples illustrates the need for firms to monitor how their products are used by their focal customers.

A variety of psychological processes unfold when products are obtained and used. For example, considerable research has shown that the simple act of owning a product enhances its valuation by the owner. Much of this research has been explored as a form of loss aversion called the *endowment effect*—a cognitive bias whereby people assign higher monetary values to owned items. The effect leads to differences between the price people are willing to accept to sell an item and the price they are willing to pay to acquire it—who hasn't had a hard time selling a used car to an interested buyer. A recent example relates to Taylor Swift fans, who refused to sell their 2024 concert tickets even when huge prices were offered by others.[41] The endowment effect can also be leveraged to encourage purchase of products by providing a sense of ownership prior to purchase (e.g., via product sampling). Returning to an earlier example, teen customers of the aforementioned makeup brand were more likely to buy product when they could try the product and see how products look on them before purchasing.

The fundamental nature of how products are used by customers has dramatically changed in recent times. One influence relates to the sharing economy, where products and services of all types can be rented and/or shared across groups of consumers, including ride-sharing (Uber and Lyft), car rentals (Turo), clothing (By Rotation), and accommodations (Airbnb), to name a few. Another major influence is what some call a circular economy, which aims to eliminate waste and continuously reuse resources. A major goal of this framework is to keep materials, products, and services in circulation for as long as possible. Unfortunately, in today's convenience-oriented market where low cost looms large (illustrated by the dominance of fast fashion), the idea of repairing a product is not an immediate solution to one's need (indeed, it is often easier to throw the old one in the trash and buy another).

Organizations that repair products are becoming a thing of the past, as seen by the demise of the television repair store.[42] That said, some organizations do rely on renewal (aka repair) of products as a core strategic feature of their offerings. Take, for example, Allen Edmunds, which provides recrafting services to its customers' shoes. Such an approach is more than a way to participate in the circular economy; it also builds deeper and stronger relations with the organization. As noted on their website, Allen Edmunds states: "Some things never grow old, they become part of your legacy."[43] Such themes are not uncommon. Patek Philippe watches introduced its generations campaign in 1996 that argues that: "You never own a Patek Philippe. You merely look after it for the next generation." We are not surprised that the campaign has lasted for decades.[44]

Post-Purchase

Various things should be considered in terms of post-purchase customer activities related to a company's product and services. A typical consideration relates to satisfaction and dissatisfaction with the product or service experience. Organizations have historically spent considerable resources to understand and build customer satisfaction after the purchase and use of a product or service. Forty years of research on the topic has shown us that satisfaction leads to positive outcomes related to customers (e.g., retention, spending amount) and organizations (e.g., financial performance).

A great example is provided by Rolls-Royce, which prioritizes post-purchase customer satisfaction through personalized service and bespoke customization, both of which are integral to its customer experience.[45] Services range from personalized design consultations to customize one's vehicle (e.g., with options like rare woods and hand-stitched leathers) to a luxury in-dealership experience (e.g., with private access, consultations, and gourmet refreshments). Similar examples are seen in luxury goods. One of us recently needed the band of his Omega watch adjusted and while he waited at a SoCal location, the employee asked about enjoying some high-end whiskey to pass the time.

Returning to the idea of the circular economy, once products have become past their useful lives and cannot be repaired, there are options for their continued use that do not require immediate disposal (e.g., recycling, gifting, donating). A recent trend among U.S. Gen Z consumers is *thrifting* (purchasing used products in thrift stores) in what some call "recommerce."[46] Such practices can be seen throughout the globe, and the thrifting scene in Los Angeles is something to witness.

This is not only a U.S. phenomenon; thrift stores are now part of the fabric of most major European cities.

An incredible example is that of Filipino *pagpag*, whereby people salvage food waste (often discarded by food establishments into the waste stream), which is then cleaned and recooked to be served once again to new customers.[47] No matter the desperate need for food and resources in developing economies, the unfortunate reality is that a great deal of the world's products (particularly from developed countries) end up in landfills or as pollution in our environment. While one can argue which of the UNSDGs (United Nations Sustainable Development Goals) are most important, there is no doubt that the production, consumption, and disposal of consumer goods has had an indelible impact on the globe and continues to do so to this day.

Issues surrounding product purchase, use, and disposal not only impact customers but also play an interesting role in how firms develop and execute customer-centric strategy. Examples in the 20th century of firms that failed to make such considerations (e.g., cigarette manufacturers, producers of forever chemicals) are sobering. Indeed, it is a complex balancing act for organizations, which need to weigh the needs and wants of their customers and stakeholders against regulations, actions of the competition, corporate social responsibility, and societal expectations, along with considering any potential long-term negative impacts of the organization's actions.

Organizations can mitigate some of these factors via customers themselves by taking back products from them. Such "take-back" programs support the circular economy by extending the useful life of a product and are used by firms offering an array of products (e.g., IKEA, H&M, Apple).[48] Beyond benefits to the circular economy, such programs can also increase customer loyalty with the firm and differentiate firms within the market.

Managing the Journey

As detailed throughout this chapter, many factors influence how consumers behave. As a result, there is so much research, thinking, and commentary on consumers that it can be overwhelming for a business to appreciate how and why customers have the needs and wants that they do. A central means by which organizations can understand their customers and frame important details of the purchase process is customer journey mapping. The customer journey reflects the entire process by which consumers interact with a product or service, including all touchpoints from initial awareness of a need to disposal of the item.

By understanding the journey, it is possible for the organization to manage, influence, and direct how it unfolds. Many organizations have well scripted journeys, similar to a movie script. Disney meticulously crafts the guest experience in its parks through mapping, ensuring seamless and immersive interactions. But the value of a journey need not only be useful for Disney; indeed, the concept can be readily used by all firms, whether B2B or B2C for anything from cooper ore to new homes. For example, Airbnb used a Disney-inspired technique to map the ideal customer experience—an effort dubbed "Project Snow White" by its CEO. This allowed the firm to visualize and enhance touchpoints from the initial booking to interactions after the stay was complete.[49]

Need Recognition and Beyond

Central to the customer journey is the decision-making process of one's customers. The nature of decisions can range from the ridiculously simple (e.g., ordering what you always eat at your favorite Mexican restaurant) to more complex decisions (e.g., buying a new car). The typical steps in a customer decision-making process include: need recognition, information search, evaluation of alternatives, purchase, consumption, post-purchase evaluation, and disposition. Almost every decision (whether simple or complex) will include all of these steps but will vary in terms of the amount of attention each step gets. A variety of factors can influence whether the decision-making process is limited or extended. More complex decisions are typical when they are highly and involve choice alternatives with greater differences.

We believe that understanding steps in the typical customer decision process is a critical part of understanding the customer journey. Another benefit of understanding decision processes is the ability for an organization to influence steps within the process to shape customer behavior. For example, activating a specific need and showing customers how an organization's product or service meets that need can result in purchase of the offered item. A good illustration of such need activation can be seen with the 2025 Super Bowl ad for Hims & Hers Health (which some have described as "strikingly dark," with its underlying critique of the U.S. healthcare system) that was designed to activate weight loss needs from a cost perspective.[50] The one-minute ad likely cost $14 million for the company to make the case to viewers that they are the alternative health option for saving money.

Pretty much any step of the decision-making process can be influenced by firm actions, assuming the customer decision-making process is clear. A key step in the decision-making process relates to how customers decide which alternatives will be considered for purchase. Considerable research has focused on this issue, justifiably so, given the critical nature of this within the customer journey. As noted earlier, a concept of importance is the notion of the consideration set—the set of choice alternatives that are actively being considered by a customer to select from. It is critical for organizations to be within the consideration set, as research has shown that purchase likelihood increases for any alternative included in the consideration set. There are several once well-renowned brands that have disappeared, because they were simply not often in the consideration set of customers. The two of us grew up with Oldsmobile and Pontiac, but those brands are now relegated to the pages of Auto Trader. Firms can increase the chance of being part of the consideration set via brand-building activities by enhancing recall and recognition of their brands.

Mapping the Journey

Researchers, practitioners, and consultants alike have provided considerable information regarding how to map the customer journey along with best practices to do so. There is value in doing so—we strongly believe that mapping the customer journey is critical for understanding and enhancing the customer experience and customer-centric strategies. A recent study by *Forbes* magazine found that approximately 80 percent of surveyed firms are either mapping (or planning to map) customer journeys. As noted in the article, journey mapping should be considered as "table stakes for brands to compete for customer loyalty."[51] One thing to keep in mind is that journey mapping is an ongoing (never-ending, if done correctly) process driven by market intelligence that is continually changing and evolving.

An underlying goal of the journey is for the organization to be able to create a positive meaningful experience between the organization and the customer. With customer journey mapping, the organization can understand the many touchpoints at which there is an interaction between the brand and the customer. Thus, an ideal goal for customer mapping is to broaden the view of customer experience to include the entire ecosystem of touchpoints that contribute to positive outcomes of the customer journey that will likely lead to enhanced satisfaction and increased willingness to purchase products. During each stage of the buying process, therefore, organizations have opportunities to create positive experiences or negative ones, with the product service or brand. Some of the touchpoints may have more or less control by the organization; nonetheless, the message from us here is that they all need to be mapped and understood as part of the customer journey.

There are several best practices associated with customer journey mapping. These include defining clear objectives, using sufficient qualitative and quantitative data to understand all the touchpoints, the use of customer personae, and regular updating of the journeys over time. One critical consideration is that a single journey map is unlikely to be sufficient for most organizations. Ideally a map should be created for each of the major market segments served by a particular organization. Take for example the various market segments that fly on Delta jets. The businessperson, who typically travels in business class and takes advantage of the Delta Sky Club, is going to have a dramatically different customer journey and experience compared to a young family, who is more concerned about cost than luxury when they travel. It is therefore critical to map both journeys (and more) to understand the critical touchpoints for each customer type so that the touchpoints can be influenced by the organization to shape customer behavior.

A New Journey Awaits

The nature of customer journeys, and how they are mapped and influenced by organizations, is undergoing tremendous change in the 21st century primarily due to technological advances. In many ways we are about to embark on a new journey, one enabled by AI, increased computing power, and amazing amounts of data. It is critical therefore for organizations to continually work on their journey maps of customers and integrating technology as resources allow.

Returning to Disney theme parks, the company uses interactive technologies to enhance the customer experience journey. As one knows from a visit to the park, immersive storytelling and incredible attention to detail are hallmarks of the customer experience. Building on technological innovations, Disney can shift customers from simply being guests to active participants in the story and experience. A great example is an attraction named Star Wars: Galaxies Edge that allows visitors to engage with and participate in the story's narrative.[52] Several technologies and data streams allow Disney to tailor customer experiences to individual guests within the park. A key dimension of this is Disney's MagicBand (an RFID-enabled wearable device that integrates park entry, purchases, ride access, and personalized experiences). In addition to supporting an enhanced customer experience, the device provides numerous benefits to Disney, included enhancing its ability to collect data, personalize experiences for guests, enhance park efficiency, save costs, and build customer loyalty.[53]

We contend that organizational strategists must have a nuanced understanding of customers as a starting point to setting strategy, rather than as a consequence of doing so.

As illustrated in the example of Disney and the MagicBand, the ability to understand and influence a customer's experience journey will only increase along with advances in technology. Returning to Chapter 3 of this book, recall that the rise of the consumer in the 21st century has been driven, at least in part, by a desire of consumers to have a focus on themselves, each as an individual customer. While this situation may be contained within developed economies at the moment, there is no reason to believe that customers from around the globe will not have a desire to have their own unique customer journey for whatever particular product or service they have in mind. Technology will undoubtedly help this occur and is likely to only accelerate in the coming decades, as chip processing power and artificial intelligence start to mirror that of humans.

Conclusion

Understanding what motivates one's customers—including their needs, wants, and desires—is critical to setting a customer-centric strategy. Consumers are anything but simple or static, rather (as illustrated in this chapter) they are dynamic, complicated, and increasingly empowered by technology and information. Driven by cognition, emotion, and physiology, customers make copious decisions regarding what to buy in the market every day. Thus, the goal of any organization is to understand what drives its customers and to manage the customer journey taken to make a purchase.

However, as the landscape of consumption continues to transform with AI, societal challenges, and environmental disruptions, it is even more critical for organizations to deeply understand their customers to be best positioned in the market. In sum, we contend that organizational strategists must have a nuanced understanding of customers as a starting point to setting strategy, rather than as a consequence of doing so. The content in this chapter will be critical to building true customer advantage in the marketplace.

Building a Customer-Centered Organization

IN PART III of this book, we show you how to build a customer-centered company around four key issues related to leadership, the structure and systems of the organization, customer intelligence requirements, and the discipline to innovate and abandon.

In Chapter 7, we explore the leadership imperatives required to build and sustain a customer-centric organization and emphasize two levels of leadership. At the organizational level, top management must define a clear mission, vision, and purpose that centers on customer benefit and establish a culture that aligns with this strategic approach. We illustrate how companies do so with examples such as Amgen, Costco, and Netflix. At the individual level, senior leaders must embody customer-centric competencies. Among other traits, leaders must be ambidextrous—balancing present performance with future innovation, formal systems with informal networks, and courage with consistency. Ultimately, customer-centric leadership is not only about strategic design, but also about leaders who embed customer value into the daily decisions, behaviors, and mindset of the organization.

In Chapter 8, we examine how organizational design and reward systems influence an organization's ability to deliver on a customer-centered strategy. We frame this around seven principles of effective structure, such as communication and role clarity. The core of the chapter is our evaluation of four (common) global structures for an organization—divisional, matrix, geographic, and product-based. Our experience suggests that no structure is perfect, but organizations need to consider how their structure either impedes or facilitates a customer-focused approach to strategy formulation. A final aspect for organizations to consider is how to motivate customer-centered behavior within the organization. While financial (extrinsic) rewards matter, we contend that to make a company truly customer centered it takes intrinsic rewards where employees are driven by meaning, autonomy, and shared purpose with the organization.

Customer intelligence is the foundation of any effective customer-centered strategy and the topic of Chapter 9. Any such effort starts with collecting data but the real value comes from transforming that data into actionable insights. As Drucker noted, "The purpose of information is not knowledge. It is being able to take the right action." We dig deep into a three-step model that includes: (1) the generation of intelligence, (2) sense-making of the information, and (3) dissemination of data and its use by the organization. We illustrate intelligence tools including traditional methods (such as surveys and focus groups) and advanced technologies (such as AI and machine learning), with examples from companies like Capital One, Nike, and Sephora. Critical to an intelligence system is an organization-wide process to sense-make the data to ensure insights are relevant and context-rich—a goal that can be challenging due to bias, AI hallucinations, and siloed communication. Ultimately, we argue that for organizations to be successful, they must embed a focus on customer intelligence and share it widely across the organization.

In the final chapter of this section, we argue that customer-driven organizations must not only innovate for the future but systematically abandon the past. Drawing from Drucker's work, we introduce innovation and abandonment as twin disciplines essential to organizational growth and adaptation. To start, we argue that innovation is everyone's responsibility—not just R&D—and should be a structured effort rooted in everyday activities of the organization. Building on Drucker, we outline seven sources of innovation—ranging from unexpected success to demographic shifts and new knowledge—that organizations can draw upon. Equally important to innovation is systematic abandonment—the intentional, organization-wide practice of ceasing products, services, or practices that no longer create customer value. We profile companies like Amazon and Microsoft as leaders not just in innovation, but in letting go of outdated offerings and approaches. Ultimately, innovation without abandonment leads to clutter and inefficiency; abandonment without innovation results in decline. To lead in dynamic markets, organizations must create space for new ideas by actively letting go of what no longer serves customers—or the business.

7

Leadership and Customer Centricity

"Economic forces set limits on what management can do. They create opportunities for management's actions. But they, by themselves, do not determine what a business is or what it does. Nothing could be sillier than the oft-repeated assertion that management only adapts the business to the forces of the market. Management not only finds these forces; management creates them by its own actions. The more management creates economic conditions or changes them rather than passively adapts to them, the more it manages the business."

—Peter Drucker, 1954[1]

Introduction

The essence of a customer-centered enterprise is driven by the organization making a series of choices related to the choice of target segment, value proposition, profit model, and capabilities to deliver value. Customer-centered organizations must be keenly aware of their competition, possess a deep understanding of their customers, and keep an eye on both current and future markets. Together, these choices and knowledge will drive key market-facing decisions. If successful, the enterprise will be able to take a leading role in shaping the evolution of markets. Per the Drucker quote, leading organizations do not take the existing industry structure as a given—rather, they shape the behavior of players in the industry (including customers) and the structure of the industry itself. But none of this can occur without leadership within the organization.

In this chapter, therefore, we turn to the leadership considerations in building and nurturing a customer-centered organization. There are two levels of leadership that are important to consider—one focused on leading the organization and the second on leading oneself as a member of the top management team. The top management team must lead the effort to be more customer-driven. Here we discuss five critical decisions and activities for the senior leadership team. These include setting the direction for the organization (e.g., mission, vision), setting a customer-driven culture, crafting and communicating the strategy, building the best bench of talent, and managing in two time periods—the present and the future.

After our discussion of organization-level leadership, we turn our attention to the individual competencies that senior leaders need to develop to accelerate the journey to be more customer-driven. Not surprising, this set of competencies begins with the ability to be ambidextrous—to deliver business performance in the short run *and* transition the organization to the future. This is grounded in a commitment to an outside-in, market-based orientation. An outside-in orientation balances two individual behaviors that go hand in hand—curiosity and the need to lead under conditions of uncertainty. An outside-in perspective encompasses the ability to explore, test, experiment, and learn about markets and how they change. This requires curiosity. Since the future is uncertain, leaders must be comfortable with this ambiguity. That said, we return to the opening quote—that the best way to get to the future is by managing the evolution of the industry structure.

Leading the Organization

In this section, we are focused on the activities and choices of the top management team. Not surprisingly, it is this team that sets the context for all of the customer activities to follow. The starting point is the crafting of mission, vision, and purpose (MVP) statements. Collectively, these set the north star for the organization. As Drucker noted several decades ago, a major cause of business failure is the lack of understanding of outcomes provided by an organization's products and services offerings. So, to build a customer-driven organization, you must ensure that the mission is focused on the customer benefits and outcomes—not the products of the organization. Next, the organization needs to set the guardrails for the culture of the company. There is no one "right culture" for every organization. The choice of culture needs to fit the mission, strategy, and industry context. Costco's family-oriented culture is a perfect fit for their strategy, while Netflix states categorially they are not a family culture. They are much more competitive, less nurturing, and all about results. It works for Netflix, but it would be a disaster for Costco.

The third leg of the stool is strategy. While the MVP statements set the broad direction and address "how the work gets done," the strategy lays out the five choices of a customer-centric strategy. The MVP, culture, and strategy all work together to form a coherent "whole" for the organization. Amgen, the world's largest independent biotechnology company, has a stated mission to serve patients by transforming the promise of science and biotechnology into therapies that have the power to restore health or save lives. Amgen's culture reinforces the need for continually innovating in bringing these therapies to market. Hence, one key value is to be "science-based"—using the scientific method to guide critical drug discovery methods. Amgen also notes that they need to compete intensely and win—but to do so in a high integrity, team-based, collaborative environ-

> *Since the future is uncertain, leaders must be comfortable with this ambiguity.*

ment. Their strategy follows from this mission and set of values—namely, develop and commercialize innovative therapies in specific areas (e.g., oncology) and build a strong pipeline of new, differentiated drugs. Amgen balances this innovative portfolio with a robust line of biosimilars to address affordability concerns. Furthermore, they are a global player, so expanding and winning in developing markets is also a key aim.

Since talent is the key asset to help execute the mission, strategy, and culture, it is obvious that management time needs to be devoted to selecting, developing, and retaining talent. The key message here is that it is not "talent development in general"—rather, it is talent that fits the mission, culture, and strategy of the organization. A company like Netflix must focus on agility, speed, and adaptability. In contrast, a company like Cargill—which is one of the dominant players in the agribusiness industry—must focus on operational excellence, efficiency, and scale. Indeed, the leadership competencies of Cargill are the opposite competencies of Netflix. Too often organizations accept popular trends in leadership competencies (e.g., we need "grit") rather than do the hard work to match the talent management activities to the strategy and mission of the organization.

Finally, a key message throughout this book is the need to balance continuity and change in order to be customer centered. Leaders need to be comfortable with the need to experiment about the future and provide budget to pilot various ideas to "test the future." The future does not just happen—it is created by industry leaders. We address each of these five decisions in the following sections.

Setting Direction: The Mission, Vision, and Purpose

Most organizations have a mission, vision, and purpose—so, you could be asking why this decision is covered in this section on leading the organization. There are two basic reasons for us covering this topic. The first is Drucker's observation that the mission of the organization needs to be constantly tested, examined, and challenged. Changes in the needs and wants of consumers (as delved into in Chapter 3) should be considered when adjusting the mission; for example, what are the implications of the rise of interest in thrift stores for traditional retailers? Markets often change quickly—where there is an inflection point, where there is a "step change" in configuration of the industry structure. Many professional services firms are experiencing this shift, with a blurring of traditional industry boundaries, the role of near and offshore, and the emergence of generative AI. For example, global law firms are experiencing a race to scale globally in the face of an influx of nontraditional practices and shifts in legal-tech. These forces require law firms to rethink the nature of "what business are we in?"

A second reason is that many mission statements are focused on products and technology rather than the underlying benefits or outcomes that customers are looking to receive. Tesla's mission is to accelerate the world's transition to sustainable energy. Telsa could have identified their mission as transportation or mobility, but they chose to select sustainable energy. This leaves them with a very broad playing field—including solar energy, batteries, charging stations, and other sustainable energy products.

Let's consider the mission, vision, and purpose in turn. A mission statement answers the simple question, "what business are we in?" from the point of view of the customer. Disney is in the business of storytelling that entertains and inspires people. Their mission is to "entertain, inform, and inspire people around the globe through the power of unparalleled storytelling, reflecting the iconic brands, creative minds, and innovative technologies that make them the world's premier entertainment company."

This statement scores well on mission statement criteria.[2] Most notably, (1) it focuses on the underlying benefit, (2) it identifies its target market (in this case a global market), (3) it is inspirational, and (4) every employee can see how they can contribute to the mission. One could argue it is too lengthy—since mission statements should be easy to recall for all key stakeholders. One other key point—if you saw this on a wall poster, you would probably know it was Disney. This is quite important since some mission statements are so lofty that you do not know who the organization is and what business they are in.

A vision statement follows from the mission statement. It answers the simple question—what does the world look like when the organization has accomplished its mission? For Habitat for Humanity—an organization that provides homes for those with limited financial means—their vision is to create "a world where everyone has a decent place to live." For Caterpillar, their vision is a world in which all people's basic needs—such as shelter, clean water, sanitation, food, and reliable power—are fulfilled in an environmentally sustainable way, and a company that improves the quality of the environment and the communities where we live and work.

Both of these vision statements have a clear end state in mind, and they are both inspirational for the workforce. Habitat's is more concise and hence more memorable than Caterpillar's. Moreover, both use image-based language—we can imagine a world where everyone has a decent place to live. There is an issue about achievability for both. Is the vision statement too aspirational? Finally, both are centered on core customer issues—basic needs such as housing. In this sense, the visions are customer-centric.

While mission statements articulate the fundamental customer benefit and vision statements provide the desired end state, neither illustrates how society benefits from the presence of the organization. Yet, it is the societal benefit that is most motivating for employees, customers, and other stakeholders in the community. This is normally accomplished with a purpose statement.

For Mars Petcare, their purpose is a "better world for pets." What is interesting about this purpose is that the customers—the pets and pet owners—are key stakeholders. However, every other player in the industry—the veterinarians, the shelters, the city governments—are also part of the pet ecosystem. Hence, to create a better world for pets—so the world is a better place—they have to focus not just on customers, but on the mutual value that is created for all players in the ecosystem. Everyone must win.

Customer-Centric Culture: Setting the Guard Rails

In creating a customer-driven organization, Jim Sinegal, co-founder and former CEO of Costco, noted that "culture isn't the most important thing—it's the only thing."[3] We understand he is understating a key point, but also recognize that culture is one lever in building a customer-centered organization. There are numerous definitions of culture, but a key underlying element is that it shapes "how work gets done." It is a shared set of values, beliefs, norms, and attitudes for how to approach and complete work activities.

We tend to think of strong versus weak cultures rather than "good" or "bad" cultures. A good culture is one that "fits" the strategy and enables the organization to achieve its mission. Some cultures are family oriented while others are more like sports teams. One is not better than the other—they are simply different philosophies or orientations that serve different organizations.

A strong culture is a great fit for one segment of employees and a terrible fit for a different segment of employees. One CEO told us that he spoke with every potential new employee of his mid-sized organization and told them, "This will either be the best place you ever worked or the worst place." A strong culture reflects how the company believes it will succeed and why. Importantly, culture drives specific types of behavior, and all rewards and systems must support the culture.

Cisco describes their conscious culture as "We are self-aware of ourselves and our environment. We feel accountable and empowered to contribute to a culture where everyone thrives and where we intentionally seek out, learn, understand, and appreciate who and what surrounds us."[4] Chuck Robbins, the CEO of Cisco, notes, "Our people are what make this company great. They have an incredibly competitive spirit, but they also have a commitment to doing what is right—for our customers and partners, their communities, and for each other."[5]

Crafting the Strategy

The top management team is responsible and accountable for the strategy of the organization. A firm strategy is a long-term plan that outlines how a company will achieve its goals, gain a competitive advantage, and create value for stakeholders. Whether you use the customer choice cascade in Chapter 5 or another strategy framework, the choice of "where to play" and "how to win" rests with the executive team. Consistent with the theme of this book, all relevant stakeholders must be able to easily see how customer insight has shaped the strategy choices. With the customer choice cascade, this begins with a rich description of the target segment—who they are, why they buy, what experience they desire, and what outcome they are looking for in the offering. The more comprehensive the description, the easier it is for employees to align their contribution to the strategy.

In practice, we have observed three approaches to crafting the strategy:

- **The first approach is when the CEO takes charge of the process.** This approach has two major advantages. The first is that everyone in the organization knows the CEO owns the process, so there will be no ambiguity regarding the organization's commitment to the outcome. Second, if the CEO is driving the process, it signals the importance of the activity—not just to employees but all stakeholders, including investors. The one potential downside is when the CEO has prematurely locked in on a strategy without considering the various legitimate alternatives. For important decisions, there must be a clash of opinions—based on evidence from the customers and the market—to find the best outcome. In this case, you must challenge both "groupthink" and the strongly held assumptions of the industry.

- **A second approach is assignment of the strategy process to senior executives—often with the title of SVP or VP of strategy.** The top management team maintains all decision rights, but the analytical work is led by the SVP and their team. This has the advantage of both freeing up the CEO and allocating a large portion of the senior executive time to the activity. Often an internal team is also allocated to collect the market data, run the pro-forma financial analysis, and craft the overall storyline. Sometimes, the CEO and a couple of additional top management team members form a steering committee to oversee the process. The principal upside of this approach is the time, resources, and commitment of an internal team to shape the process. Similar to the first approach, the team must examine several legitimate alternatives, to be comfortable that the right strategy emerges.

- **A third approach is to enlist the help of external strategy advisors.** The major upside of this approach is the external perspective. Namely, the advisors have no (or much less) vested interest in the various outcomes. There is typically a steering team (CEO, other C-level executives, and a few others) and a working team (comprised of both advisory consultants and internal team members). The external team is "evidence-driven," with teams allocated to customer understanding, market/industry evolution, and financial modeling. The major downside is when the team "boils the ocean" with hundreds if not thousands of slides on various topics. What sometimes gets lost in the analysis is marshalling the evidence on the three to four key strategy options. Instead, the slide decks take on a life of their own—overwhelming the client organization. To mitigate this situation, the client must focus the team early on in the process on identifying legitimate alternatives and let those alternatives drive the market/customer intelligence gathering process.

Regardless of which approach is used, the top management team has to screen, approve, and make the final decision on the strategy of the organization. The strategy roll-out process typically has two key steps: (1) communicating the plan inside the organization and to the external marketplace (i.e., investor meetings) and (2) conducting alignment workshops to ensure that all functions, regions, and countries are able to synchronize their goals, activities, and budgets to support the corporate strategy.

A few words about each of these workstreams. The communication plan should include as many voices as possible. Ideally, the rollout requires "many" executives to communicate the strategy as realistically as possible. This lets the troops know that there is buy-in at multiple levels. Second, alignment workshops are key to the enactment of the strategy, as the communication plan is necessary but not sufficient to embed the strategy into the daily activities of the organization. In these workshops, it is best to ask each person what they can do to contribute to the strategy, rather than provide top-down direction.

Developing Customer-Centered Talent

In the Microsoft transformation led by Satya Nadella, there was a pivotal senior executive off-site that included customer visits for the first time. As the story is told, there was push-back and disgruntlement to allocate time to this activity. Despite their "eye rolling and groaning," the executive

> *In a competitive economy, above all, the quality and performance of the managers determine the success of a business . . . For the quality and performance of its managers is the only effective advantage an enterprise in a competitive economy can have.*
>
> —*Drucker, p. 3*[*]

---

[*] Drucker, P. F. (1954). The practice of management. New York, NY: Harper & Row.

ended up talking for days about what they learned and what it meant for Microsoft's future. In Nadella's eyes, the transformation of Microsoft had begun.[6]

Beyond for-profit firms, Catholic Relief Services (CRS) demonstrates customer-centered talent development in a religious-based organization. Operating on the principle of subsidiarity—making decisions as close as possible to those affected—CRS requires leaders to spend significant time directly with the communities they serve.[7] For example, country directors participate in village planning sessions and community meetings, developing deep "customer knowledge" of local needs. Like Microsoft's executives, this direct engagement transforms how leaders of the organization approach their work. A great example of Drucker's principle that proximity to customers creates sustainable competitive advantage.

Almost every organization has some form of talent development in place. Indeed, most firms have programs for every talent level within the organization (e.g., onboarding of entry-level employees to executive education programs for the C-suite). These programs are absolutely essential to refresh talent. Drucker's view was that all talent needed to be developed—not just "next generation" leaders. He did not see a middle ground—organizations either invested in talent or they stunted the development of their talent.

Our key question in this section is: "What does it mean to develop talent from a customer-centered perspective?" Here we have been fortunate to work with many top organizations on their most senior programs and believe three design parameters for these programs. How these design parameters translate into education or development experiences can vary greatly by organization and industry. However, the three design parameters themselves remain stable across organizations.

- **First, there must be common understanding of the evolution of the marketplace.** This begins with a clear narrative of how the industry, marketplace, and customers will evolve. Unless the organization has similar perspectives on the future, resources will be directed haphazardly, often in the interest of the business units or functions. If you can arrive at a common viewpoint, then resources can be targeted to this future state.

- **Second, the voice and care-abouts of the customer are embedded in the design of the talent-development programs.** Often this is the starting point of the program, but it need not be. The key is that everyone attending the program understands that all actions—whether it is leadership behaviors or specific program initiative—must be tied back to the voice of the customer. Our point here is that the voice of the customer has to be a red thread that ties the entire program together.
- **Third, how is the customer experience improved as a result of the program?** What specific changes are going to be made to better serve the evolving needs of the customer? What is the impact that you expect post-program? And how do you track this impact?

Finally, beyond talent development programs, the organization must be asking how to embed customer insight and understanding on a continual basis in the role of every employee. From a Drucker perspective, it is the employee who should be asking this question—what can I do to better serve our customers? Indeed, in each yearly evaluation and performance assessment, it would be a good idea to start with the questions: "How have you helped improve the customer experience and customer satisfaction this past year?" and "What new actions can you take this coming year to improve customer relations?"

Managing Continuity and Leading Change

The final "leading the organization" characteristic is balancing of continuity and change. We address this issue further when we discuss leadership competencies later in this chapter, for now we are concerned with the ability of the top management team to deliver results in the current time period and ready the organization for the future. Recall, this is the final choice in the choice cascade in Chapter 5. Moreover, this was a continual theme of Drucker's work; the starting point for this journey is the principle of abandonment. Drucker felt that organizations had enormous difficulty in giving up products, work routines, and culture that made them successful "in the past." Here, he offers one of his most cited insights—if you were going to start your business all over again today, knowing what you now know, what would you do different?

When we have asked this question of top management teams, they often have a number of ideas about what to abandon. However, they often struggle with stopping activities. This is due to a variety of reasons—turf protection, vested interest, organizational politics, and the lack of certainty of performance outcomes. We will explore this issue in more detail in Chapter 10. However, from a Drucker view, this is the first principle of leading change.

> *A key message throughout this book is the need to balance continuity and change. Leaders need to be comfortable with experimentation. The future does not just happen—it is created by industry leaders.*

Next, Drucker argues that top management teams need to allocate 20 percent of their time and budget to the future. This, of course, is rarely the case. Keep in mind, we are not simply talking about R&D spend. Here, life science and technology-based organizations often do a good job on this budget item. However, we are referring to something much broader—the entire business that must be aligned to the future. Hence, how do you allocate talent, what are the "solutions" of the future, and what markets are most important? What new segments will emerge? What existing segments will disappear? It is this holistic view of the business that must be front and center of any discussion of the future.

Finally, returning to our quote at the start of the chapter, managing change is not simply predicting the right industry and market trends, it is actively managing those trends to shape the behavior of customers. The academic literature has made the distinction between market-driven organizations and driving markets.[8] Market-driven organizations spend a great deal of time and effort learning about current customers and current markets. They take this understanding and deliver products and services that compete very well in the present time period. This is absolutely necessary—to take a leadership position in the current industry environment. At the same time, leading organizations do not simply take the industry structure as a given; they shape the behavior of actors in the industry. This could be regulators, channel members, and key opinion leaders. This is also about shaping customer behavior. This is about changing customer behavior. Market leaders change the behavior—or as Drucker notes, management does not simply accept economic or industry conditions; they shape their evolution.

Leadership Competencies

In the previous section, we focused on what leaders need to do to lead the overall organization. Here we shift the unit of analysis to individual competencies for the top management team. These competencies include behaviors as well as mindsets regarding customer-centered leadership. In particular we address four leadership competencies.

First, as you might expect, customer insights is at the top of the list. Here we are specifically referring to taking bold action based on the unique insights that the organization has gathered and processed. Think of this as "customer evidence-based" decision-making. More broadly, these senior leaders are taking into account the entire marketplace and how it is changing. We term this an outside-in perspective. Second, customer centricity leaders are driven by curiosity—the desire to learn and know. Yet, curiosity also has a very specific business application—the willingness to challenge the status quo. Third, it follows therefore that customer-driven leaders need to drive change under conditions of uncertainty.

Finally, these three characteristics—outside-in, curiosity, and leading under uncertainty—all share an underlying "mindset and orientation," namely, balancing an ambidextrous approach to leadership.[9] That is, the ability to hold two competing perspectives in one's leadership capabilities and selectively deploy them given the situation at hand. The following sections describe each of these leadership competencies in more detail.

Outside-In: Exploit Unique Customer Insights

In Chapter 5 we focused our attention on unique, differentiated insights that could be exploited to gain competitive advantage. While it is possible to gain competitive advantage with similar customer insights, it is the novel insight that provides a runway for longer term advantage. So, what is a unique customer insight? While there is no guarantee that competitors have the same insight, leaders must be inquisitive and open-minded to challenge strongly held beliefs about customers. These strongly held beliefs often get in the way of innovation. They are a form of "groupthink" within the organization. The most fundamental question is "what do we know that others' don't know that can enable us to deliver greater value to customers and to our organization?"

You may be thinking right now about what experiences that customers desire, or what new benefits or outcomes they may be willing to pay for. However, we encourage you to think about the "where to play" question, since alternative ways to view the market provide more growth opportunities than accepting the conventional, industry-standard segmentation. Another way to think about segmentation is to consider alternative ways of extracting value from "difficult to service" or formerly "unprofitable" segments.

So, what is required of leaders? First, be inquisitive about the evolution of customer needs and desired outcomes. As detailed in Chapter 3, consumers continue to evolve particularly in the current era. That said, customers are often trained over time by the market to have certain expectations about what they will receive from any particular organization. Indeed, when several organizations provide largely the same services and offerings, customer expectations are "locked in" to a certain pattern, set of beliefs, and expectations. Consider, for example, one of your recent hotel experiences—whether it is Sheraton, Hilton, Marriott, or another experience with similar priced hotels. These are all largely the same experience, with customers largely having the same expectations. In our experience, there can even be a sense of déjà vu when traversing the halls of a Courtyard hotel built during a certain era; indeed, a customer can reasonably ask: Where is it that I am again?

Here the question to be asked by the organizations is: "What is the next benefit that can be delivered to this customer segment?" Our point is that the customer is "ready" for something new, since they have been receiving a similar experience over an extended period of time. For example, many years ago, Wi-Fi was introduced for international air travel. This was a revelation at the time and very loyal customers switched airlines in order to have communication access. What is the "next logical benefit" to offer your customers, whereby very loyal customers of competitors will switch to your offering?

Second, and relatedly, we are big fans of observing customers in their natural setting (more on that soon in Chapter 9). Years ago, Paco Underhill observed customers shopping in retail environments.[10] He was able to uncover a number of novel insights that would not be obtained by surveys or interviews with customers. For example, he found that retail establishments frequently have a "runway" where customers enter the store and "stop" to orient themselves at a logical stopping point—about 20–30 feet into the store. The interesting question therefore is where to put store signage—at the front of the store or at this natural stopping point? Also, where should stores put shopping carts—outside the store or at this natural stopping point?

Third, it is not enough to have an insight; the organization must be able to "make money" on the insight. For example, for many tourist destinations there is a standard line to enter the site (e.g., museum, ski resort) and a VIP line. The VIP line is often much more expensive, but customers are willing to pay for this service. Interestingly, it is often the case that there are "multiple options" from these destinations—from standard, to VIP, to bespoke one-on-one services. These bespoke options (private access, tour guides) are often much more expensive—but a segment of the customers is more than willing to pay for these services.

Beyond a focus on customers, leaders need to be thinking about the evolution of the industry and the broader economic environment. Clayton Christensen's work on *The Innovator's Dilemma* is a case in point of how an overzealous focus on current customers can lead a company to "miss" the evolution of the industry as a result of new emerging technology solutions or new-to-the-world competitors who provide better solutions.[11] Hence, the outside-in mindset.

Curiosity

Curiosity has been defined as "taking an interest in ongoing experience for its own sake; finding subjects and topics fascinating; exploring and discovering."[12] William James differentiated between two types of curiosity. The first entailed an emotional blend of excitement and anxiety with respect to exploring and enjoying novelty. The second was scientific curiosity or metaphysical wonder, evoked by "an inconsistency or a gap in . . . knowledge."[13]

It is this second form of curiosity—willingness to explore new information or experiences that are related to either the external environment of the organization or to the "fit" of internal resources to the evolution of the marketplace—that is most relevant for our purposes. Here, there are three specific characteristics that are associated with this "specific curiosity"—openness to new ideas, a future orientation, and the enjoyment of problem-solving.

Customer-centric orientation requires constant vigilance of the evolution of the marketplace and customer needs. A genuine openness to new ideas—new ways of serving customers, the emergence of new segments, or abandoning previously successful services—is paramount. These leaders are accepting of new ideas. Rather than quick dismissal or rejection of new ideas, they actively try to find new ways of thinking and new ways of working. They are inquisitive—asking questions and thinking creatively about various options.

A second driver of curiosity is a future orientation. This means that leaders are not simply delivering results in the current time period, but are actively thinking about how to compete in the future. It is an aspect of ambidexterity that we discuss later. That said, curiosity recognizes that the "status quo" of strategy must be constantly challenged. In particular, you should be concerned about the evolution of customers—so, both a "present" and "future" customer orientation. What do the customers of the future desire, expect, or want? What changes will this require of your organization? How do you "get ready" for the customers of the future?

A third factor is enjoyment of problem-solving. Research has shown that this third factor increases the curiosity of leaders.[14] A significant part of being a leader is solving problems. As noted earlier, problem solving is not simply correctly defining the problem; it is accurately "balancing" several legitimate options at the same time. We often observe leaders rushing to a particular solution without thinking through the various options to solve the problem. Being comfortable with alternative solutions—indeed, seeking out minority views—is essential to reaching optimal solutions.

Lead Under Uncertainty

Leading under uncertainty is a third competency of being a customer-centered leader. The starting point of leading under uncertainty is to establish a point of view about the evolution of your industry. It is relatively easy to identify 100 trends that are shared by your industry. The challenge, therefore, is to reach agreement on the five to six trends that are the most important in shaping the evolution of the industry. We referred to this early as a point of view statement. Consider this point of view of a CEO of a top 20 B2B firm in 2010[15]:

- The reordering of the global economy toward emerging markets as the main sources of growth.
- The need for new products at more price points to compete across diverse global markets.
- The geopolitical and business impact of a resource-constrained future.
- The role of substantive and strategic collaboration in a highly networked world.
- The growing intersection of dysfunctional governments with business in both mature and emerging countries.

Each of these requires a bit of explanation, but in general, you can likely see the implications for the firm. For example, the firm needed to develop new products at different price points to meet the needs of emerging markets. The emerging markets would pay 25 percent of the price of a developed economy. However, the volume had the potential to double revenues. That said, the products needed to have the same margins as the first-world products. The organization also noted that governments were going to be very dysfunctional. Therefore, they had to increase their lobbying and government relations efforts.

In general, point-of-view statements should be evaluated on four criteria.

- **Easy to comprehend.** They should be short and easy to understand.
- **Evidence-based.** They should be data-rich, grounded in real-world events, and make sense of those events. These are not opinions—there are facts to support each observation.

- **Choiceful.** Each statement has to take a position, where there could be opposite positions. For example, this CEO believes that digitization and platform businesses would reshape the industry. One could argue otherwise.
- **Actions and resources can be applied.** Each point of view statement can be accelerated if the firm invests in efforts.

Once a point of view has been established, the leader can then begin to "vision" a future state of the industry. What does the firm do to compete in this new world? What customers will emerge? What strategy should be pursued? What is going to create a competitive advantage for the firm?

Ambidexterity

This refers to the ability to juggle two different perspectives—and opposing behaviors—depending on the situation. Research has identified five distinct balancing abilities of ambidextrous leaders[16]:

- **Balance existing and future strategy.** Leaders need to be able to take advantage of short-term market opportunities within the confines of the existing strategy and, at the same time, they must actively build the new strategy.
- **Balance operational excellence and experimentation.** This is the ability to drive flawless execution, while at the same time being able to let go of those routines in order to experiment.
- **Balance formal and informal networks.** This is the ability to know how to follow formal procedures for dealing with stakeholders but possess the capacity to work this informal network to achieve mutual goals.
- **Balance centralized and decentralized decision-making.** When managing people, ambidextrous leaders have the capacity to lead from the front, telling their people what to do, but can also step back and function as a coach.
- **Balance courage and consistency.** This is the capacity to make big courageous leaps, while also having the ability to put yourself back in an equilibrium and find your quiet center.

Each of these five features of ambidexterity needs to be considered and acted upon for the organization to compete in the future. Per our observations, a seasoned ambidextrous leader is able to read the situation and "dial up or down" a particular competency given the environmental demands.

Conclusion

Our aim in this chapter was to overview the leadership capabilities of customer-centered leaders. We introduced the idea that there are two levels of leadership—one focused on the organization and the second on individual competencies of the leader. The organization level focuses on the basics of mission, vision, purpose, as well as the strategy. It also focuses on the culture of the organization and the need to develop customer-centered talent. At the same time, customer-centered leaders have to lead themselves in particular ways. The first, and most important, is to use customer insights to drive four key choices (Chapter 5)—where to play, how to win, how to shape markets, and abandonment. We also noted that these leaders share a curiosity about the future; they are always questioning the status quo. And finally, customer-centered leaders are comfortable with uncertainty and establish a point of view and "vision" to lead the organization to the future.

8

Structure and Systems

"Instead of searching for the right organization that fits the task, the organization needs to learn to look for, to develop, to test 'the organization that fits the task.'"

—Peter Drucker

Introduction

While leadership is central to being customer centered (as we laid out in Chapter 7), it is imperative to consider the overall structure and systems of the organization. In this chapter, we shift to two organizational considerations that have implications for the nature of how organizations and their leadership deliver on the promise to be more customer driven. These include choices on the structure of the organization and the systems to reward customer-driven behavior.

As Alfred Chandler noted more than 60 years ago, organizational structure follows from the strategy decisions of the firm.[1] Hence, given the focus on customer strategy choices in Chapter 5, we can now turn to the organizational structure. It is very important to note that there is no one perfect structure of an organization. Every single organization structure has strengths and limitations, which have been noted in the academic literature.[2] What is less well-known is how various structures impede or accelerate customer centricity. Indeed, even for structures

157

that are clearly designed to be customer driven, the financial outcomes are not always positive.[3] We take the point of view in this chapter that your organization has already committed to a particular organizational structure. Thus, trying to convince you to change your entire structure is not the best approach. Rather, we focus our attention on how to enhance customer centricity given that you have a particular structure in place.

We begin by discussing seven key principles of organization design that should be considered by any organization. Next, rather than discussing all potential configurations, we focus instead on the four dominant structures of global firms: divisional, matrix, geographic, and brand/product structures. Each subsection is organized to cover a description of the structure, a case study of an organization that has adopted the structure, the advantages and challenges of the structure, and recommendations to enhance customer centricity. This is the portion of the book where you can comfortably focus only on your structure—or you may decide to read all sections to see what you are missing. Finally, we also address issues related to the structure of the commercial organization as it relates to building a customer-focused strategy.

In addition, we also explore in the chapter two schools of thought regarding the reward and incentive systems that are deployed by organizations to enhance their customer orientation. The first school of thought is an externally motivated, financial perspective while the second is an internally focused, purpose-driven viewpoint. Obviously, these can work in combination. However, it is more likely to accelerate customer centricity by adopting a single school perspective.

Principles of Organizational Design

Designing an organization involves a mix of elements to ensure that it functions effectively, achieves its goals, and adapts to changing environments. In this section, we discuss seven core principles that guide organizational design.[4] The first two are related to the strategic direction and work styles of organizations, the

Organizational structure follows from the strategy decisions of the firm.

next three are related to relationships and workflow, and the final two relate to employee behavior.

Principle 1: Derived from Organizational Mission, Purpose, Vision, and Strategy

This principle follows from Chandler's observation that structure follows strategy. However, most organizations begin with their mission, purpose, and vision, as outlined in the preceding chapter. For example, if the organization's mission is to deliver services in every country in the world, that implies a very different structure than if the organization was serving a single country. Various strategies (e.g., low cost or differentiated) also have implications for the choice and prominence of various functions. The long-term goals of the enterprise (e.g., vision) also influence the choice of structure. The aim of principle 1 is to gain alignment on the "fit" between mission, purpose, vision, strategy, and structure.

Principle 2: Reinforces Culture and Values

For most companies, the key to success is the cultural norms and behaviors that drive their competitive advantage. Values are one element of culture, albeit a very important one. We covered this in detail in the last chapter. For cultures that are very development and growth oriented (like Costco), their structure needs to nurture "growth of talent from within." In contrast, the sports team, best athlete culture of Netflix should be reinforced by a structure that celebrates individual autonomy and results (vs. process). Furthermore, Netflix does not have professional development plans. In sum, the way people interact, communicate, and work together should align with the core values and principles of the organization.

Principle 3: Establishes Reporting Relationships

Defining the hierarchical relationships in an organization establishes the reporting and authority relationships. There needs to be a clear designation of decision rights and decision processes. In recent times, organizations have moved to "de-layer" their structures, in favor of flatter structures, to encourage communication and decision-making at lower levels.

Indeed, the same is true for individuals to direct themselves—a concept Drucker referred to as management by self-control. As Drucker noted, "Management is not an end in itself. It is an organ of the business enterprise. And it consists of individuals. The first requirement in managing managers is therefore that the vision of the individual managers be directed toward the goals of the business, and their wills and efforts be bent toward reaching these goals."[5]

Principle 4: Efficient Communication Flows

The efficiency and speed of information flows within organizations can be a source of competitive advantage (e.g., Zara). Hence, companies need to design the organization so that information flows efficiently across all levels. This can be vertical (up and down the hierarchy), horizontal (across departments or teams), or diagonal (across different areas of the organization). Open communication, feedback, and collaboration should be encouraged to ensure that information doesn't become siloed in a function, division, or layer of the organization.

Principle 5: Process and Workflow Efficiency

Modern organizations are built on core processes and workflows. Organizing the workflows in a way that minimizes redundancies and maximizes efficiency is essential. Processes should be streamlined to improve productivity and ensure high-quality output. The design should consider workflows across departments, ensuring smooth handoffs, timely decision-making, and fewer bottlenecks.

Principle 6: Role Clarity for Every Employee

Every person or team within the organization should have a clear understanding of their role, responsibilities, and expectations. Well-defined roles help avoid duplication of efforts and minimize confusion. As Drucker noted decades ago, jobs should be designed to provide employees with meaningful work, opportunities for growth, and a sense of autonomy. Empowering employees to take ownership of their tasks and contribute to the decision-making process can drive innovation and engagement.

Principle 7: Accountability and Performance

The organization's design should include mechanisms for holding people and teams accountable for their work. This includes clear performance indicators, feedback loops, and a transparent review process. Measuring performance at both the individual and organizational levels helps ensure alignment with the overall strategy.

By considering these principles, organizations can design a structure that is efficient, responsive, and capable of achieving long-term success. Every design choice should be intentional and serve the broader strategic goals of the organization. That stated, there are many different ways to design an organization. In the next section, we consider four distinct structures for global organizations and how they support (or fail to support) customer-centered outcomes.

Structures for Global Organizations

In this section, we consider four dominant designs for global organizations. While there are a number of additional designs to consider, the four that we review cover the overwhelming majority of global organizations. Importantly, as the previous quote notes, organization structures are fluid and redesign is frequent. Thus, the case studies we use to illustrate a particular structure may change this year or next year. The key therefore is to focus on the structure—its strengths, challenges, and how it supports a customer orientation.

We structure each as follows. We first describe the global structure. Next, we identify a well-known organization that is currently deploying that structure. We then turn to its general advantages and limitations. We conclude

Organization redesign is inevitable—half of organizations have gone through a redesign in the last two years and the other half expect to in the next two years. The benefits of a successful redesign are clear: faster growth, better decision-making, and greater efficiency. But fewer than a quarter of redesign efforts actually improve performance. Small structural changes or off-the-shelf approaches for de-layering rarely result in lasting value.[6]

with a focus on the challenges of the particular structure for customer centricity and recommendations for how those challenges can be mitigated.

Divisional Structure

This divisional structure divides the organization into semi-autonomous divisions based on product lines, markets, or geographic regions. Each division operates like its own company, with its own functional departments (marketing, finance, etc.).

Case Study: Siemens   As of 2024, Siemens's organizational structure features three main operating and three strategic companies. The operating companies are based on the historical industrial foundation of Siemens. They include (1) mobility and transportation solutions, (2) infrastructure (including smart infrastructure), and (3) the industrial digitalization platform. The strategic companies include (1) Siemens health, including a leading medical technology provider, (2) Siemens Gamesa Renewable Energy, which is part of the Siemens Energy group and focuses on renewable energy, and (3) Siemens Energy, which is a separate company spun off from Siemens, focusing on energy technology. Another component of its structure is its portfolio businesses and other business units. This includes Siemens technology, corporate real estate, consulting services, and the shared business services unit.[7]

Advantages   There are a number of advantages to a division structure. First, there is a clear focus on specific products, markets, or regions. Second, P&Ls are often division based, making it very clear who is accountable and responsible for key financial targets. Third, an organization can develop deep expertise in the industry. This know-how can be a source of competitive advantage, thus speeding up product lifecycles, product launch expertise, and industry-specific innovation. Fourth, companies can develop talent with specific knowledge and tradecraft in the industry. Finally, by focusing on one area of expertise, an organization can enhance its overall brand and reputation inside and outside of the industry.

Challenges   There are a few key challenges in operating in a division structure. One is simply the gravitational pull of the P&L. Many organizations attempt to provide solutions that involve two or more divisions but face enormous challenges in making this work. First and foremost is the reward system of the division structure. Rewards are often limited to within-division key performance indicators versus cross-division indicators. Indeed, our experience is that cross-division solutions only work if both divisions "win" financially from the solution. Even if they both win, it does not guarantee success since the cultures and ways of working in each division may not be compatible. Furthermore, employees in a given division may not know the business of the other division—or might not know key people to contact to make cross-divisions solutions a reality.

Finally, the strength of the division structure is its autonomy, but this must be traded off against the duplication of resources across divisions. Organizations often attempt to balance this tradeoff by setting up centers of excellence at the corporate level, to help them share services, know-how, and talent.

Strengths and Limitations of Customer Centricity   Division structures have a key advantage of enabling deep expertise and knowledge of key stakeholders, including customers of a particular division. As such, divisional structures often enable organizations to stay "close to their market and customers." This is a major—and perhaps *the* major—advantage of this form of organization design. However, we have observed two major challenges related to customer centricity. First, as noted, the single-minded focus on division products and solutions means that "new to the world solutions" that solve fundamental customer pain points and require cross-division collaboration are hard to achieve. Per Chapter 7, this underscores the importance of an outside-in and curiosity of the leadership team to recognize solutions that do not reside in a single division. Second, organizations can get stuck in a "product mindset" rather than a customer mindset. Rather than look at the outcomes or benefits that are provided by their products or solutions, they focus on their current offerings and technology and make incremental product modifications. This relates, in part, to the innovator's dilemma of not being aware of fundamental technology or market shifts.

So, how can organizations overcome these inherent challenges? First, rather than focus on cross-division collaboration, they need to focus on the evolution of customer needs. That is the starting point. For Siemens healthcare, this means focusing not on its various medical solutions, but on the patient, physician, and hospital needs first. Too often, firms rush to provide integrated, digital healthcare solutions without first understanding the stakeholder problems at a deep, visceral level.

Second, organizations need to pilot solutions. Think minimally viable pilots and offerings. For large companies, they often stifle cross-division solutions by requiring stage-gate processes, steering committee oversight, and financial metrics that are unreasonable at the startup stage. Drucker made the argument that organizations need to continually experiment and "pilot" offerings to test the evolution of the marketplace. This needs to be small in scale, resource light, and unconstrained by the bureaucracy of large organizations.

Third, divisions need to get to know the business of other divisions. We would be surprised if the healthcare division of Siemens knows the fundamental business operations of the transportation division. There is likely to be little cross-division collaboration if one does not have the "know-how" and "know-who" of the other divisions.

Fourth, senior division executives wear two hats—the enterprise versus division hat. Our experience is that 99 percent of the time, the senior division executives wear the division hat, not the enterprise one. This works well because their rewards are based almost entirely on the P&L of the division. Moreover, it keeps the executive single mindedly focused on their current and evolving market. However, at the C-suite level, the CEO needs the team to focus on both the enterprise performance and the results of their specific divisions or functions. In working with these teams, we have found it useful to introduce the two hats terminology and to declare in key debates which hat the senior executive is wearing.

Fifth, and perhaps most obviously, companies need to align incentives to accomplish cross-division collaborations. Obviously, if they are designing win-win solutions for each division, incentives are aligned. Hence, we often recommend starting with solutions that are win-win. Indeed, this is perhaps our strongest recommendation since the pull of the divisional P&L is so strong.

Matrix Structure

The matrix structure combines elements of functional and divisional structures. Employees report to two managers: one based on their function (e.g., marketing or finance) and the other based on product, region, or project. This structure is often used in organizations where there is a need for both functional expertise and global or product-specific focus.

Case Study: Nike Nike employs a matrix organizational structure, combining functional and divisional (geographic) structures, which allows for global integration and local responsiveness. This structure involves global headquarters, regional headquarters, and business units, with employees reporting to both functional and product/ regional managers.

In particular, global headquarters set overall strategy and global standards. Regional headquarters adapt and localize the strategy to their specific geographic areas. Nike also has divided its businesses into major segments. Each segment is responsible for managing the manufacturing, distribution, and marketing of relevant products. The company's primary business segments include (1) the Nike Brand designs, distributes, and markets Nike's footwear, apparel, and equipment; (2) Converse, a subsidiary of Nike, oversees the design and marketing of Converse footwear and apparel; and (3) Jordan, overseeing the global marketing, design, and distribution of Air Jordan athletic footwear (mainly basketball). These segments operate within the boundaries of the regional strategies.

With respect to the matrix structure, there are functional departments and regional teams. Employees belong to functional departments (e.g., innovation, manufacturing, finance, sales). Employees also belong to product or regional teams. As such, they have a dual reporting structure, reporting to both a functional manager and a product/regional manager.[8]

Advantages   The principal advantage of this form of structure is the alignment across functions, divisions, and regions. Communication is fluid and, as a result, it promotes collaboration across functions and divisions. In theory, this type of structure should facilitate faster decision-making, flexibility, and adaptability. It is also designed to enhanced sharing of knowledge and resources.

Challenges   While this structure has the potential to provide synergistic integration, it is complex and has the potential for conflicts due to the dual reporting lines. Philips moved away from its matrix structure, which was no longer effective, primarily due to issues with accountability. Specifically, the matrix structure, where employees reported to both functional managers (e.g., country heads) and product managers, created confusion regarding profit-and-loss (P&L) responsibility. Philips implemented a reorganization in the early 1990s, creating units with worldwide responsibility for groups of the company's businesses, such as consumer electronics and medical products. The national offices then became subservient to these new units, which were built around products and based at the firm's headquarters. In more recent years, Philips has continued to draw back from this structure without a radical reorganization, implementing changes such as appointing a chief marketing officer to focus more on customers.[9]

Strengths and Limitations of Customer Centricity   There are two key strengths from a customer perspective. First, the matrix organization enables more comprehensive communication flows. Hence, once an organization has made an evidence-based customer decision, they can align behind that decision. Second, it enables integrated customer-facing decisions since all key parties provide input to the decisions. However, its complexity can create two major challenges for customer centricity. The first is speed to market. The key tradeoff is coordination versus time to market. While the matrix structure provides better coordination, the multiple touch points slow decision-making and impede the time to market for new or updated solutions. Hence, competitors can move more quickly to respond to evolving customer needs, assuming they have a simpler organizational structure.

The second is that its complexity leads companies to focus inward versus outside. Several years ago, we were working for one of the world's largest business-to-business organizations. A key challenge for them was the complexity of the business and the need to be more agile and "simple." In the course of our discussions with them, they noted that key senior executives needed to have the courage to overcome the matrix organizations. We found this a curious phrase since the entire point of a structure of the organization was to help individuals achieve their objectives! Instead, the structure became a major obstacle to overcome.

Geographical Structure

In this structure, the organization is divided into regions or geographic areas. Each region operates with a high degree of autonomy, allowing for localized decision-making and strategy implementation.

Case Study: Coca-Cola   The Coca-Cola Company's operational structure includes five geographic operating segments: Europe; Middle East & Africa; Latin America; North America; and Asia Pacific. The company's reporting structure also includes the non-geographic segments of Global Ventures and Bottling Investments.[10] The aim was to combine the benefits of a global scale with the deep local intimacy to win within regions/markets.

Advantages   For large organizations that are focused on a very narrow product line (like Coke)—as compared to the conglomerate Siemens we discussed earlier—the geographic structure makes a great deal of sense. First, it enables greater understanding and responsiveness to local markets and cultures. And as such, companies are able to tailor products and services to regional needs. Second, it recognizes that there are variations by region—both in terms of the context and the customer behavior.

Challenges   There is a tradeoff when an organization decides to give the decision rights on localization to the regional team. The first is the risk of duplication of resources across regions. Region A and region B might use the same agencies, partners, and software systems (e.g., ERP, CRM, Salesforce) but not take advantage of potential cost reductions of partners as a single organization. Second, there is the risk of less standardization across the organization. This may not be a challenge in certain areas, but if the brand is markedly different across regions, it can be a major problem.

Strengths and Limitations of Customer Centricity   On the one hand, the ability to understand the unique regional and/or country needs of customers and deliver against those needs is an excellent example of being customer driven. Needs, wants, and expectations vary from region to region, thus this is perhaps the key customer strength of this form of organization. On the other hand, it is often the case that regional divisions do not get together on a regular basis to discuss their evolving market needs. As a result, the "common thread" of needs across regions may be missed. Second, there may be "lead countries" where the customers in those regions represent the "early signals" of shifts in customer preferences. Again, the lack of this knowledge transfer across regions means that a given region may be slow to adjust to trends, even though the insights were available in the lead region. Third, if as a result of customization, the brand has a different image in the various regions, it could lessen its overall global value.

Product-Based Structure

A product-based structure organizes the company according to its product lines. Each product line or brand has its own functional departments, such as marketing, sales, and operations, to handle its respective business needs.

Case Study 1: P&G   P&G operates through five industry-based Sector Business Units or SBUs: Baby, Feminine and Family Care; Beauty; Health Care; Grooming; and Fabric and Home Care.[11]

The SBUs have sales, profit, cash, and value creation responsibility for P&G's largest and most profitable markets, termed Focus Markets—accounting for about 80 percent of sales and 90 percent of after-tax profit. In each Focus Market, market operations work across the five SBUs on scaled market services and capabilities, including customer teams, transportation, warehousing, logistics, and representing P&G externally.

The rest of the world is organized into Enterprise Markets—a separate unit with sales, profit, and value creation responsibility. The SBUs provide innovation plans, supply plans, and operating frameworks for the Enterprise Markets to deliver these mutually agreed business goals. Enterprise Markets are important to the future of P&G because of their attractive market growth rates, and the intent is to accelerate this growth and value creation.

Supporting the SBUs, market operations, and Enterprise Markets are key corporate resources focused on scaled services, governance, stewardship, and areas requiring high mastery. This structure enables a more empowered, agile, and accountable organization to accelerate growth and value creation.

Case Study 2: Unilever   Unilever is a major competitor of P&G. It is interesting to compare its operations to P&G. It operates around five distinct business groups, including Beauty & Wellbeing, Personal Care, Home Care, Nutrition, and Ice Cream. Each business group is fully responsible for its own strategy, growth, and profit delivery globally, and thus is held with more accountability. These are not identical to P&G, but there is significant overlap.

Each business group contains particular categories and manages well-known brands. For example, the Beauty & Wellbeing business group includes categories like Hair Care, Skin Care, and Prestige Beauty. The Personal Care group, for instance, includes brands like Dove, Rexona, and Axe. Again, this is similar to the brand orientation of P&G.

The five groups are supported by Unilever Business Operations, which provides the technology, systems, and processes to drive operational excellence across the business. By organizing around product categories, Unilever aims to respond to consumer and channel trends more effectively. The organizational model is designed to reduce complexity and enable faster responses to consumer demands. Again, both operate with this shared services and operations model.

Advantages   The key advantage of this structure is that it enables brand and category managers to maintain a consistent brand meaning and image across the globe. As compared to other structures, it is easier to manage product-specific strategies and initiatives. Third, the brand management structure is a training ground to manage the end-to-end business. Hence, it facilitates talent development, management, and growth. Fourth, know-how can be transferred across the brand structure.

Challenges   At times, the number of SKUs can be overwhelming, leading to duplication and cannibalization within the product category. When managing large global brands, companies may be less focused on regional or functional synergies.

Strengths and Limitations of Customer Centricity   On the positive side, the good news is that strong brands often are tied to specific segments and their needs. For example, the Axe brand is targeted to young men, with a similar brand positioning globally. One limitation of the brand organizational structure is that each brand is its own P&L. As such, it raises an issue that is similar to the cross-division challenges noted earlier in the chapter. Namely, it is hard to gain cooperation across brands—to provide "bundles" of solutions, for example, in healthcare or beauty.

In summary, there is no one best organizational structure. All have their strengths and limitations related to customer centricity. The key is to identify the challenge—and make sure everyone is aware of the challenge. Then, the next step is to address the challenges as best as possible—given various constraints faced by each organization.

Commercial Structure: Observations and Recommendations

In recent years, firms have started to group all customer-facing functions into what has been termed the commercial organization. The commercial organization is the business unit responsible for driving revenue, profitability, and market share through customer acquisition, relationship management, and go-to-market execution. It typically encompasses functions such as sales, marketing, business development, pricing, customer success, and sometimes even product management. In this section, we address issues related specifically to the commercial organization. While there is literature that has emerged in marketing on the structure of marketing organizations and customer-focused structures, we turn our attention in this section to specific commercial structures that organizations have employed to become more customer driven. Since we have had the good fortune of being involved in many customer-centered transformations, we rely on our first-hand observations of these client journeys.

Vertical Markets

Many B2B companies organize their sales activities by vertical markets (e.g., government, automotive) and develop a client-centered approach based on the belief that these customers have similar preferences, buyer behavior, and needs. As such, dedicated salespeople and marketing collateral that is specific to these vertical markets is the best way to deliver a customer-focused experience. This approach does have merit. As the sales rep serves a vertical segment, they are able to develop expertise and tradecraft regarding the unique characteristics of the vertical market (e.g., how they buy, who are the stakeholders, the unique vocabulary and processes that are related to the industry). The deep vertical expertise enables the salesperson to develop industry-specific credibility, and they develop and serve clients.

That stated, there are a number of challenges that need to be acknowledged with this vertical approach. First, we have observed significant variation in the buyer behavior within the vertical markets. Our key question to clients is, "do all customers in the vertical segment have the same needs and care-abouts?" If not, then the company needs to think about segments within the vertical. Indeed, we often observe more commonalities across verticals (e.g., desire for low-cost solutions emerges in every vertical) than within.

Second, salespeople develop strongly held assumptions about the vertical market that may not be true. Here is where curiosity is critical. While the tendency is to look for situations where current products can be sold, the salesperson needs to balance this "sales orientation" with a curiosity orientation around the evolution of customers in the vertical.

Third, organizations tend to lock in on the vertical markets. By structuring the organization to serve verticals, it is hard to see the industry evolution. When does a new vertical emerge? When should they stop serving a vertical market? Once an organization locks in on a vertical, it is hard to abandon that vertical even if it is no longer economically viable.

Key Account Management

The entire purpose of a key account management structure is to recognize that organizations have different-sized accounts (e.g., large, medium, and small customer accounts) and they need to be managed differently. That is, large accounts will have dedicated sales teams that serve that single client while smaller accounts may be served by call centers or distributors. Here the organization recognizes that large accounts provide the most economic value to the organization and should therefore be served with dedicated resources that match the value capture.

While we agree with this form of commercial structure, we want to point out three issues that we have observed in practice. First, organizations need to think carefully about the "unit of analysis" within their largest accounts. A customer is not a company; it is a collection of people in roles. Purchase decisions are made by people, individually and collectively, who share the same heuristics and biases as consumer markets. As such, companies need to deeply understand the buying collective and how their needs vary by role. Also, companies need to be very clear about whether the unit of analysis is a whole company, a division of a company, or something less than that, such as a plant.[12]

Second, who is accountable and responsible for the performance of the account? While this may seem like an obvious answer, the reality is that it is best to have multiple organization personnel involved with multiple customer personnel. There may be a role for the salesperson to be the orchestrator of all the various relationships, but the account becomes a sticky relationship account when there are many different relationships (e.g., our supply chain team works with their supply chain team, our R&D folks work with the client R&D team).

Third, customer centricity is about providing mutual value to both the customer and the organization. One challenge with large accounts is that they are frequently very demanding, and there are often "hidden costs" of serving these accounts. Once these hidden costs (e.g., time, changing requirements, client management) are fully accounted for, firms often discover that their largest accounts are not their most profitable accounts.

Finally, firms need to think carefully about customer migration—both deterioration and growth. Small accounts can become large accounts and large accounts can become small accounts. This happens for a variety of reasons related to economics of the client organization, industry trends, change in key senior client personnel, and account management approaches. Firms need to have a standing committee who is able to take an enterprise-wide view on the movement of accounts and think strategically about the mix and evolution of these accounts.

The challenge for the commercial organization in managing key accounts is to manage continuity and change. Key accounts are an excellent structure to enable customer centricity. However, firms need to be keenly aware of account transitions—mid-size accounts transitioning to large accounts and large accounts that "disappear" for a number of reasons (often due to competitors better serving the account's needs).

Reward, Incentive, and Recognition

As organizations focus attention on customers, there is a need to design reward and recognition systems to drive customer-centered thinking, motivation, and behaviors. While there are many perspectives on human behavior, we focus on two prominent schools of thought that contrast perspectives on what drives employee behavior: an externally motivated, financial school and an internally motivated, purpose-driven school. While both acknowledge the importance of motivation, they diverge sharply on their source and nature, often leading to different organizational cultures and strategies.

The externally motivated, financial school of thought, rooted in classical management theories and economic principles, posits that humans are fundamentally driven by extrinsic rewards, primarily financial compensation. This perspective finds its foundation with Taylor's scientific management and emphasizes efficiency and productivity achieved through clearly defined tasks, standardized procedures, and performance-based pay.[13] It is also the ground from which Friedman's ideas on shareholder value maximization sprung to life.

The key assumption is that people are "rational actors" who seek to maximize their economic gain. But as noted in Chapter 6, humans (whether consumers or employees) are not rational actors. Under this paradigm, motivation becomes a matter of designing incentive systems that directly link customer-centered behaviors to financial rewards. Bonuses, commissions, and promotions based on customer centricity become the primary tools for driving performance, while potential disincentives, such as the fear of job loss or reduced pay, are used to deter undesirable behaviors.

Financial incentives can indeed boost a customer-centered culture. However, their limitations become apparent when dealing with complex customer issues that require curiosity, creativity, and collaboration. Think a car salesperson at the end of the month where "sell, sell, sell" is the dealership's mantra of the moment. Focusing solely on financial rewards can lead to a narrow, transactional relationship between employees and the organization, where loyalty and intrinsic motivation are sacrificed for short-term gains. Furthermore, this approach can foster a culture of competition and individual achievement at the expense of teamwork and shared goals. This is the exact opposite of an enterprise-wide view of the customer. The emphasis on extrinsic rewards can also crowd out intrinsic motivation, diminishing the inherent satisfaction derived from meaningful work serving customers (like one would see at Trader Joes, Nordstrom). When employees perceive their efforts solely as a means to a financial end, they may become less engaged and less likely to go the extra mile.

In contrast, the internally motivated, purpose-driven school of thought emphasizes the power of intrinsic motivation, stemming from a sense of purpose, meaning, and alignment with the organization's mission. We explore this approach to organizational purpose in Chapter 11, but here we want to draw attention as to its critical role in incentivizing customer-centered behavior within the organization. This perspective, ignited by writers like Viktor Frankl and more recently by Simon Sinek, recognizes that humans are driven by a deeper desire to contribute to something larger than themselves. It suggests that people (whether employees or customers in an organizational context) are more likely to be engaged, committed, and productive when they feel their work has a positive impact and aligns with their personal values. This school of thought posits that organizations should focus on creating a customer-centered culture that fosters a sense of purpose, where employees understand how their work contributes to the overall mission of serving customers. This involves clearly articulating the organization's values and goals, providing opportunities for employees to develop their skills and grow, and fostering a sense of community and belonging.

Returning to Habitat for Humanity, they have a stated purpose to provide everyone with a decent place to live. This purpose is what motivates people to willfully volunteer their time and effort to deliver this purpose. While Habitat is a nonprofit, there are many for-profit firms—like REI, Patagonia, and Johnson & Johnson—whose mission and purpose enable society to function better.

Organizations that embrace this approach often prioritize mission-driven initiatives, invest in employee development, and create a culture of transparency and trust. They understand that intrinsic motivation can lead to higher levels of customer centricity. Employees who feel a sense of purpose are more likely to be proactive, take initiative, and collaborate effectively. They are also more likely to be resilient in the face of challenges and setbacks, as they are driven by a deeper sense of meaning. This school of thought acknowledges that financial compensation is important, but it views it as a necessary condition rather than the primary driver of motivation (think shareholder vs. stakeholder views). It recognizes that people are motivated by a complex interplay of factors, including autonomy, mastery, and purpose.

However, implementing a purpose-driven approach requires a fundamental shift in organizational culture and leadership. As expanded upon in Chapter 11, such an approach demands a genuine commitment to values-based leadership, open communication, and employee empowerment. It also requires a willingness to invest in employee development and create a work environment that fosters a sense of customer centricity. Furthermore, some critics argue that the purpose-driven model can be hard to implement in some industries that are highly competitive and have very tight margins. In those cases, financial incentives may be the only realistic, immediate motivator.

BRAC, an NGO operating across Bangladesh, Uganda, Liberia, and Sierra Leone, motivates employees with a hybrid model. Local teams have the freedom to adapt services to community-specific needs, which enables employee empowerment and local responsiveness. In contrast, centralized systems exist for training, data management, and operational oversight—an approach that maintains consistency and enables knowledge sharing across regions. Such an approach prevents fragmentation that often comes with decentralized structures, proving that organizations can remain locally responsive without losing coherence.[14]

Employees who feel a sense of purpose are more likely to be proactive, take initiative, and collaborate effectively.

Ultimately, the most effective approach to motivating human behavior in organizations likely lies in a synthesis of these two schools of thought. While financial compensation remains a crucial factor, organizations that prioritize purpose, meaning, and employee development are more likely to cultivate a highly engaged and productive workforce. By creating a customer-centered culture that balances extrinsic rewards with intrinsic motivation, organizations can unlock the full potential of their employees and achieve sustainable customer satisfaction and loyalty. The key is to recognize that humans are not simply economic actors, but complex, multilayered individuals driven by a desire to contribute, grow, and find meaning in their work.

By understanding and addressing these fundamental human needs, organizations can create a workplace where people thrive and the organization flourishes.

Conclusion

The aim of this chapter was to introduce organizational design mechanisms that can foster a customer-centered culture. The structure of the organization as well as the design of the commercial organizations are key levers in shaping employee commitment, engagement, and enablement. Moreover, the reward systems that organizations put in place can accelerate employee behavior to respond to customer needs and pain points. As we suggest, it is often a combination of external and internal rewards that create the most sustainable customer-centered culture.

9

Customer Intelligence and Insights

"The goal is to transform data into information and information into insight."
—Carly Fiorina, 2004[1]

Introduction

Why customer intelligence? At the heart of any customer-centric strategy is going to be data or information about an organization's customers (which we call *customer intelligence*). We contend, as detailed in this chapter, that to develop such a strategy, companies must create, gain insights from, and disseminate customer intelligence. As noted in the opening quote, this process is more than just collecting data, but rather turning that data into information and insights that can drive strategic direction in the marketplace. As noted by Peter Drucker, "The purpose of information is not knowledge. It is being able to take the right action."[2] Aligning with Drucker's view, we argue that organizations must have customer intelligence (generated from reliable and valid data) to develop market insights, and that such information must be diffused throughout the organization to take the "right action." Any other approach would simply be limiting, particularly for organizations aiming to develop an enterprise-wide, customer-centric strategy.

A critical aspect of customer intelligence is the concept of feedback, which in this context is from buyers of an organization's products or services. The process of feedback has been identified by numerous academic fields as being central to human evolution (including biological, psychological, social, and cultural dimensions). Such a mechanism is critical as it allows organisms to adapt in response to environmental challenges, thereby increasing chances of survival and reproduction over time. So perhaps it is not surprising that soliciting customer feedback (aka intelligence) emerged alongside the development of commerce.

Feedback from customers is often solicited by marketers. As detailed in Chapter 6, the current view of marketing emerged during the industrial revolution; however, evidence of marketing-related activities, such as branding, date back many thousands of years with evidence from early Mesopotamia and ancient Egypt.[3] Other documented marketing activities (prior to the industrial revolution) can be found throughout the world, including ancient Greece, the Roman empire, China, South America, and Africa.[4] It seems natural that these activities were supported by "market research" where sellers asked customers what they thought of a particular product. Such activities became more formalized in the middle ages, where merchant guilds would gather information from customers for various purposes (e.g., observing customer demand, managing product quality, and responding to complaints).[5] The drive behind marketing and related solicitation of feedback happened alongside the development of human communication, trade practices, and general economic development.

The importance of customer intelligence exploded during the industrial revolution with the mass production of consumable products. Customers no longer had direct contact with those who produced their products and organizations had limited direct access to their customers—a situation that increased the need for producers to understand more about who was buying their goods. As we noted in Chapter 6, one of the earliest examples of such work was from the

American ad agency N. W. Ayer & Son, founded in 1869. In the late 1800s, this firm performed systematic consumer surveys to measure preferences and reactions to advertisements.[6] Such practices grew in the early 21st century with well-known names such as Gallup, Nielsen, and J. Walter Thompson. These pioneers shaped our understanding and practices related to customer intelligence.

Fast forward—emerging technologies in the 20th century and early 2000s have revolutionized the collection, interpretation, and dissemination of intelligence about customers. Such practices have become more complicated and sophisticated (now fueled by AI); perhaps the only limit to such efforts is a firm's imagination (and any applicable laws) on how to collect such information. Take, for example, the gaming industry, where Epic Games (Fortnite) and Riot Games (League of Legends) collect player behavior data, in-game purchases, social interactions, and performance metrics to optimize gameplay, balance characters, and personalize the player experience.[7] Such an approach is in an entirely different realm, compared to wait staff at your favorite restaurant asking you, "how was the food?" after you complete a meal.

In this chapter, we dig deep into how organizations collect, sensemake, and use market insights to drive strategic decision-making. We scratched the surface of these topics earlier in Chapter 4, and now deeply explore a three-phased approach customer-centered organizations need to employ to leverage customer intelligence:

- **First, companies must systematically collect detailed insights about customers, which are framed as related to the company's competitors and the broader marketplace.** Critical in this step is moving beyond confirming known information but rather uncovering unique and actionable intelligence.
- **In the second step, the organization must support the collaborative interpretation of collected information.** People should come from across the entire organization (including marketing, finance, and R&D) to discuss, debate, and make sense of the intelligence.
- **Finally, companies must put these insights directly into practice, making strategic decisions related to the company's products or services and/or how it competes.** Instead of just

gathering information, successful companies must make sure that they actually use customer intelligence to drive decision-making and set a customer-centric strategy.

Generation of Customer Intelligence

Producing actionable intelligence involves deeply understanding customer care-abouts within the broader marketplace context, including competitors, substitutes, distribution channels, and technological trends. There are two types of data-based insights available to organizations, including secondary sources made up of existing data gathered for different purposes (e.g., industry reports, government statistics, academic studies) and primary sources, which include collecting new, original intelligence tailored specifically for the organization. The message here is that both sources of information are useful in shaping business strategies, but each has its pros and cons.

Secondary research is cost effective and quick, thereby providing valuable insights on context and trends in society or a company's primary industry. One downside we have observed is that no matter the quality of the secondary data, it may not directly address issues relevant to the organization. However, this can be mitigated by applying advanced technology to large data sets that can allow organizations to realize value from secondary data. Take, for example, Levi Strauss, who partnered with Google Cloud. By applying data analytics to global secondary data (e.g., consumer purchases, online browsing behaviors, retail partner information, loyalty program details), Levi was able to identify rising global demand for looser-fit jeans. This insight informed their product and marketing strategy and resulted in a considerable increase in sales for their jean products.[8]

Primary research, the focus of this chapter, provides direct customer intelligence that is focused, exact, and timely to the needs of the organization. We contend that being effective at producing this form of market intelligence, an organization can distinguish itself by providing genuinely new and actionable insights rather than confirming what is already known. Such intelligence needs to be scientifically defensible, aptly differentiated (enough to give the organization a unique advantage), and sufficiently straightforward to implement. While most organizations prioritize short-term, immediately actionable intelligence, a balanced approach that also includes forward-looking research will better position organizations for long-term success.

The Research Process

A typical research process involves multiple steps, starting with "defining the problem."[9] This is the critical first step in the process, as it frames all the remaining activities and ultimately influences the outcome of the intelligence operation. Our view here aligns with that of Drucker who argued that focusing on the right questions is more important than jumping to the right answers. Organizations should begin by identifying specific decisions or opportunities the research will address—asking questions such as, why are sales dropping, why is customer satisfaction on the rise—and then frame these into clear, actionable research questions. Doing this in isolation is not a good idea; it is important to engage stakeholders (like those in sales, marketing, operations) early to ensure that multiple perspectives are considered. Without this step, costly misunderstandings are possible, if not likely. The key point here is that precise problem identification helps to align intelligence generation with the needs of the organization and make outcomes directly relevant and actionable to set strategy.

Next, the company needs to develop an approach to tackling the identified problem whereby goals and directions of the work are clearly mapped out. During this stage, organizations need to define key ideas, questions, and issues that must be understood to make decisions using the intelligence. Our position is that it is helpful for managers to consider outcomes they expect (not want!) and have a sense of what the research might reveal. Doing so ensures that the intelligence generation remains practical, focused, and directly tied to key business decisions. Experience tells us that having a clear approach to start with makes it easier to choose the right data, methods later and ensures the research delivers useful insights that can immediately help solve real-world business challenges. For all market intelligence projects, it is essential to understand exactly what information key decision-makers need, whether it be basic customer insights or data to resolve internal debates about strategy.

Next is formulating a research design that selects the best approach for collecting customer intelligence. At a macro level, the research design must relate to the goals of the project. For example, "exploratory research" is best to help understand new or unclear problems, while "descriptive research" is often used to quantify conditions in the marketplace or customer preferences. More advanced designs can assess "cause-and-effect relationships" (e.g., did a firm's new pricing strategies affect customer demand). The important point here is that detailed decisions need to be made regarding how the data will be collected (e.g., surveys, focus groups, web scraping), from whom (e.g., existing customers, noncustomers in the target segment, or others), and how much is needed (e.g., are 100 surveys enough or do you need 200).

Depending on the decisions made in this step, research projects can range from the relatively simple (e.g., a quick, online survey to solicit customer feedback on a new product) to more complex (e.g., in-depth interviews with customers to understand deeper purchase motivations). By carefully formulating a design to gather market intelligence, insights gained from the intelligence are more readily able to inform strategic decisions. Like any business decision, how the company formulates a research design is influenced by budgets, timelines, the marketplace context, availability of in-house expertise, and the types of decisions that need to be made using the intelligence.

The final stages of the process reflect practical aspects of executing the actual research project and getting the data in the door. While most likely these aspects of intelligence gathering will be conducted by trained professionals (often external to the organization), it is important for leadership to appreciate this final, crucial step. Data collection should be done in a way to ensure that accurate, reliable data is collected by the chosen method (e.g., via surveys, interviews, scanner data). Quality control is critical here, as poor data compromises your decision-making. The GIGO (garbage in, garbage out) principle should be top of mind during this part of the process. Finally, the collected data needs to be organized, cleaned, and appropriately analyzed.

Digits and Dialogues

Methods and analytical tools are often categorized as either "quantitative" (anything based on numbers) or "qualitative" (grounded in the written or spoken word). Let's say your company conducts a survey of its customers with the generated data being analyzed using basic regression models; this is quantitative data. This compares to you conducting customer focus groups with the data analyzed using grounded theory methods. Like many of our points, what works best is contextual. Each type of data and associated method provides its own value in setting strategy—quantitative methods provide more precise and scalable insights, while qualitative approaches deliver context and deeper understanding.[10]

More specifically, quantitative methods involve statistical analysis of numerical data, are generally precise in nature, and allow for greater scaling of results. Techniques for generating such data include surveys, test markets, customer purchase behavior, with data being analyzed using various forms of statistical analyses from the simple (correlations and cross tabulations) to the mind-numbingly complex (structural equations or hierarchical linear modeling). We have seen all being applied by firms in our experience. A great example of applying quantitative methods is provided by Capital One's "test-and-learn" approach to innovation. Since the late 1980s, the firm has conducted small experiments to help refine product design, drive marketing strategy, and support customer selection. Capital One's commitment to data-driven experimentation is a cornerstone of its business operations by continually informing and refining its strategy.[11]

In contrast, qualitative methods are based on non-numerical data and employ specific techniques to analyze the written or spoken word. Researchers will tell you that these methods provide deeper insights into a firm's customers than are likely to be generated with quantitative methods. This data is produced from focus groups, depth interviews, ethnographies, and observational methods. Data analysis uses techniques such as grounded theory to provide narrative insights related to customers. A cool and useful example is the Zaltman Metaphor Elicitation Technique (often called ZMET)—a unique, qualitative research method that helps uncover deep, subconscious thoughts and feelings of customers. Zaltman's method uses both visual imagery and metaphor; specifically, participants select pictures that represent thoughts about a topic, which are then explored through guided interviews. ZMET has been applied to various situations and companies (e.g., Batta, Coca-Cola, Disney, Nestle) typically aimed at branding issues, with it helping to reveal hidden emotional drivers behind customer behavior.

Technology-Fueled Advances

Recently, research methods that can be employed to gain customer insight have evolved significantly. Numerous emerging technologies (e.g., AI, web analytics, internet of things, machine learning, data scraping) have driven the use and wider adoption of complex methods. As detailed earlier, we have seen such advances greatly enhance the ability of organizations to gather intelligence on customer wants and needs.[12] Examples abound of how firms are using advanced techniques in this way. Sephora's "Virtual Artist" feature—a digital platform that uses facial recognition technology to allow users to virtually try on makeup—is an example of an advanced customer research that transforms data collection by capturing real-time, granular insights into consumer behavior.[13] By tracking which lipstick shades users explore, how long they interact with different products, and which items they ultimately save or purchase, the technology provides visibility into customer care-abouts.

Another example is how Domino's transformed their European market strategy. To do so, they broke down data silos through Google's integrated tools (Analytics Premium, Tag Manager, and BigQuery), thus enabling them to merge customer information across digital platforms.[14] This approach allowed them to track comprehensive customer behaviors across multiple devices, with online sales growing 30 percent year-over-year and mobile orders representing 44 percent of digital sales. By creating a holistic view of customer interactions, they achieved a 6 percent immediate increase in monthly revenue, positioning themselves as the most popular pizza delivery chain in the United Kingdom, Ireland, Germany, and Switzerland, with £766.6 million in revenue by 2014.

The takeaway here is understanding the important role of traditional qualitative and quantitative methods in intelligence gathering activities of organizations. The fundamental value of these core techniques is time tested and remains, with their value being enhanced with increased computer power that can analyze larger, more readily available customer data. In our view, adding AI into the mix is like dumping gasoline on a fire, with its ability to more quickly and efficiently dig into customer insight data to unearth patterns and explore factors affecting customer behavior.

Nike has been using Nike Fit, an innovative smartphone-based technology that uses computer vision and machine learning to accurately measure customers' feet, recommending precise shoe sizes. As Nike's chief innovation officer John Hoke described it, traditional shoe sizing was a "gross simplification of a complex problem."[15] By scanning feet and creating a 3D model with 13 visual data points, the technology transforms shoe sizing from a consumer frustration into a strategic data collection opportunity. While solving the problem of ill-fitting shoes—an issue affecting 60 percent of consumers (including one of the authors of this book!)—Nike simultaneously generates rich insights into foot morphology and consumer preferences, turning every sizing interaction into a valuable market intelligence tool. No matter the method or the supplementary role of technology, the critical issue here for you is to know that the method needs to appropriately match the specific goals of the intelligence gathering. Ultimately, when selecting a research method, companies need to ensure that it precisely addresses their existing knowledge gaps.

Sense-Making of Customer Data

So now a company has a large set of data and findings to interpret regarding its customers on a particular topic of importance to strategy. No matter the topic being covered, the research design and method employed, or how the data was collected, it is essential that results of data collection provide accurate and relevant insights into the customers and that the organization makes sense of them. Our experience tells us that there are many steps and considerations that must be addressed to move data to true marketplace intelligence that can be used by the organization.

Data Quality and Analysis

Prior to conducting data analysis, it is important to ensure quality of the data (e.g., regarding accuracy, completeness, consistency, timeliness, validity). Investment to make certain the data is of high quality is well worth it, as it will be more likely to generate information that can be usefully utilized for decision-making. We have seen numerous threats to data quality including human error, issues within data systems, data silos, no data governance, record duplication, and compliance to name a few. Organizations can get ahead of these issues with proper training of staff, system integration, data security systems, and a clear data governance policy—all of which are complex and resource intensive.

Good research needs to be scientifically defensible, aptly differentiated, and sufficiently straightforward to implement.

Even when data owned by an organization is of high quality, for example genetic data from 23 and Me, things can still go wrong. In late 2023, this genetic testing company experienced a significant data breach related to approximately seven million users. The data (including personal details and genetic information) was subsequently sold online by the thieves. The breach hurt the company's reputation so badly that financial struggles ensued, ending in a March 2025 bankruptcy.[16] Make no mistake about it, data privacy of customers is a critical consideration for nearly all firms. For example, General Motors, in early 2025, was banned from selling customer geolocation and driving behavior data. The ruling from the FTC was driven by investigators who learned that GM had been selling this data to various organizations without customer consent, resulting in increased insurance premiums for the owners.[17]

Data versus Information

"Data" is the raw facts that describe some event, activity, or object; on their own data provides little meaning. Examples include product IDs, the number of web page views, or 0/1 purchase behavior of customers. "Information," on the other hand, is data that has been transformed into something useful—by processing, organizing, and interpreting it within a particular context. In other words, information is data that has been processed, organized, and interpreted to provide meaning, context, and understanding.[18]

If data is the raw input, then information is a useful output that supports decision-making. Transforming data into information allows an organization to use it for various purposes. In terms of setting a customer-centric strategy, we have found that good decisions are not made on data alone, rather decision-making should be anchored on information that is interpretable and actionable. Take, for example, a large data set that contains customer transactions of shoppers at a retail store (e.g., Target, Walmart, Kohl's). The usefulness of this data is significantly increased after the retailer actively considers things such as customer segments, market trends, and pricing levels of products.

Peter Drucker, who introduced the concept of the information worker to the world, elaborated on the important differences between data and information. In particular, he emphasized that data in isolation does not provide sufficient meaning for the company, and therefore must be transformed into valuable information. Drucker is often attributed with the idea that information is endowed with relevance and purpose, something with which we agree. In his article "The Next Information Revolution," Drucker took it a step further and argued that information is a critical asset to any organization and essential to business success. He noted that without turning data into information, an organization can easily be overwhelmed by the sheer volume of data, particularly in today's world where big data is everywhere.[19]

Sharing and Sense-Making

Once the intelligence is ready, the next critical step is to make sense of the data and achieve consensus on a few critical consumer behavior insights. How is this done? Ideally, findings of the research are distributed to key stakeholders across the organization. The shared information kickstarts collaborative conversations among stakeholders, with the goal being to gather diverse perspectives on customer intelligence. For instance, Parker Aerospace's approach to understanding customer needs involves actively gathering customer feedback through various methods such as regular customer surveys that track the Likelihood To Recommend (LTR) scores, reviewing customer scorecards, and conducting executive-level meetings with major customers to discuss performance and future opportunities.[20] This feedback and data is then used to inform strategic direction, particularly within the "Customer experience" pillar of their "Win Strategy," which guides organizational goals and personal performance reviews. We know that Parker Aerospace also engages in quarterly meetings with key customers, such as Airbus, Boeing, GE, and Rolls-Royce, to determine their value priorities, which in turn influences their research and development efforts.[21] These discussions serve as a form of joint sensemaking within the group to interpret the information. By sensemaking, we mean a collaborative interpretation of customer intelligence and narrowing large volumes of data into a few actionable insights.

The public sector follows a similar approach. Singapore's Government Technology Agency (GovTech) is an example of how governments can build systematic feedback into decision-making.[22] GovTech uses FormSG, a secure form-building tool deployed across Singapore Government and public healthcare institutions, to collect citizen feedback. The agency also runs an analytics platform that processes user feedback to improve the government's digital services.[23] Such tools create feedback loops across ministries and agencies within the government. The data gets used to improve public services and meet citizen needs, much like Parker Aerospace uses customer input to guide strategy.

Remember, the goal here is to develop a small set of insights—a difficult task given that organizations often over collect data and produce too large a set of recommendations.

Central to sense-making efforts is involvement of representatives from a variety of functional areas within the organization (e.g., R&D, operations, finance), and not just marketing. Each of the functions brings its own unique perspective to customer intelligence, which means the overall organization can develop a deeper understanding of the data. The outcome of these discussions should be a set of key observations based on a broad, enterprise-wide perspective, rather than a narrow, functional one. To reach an organization-wide view, however, can be challenging as most companies operate with siloed functions, geographies, or business units that are not in regular communication. Despite these obstacles, disagreement, debate, and playing the devil's advocate are critical in this process. In other words, differing viewpoints should be encouraged and supported, as they help test ideas and refine insights.

When making sense of the data, it is important to watch out for potential bias—we are humans after all. For example, functional areas may have vested interests that unduly influence data interpretation. Another human tendency is known as confirmation bias—cognitive in nature reflecting the tendency of people to search for, interpret, favor, and recall information in a way that confirms or supports preexisting beliefs. The problem with this bias is that it can lead people to put more weight on information that supports their own views and to undervalue (or even ignore) evidence that contradicts them—something we have seen too often. There are numerous ways in which to mitigate the effects of confirmation bias (e.g., seeking disconfirming information, slowing decision-making). One approach to employ is appointing a devil's advocate to challenge assumptions of the group. Research has shown that dissent in group decision-making can promote more thoughtful, creative, and open-minded processing of information—exactly what is needed when sense-making within a firm.[24]

> *Adding AI into the mix is like dumping gasoline on a fire, with its ability to more quickly and efficiently dig into customer insight data to unearth patterns and explore factors affecting customer behavior.*

Returning to an earlier point we discussed in Chapter 4, sense-making can be enhanced by exploration, given that such a mindset can help break through confirmation bias and may help challenge conventional wisdom, surprise leadership, and spark debate. Classic research on how to foster human motivation finds that when people have a sense of autonomy, a sense of competence, and feeling connected to others, they are more likely to engage in self-driven exploration, learning, and creativity.[25] What this means is that when doing sense-making within a group, it is important for the organization to provide members of that group both a sense of autonomy and competence.

Dissemination and Use

Essential to developing a customer-centric strategy is communication of the key market insights and customer intelligence generated by the research. Sharing of information is critical in all sorts of industries and settings. A simple but poignant example is the Challenge-Response Checklist the military uses during flight preparations, where one crew member (typically the pilot) issues a challenge to another crewmember (e.g., "Flaps?"), and the other person responds with the status (e.g., "Flaps set 15"), confirming visually and verbally.[26] The cockpit of a plane is much smaller than a Fortune 500 company, and therefore driving information sharing and dissemination of customer intelligence can be an effortful process.

Many companies collect and circulate customer insights—but surprisingly, much of that information goes unused. There are several reasons for this. For instance, it's common for organizations to routinely track various metrics (e.g., customer satisfaction, click-through rates on a website); however, those results are often disconnected from actual decision-making. The same holds true for secondary market research (e.g., industry data on industry trends, competitor movements, and customer behavior). While such reports may be informative, our experience is that their influence on decisions tends to be minimal or indirect.

Effective dissemination of customer intelligence is essential for aligning the organization's strategy around customer needs. There are numerous operational enablers of sharing information within an organization, such as cross-functional collaboration, clear communication protocols, rewards for sharing information, psychological safety among employees, and technology that enhances transparency and communication. At the organizational level, firms with learning-oriented cultures and flatter hierarchies will likely be better at promoting broader access to and use of information. The key point is that it often comes down to leadership who models open communications and normalizes knowledge sharing.[27]

For instance, Panda Restaurant Group has used technology to promote organizational transparency by implementing 3 × LOGIC's VIGIL Trends Business Intelligence software across all North American locations. This system provides visual trends on key metrics such as revenue per hour, labor allocation, and even operational data like store opening and closing times and cleaning schedules, allowing each restaurant to compare its performance against others and its own history. Lyle Forcum, executive director of asset protection at Panda Express, emphasized that this system provides "truly actionable information" that aligns with Panda's strategy of continuous operational improvement.[28] This suggests a commitment to sharing data across the organization to drive better decision-making and meet high operational standards.

Conversely, Caterpillar has demonstrated how poor information sharing and hierarchical barriers can create significant organizational challenges. In 2013, reports emerged highlighting poor relationships with labor, including constant cuts to benefits and wages. One worker in a non-union plant reported feeling "basically expendable." CEO Doug Oberhelman's significant salary increase was met with hostility from striking workers, further exacerbated by his comments regarding wages and profitability.[29] Furthermore, the description of a preventable workplace fatality in 2022 and subsequent accusations of a lack of compassion illustrate an environment where critical safety information or employee concerns were not effectively communicated.[30] While these instances don't directly address the sharing of customer insights, they suggest potential broader issues with internal communication and a lack of psychological safety, which may hinder the effective flow of any type of information within the organization.

In a parallel fashion, there are several factors that can inhibit dissemination of information within an organization. Common obstacles include organizational silos, information overload, and lack of psychological safety, all of which can discourage easy dissemination within the organization. We believe that limits to technology and poor communication structures also are a draw on the system of information sharing. Misaligned incentives and resistant corporate cultures can further suppress the flow of intelligence. Overcoming these challenges requires commitment from leadership, clear communication structures, supporting technology, and a culture valuing transparency and cross-functional collaboration.[31]

Uses of Intelligence

To be competitive as a customer-centered organization, it is important to gather intelligence (in a rigorous and directed way), draw conclusions on key customer insights, and (most importantly) take action. To be truly effective, organizations need to be committed to an on-going process that results in a customer-centered outcome—it cannot be a one-off. Companies that excel along this dimension will be able to lead in the market, by continuously adapting and responding to customer insights. As outlined in Chapter 4, there are four decisions that organizations can make regarding market intelligence as part of developing a customer-centric strategy (see Figure 9.1).

The first choice is the decision to shape the market or not. Rather than merely accepting existing industry structures and stakeholder behaviors (which is an acceptable strategy), organizations can use insight from customer intelligence to influence one or both of the key market structures related to competitors and customers. Whether the strategy involves altering the competitive landscape, redefining customer behavior, or reshaping both, the core idea here is that organizations need to lead rather than follow in the market. Don't just compete—change the game.

The second use of intelligence is systematic abandonment. In most cases, firms use customer insight to do something new within the organization (e.g., launch a new product, extend to new markets), with little consideration of what to stop doing or abandon. This perhaps should not be surprising, given that people are particularly sensitive to losses, compared to equivalent gains.[32] The engrained nature of this "loss aversion" in humans makes it particularly difficult to change from the past, but it is possible, as we have seen. Examples of firms, ranging from Domino's to Gucci, show that it is conceivable to move past

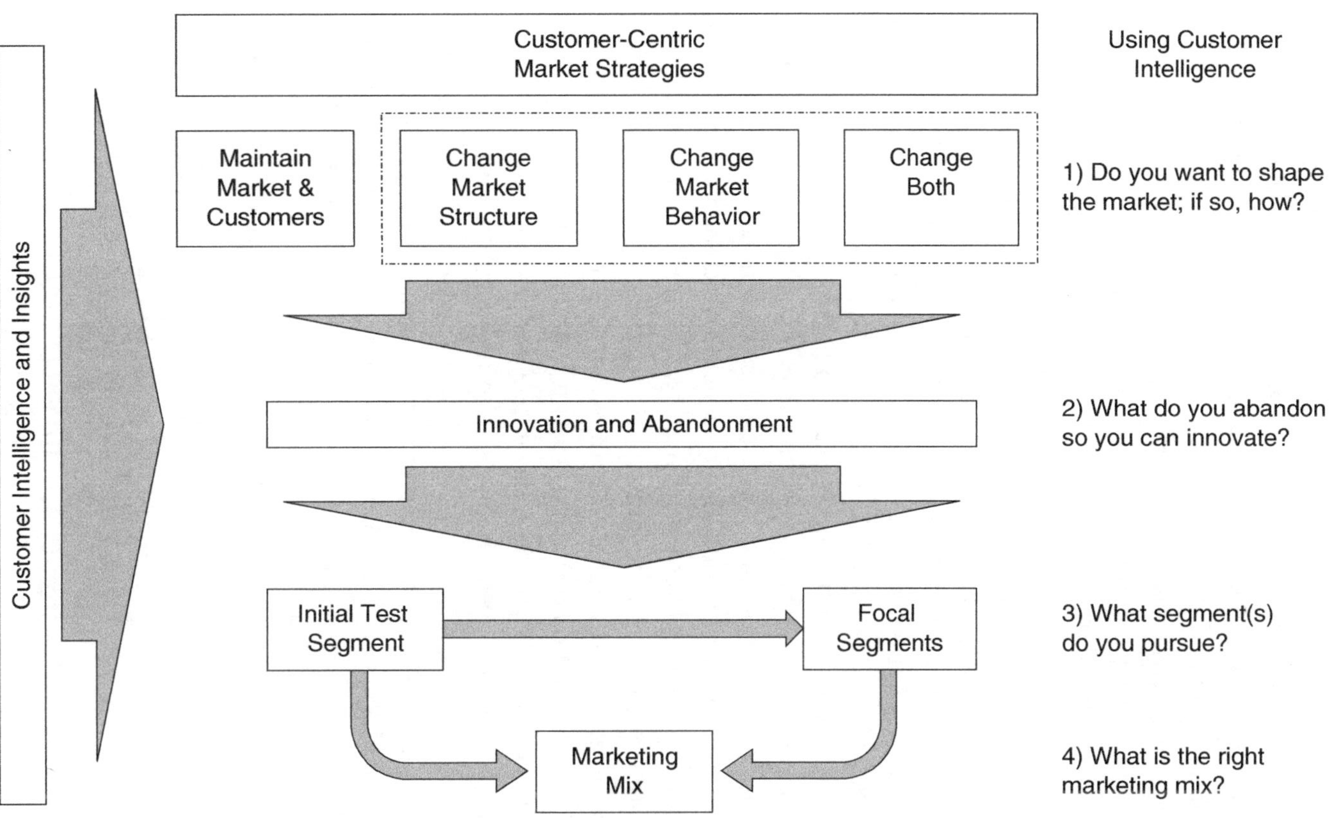

Figure 9.1 Customer intelligence and strategic choices.

calamities.[33] Gucci, in 2019, offered a sweater that was perceived as racially insensitive. To address the situation, the company apologized and also launched "Gucci Changemakers" to promote diversity and inclusion, in support of underrepresented creative communities. As part of setting a customer-centric strategy, therefore, organizations need to identify offerings, processes, or practices that no longer provide value to the organization and stop doing them. As we detail further in the next chapter, abandoning the outdated is essential for making room for new innovation and maintaining relevance in dynamic markets. In other words, innovation requires making space for the new.

Up next is the selection and sequencing of customer segments. As we noted earlier, too many organizations rely on conventional segmentation models (e.g., geographic, share of wallet). Such an approach can limit differentiation in the marketplace. It is critical that organizations leverage customer insights to view and classify markets in a different way with the goal to identify new opportunities. The choice here is whether it is best to initially focus on a single segment (which provides clarity for the organization, accelerates market entry, and strengthens positioning) or multiple segments. If the latter is chosen, then careful consideration of how segments are sequenced is important (based on market context and business goals). The takeaway for this decision is that segmentation needs to be a source of strategic advantage, not a checklist.

Finally, the organization must design the marketing mix based on the preceding strategic decisions. As we noted earlier, organizations most often think of products and services when responding to customer intelligence. But, companies cannot forget that there are 4Ps in the marketing mix, not just one. Indeed, equal attention should be given to channel selection, marketing communication, and pricing when responding to customer intelligence. No matter what part of the marketing mix is focused on, it is critical that the decisions reflect customer preferences, not just firm's convenience. Our guidance here is to start with what matters most to the customer—their care-abouts.

The Future of Customer Intelligence

Customer intelligence is critical for developing organization strategy and ultimately its market success. Our view aligns with that of Peter

Drucker, who foresaw information as the key resource of the modern organization. As he noted, "The most valuable assets of a 20th century company were its production equipment. The most valuable asset of a 21st-century institution . . . will be its knowledge workers and their productivity."[34] He specifically argues that marketplace competitive advantage will increasingly depend on how effectively organizations collect, manage, and use information. Drucker was clearly prescient about all this, but we will never know if he would be surprised by how the role of information has exploded in the unfolding AI-enabled world. While the future of using customer intelligence is rosy, there are three areas of concern that should be kept in mind.

The first concern relates to interpreting customer intelligence. An example is the classic issue of confusing correlation with causation—an errant inference that can be costly for organizations. As you likely learned in college, correlation indicates a relationship between two variables, but a correlation does not prove that one variable causes the other. For example, increasing sales and advertising may be correlated, but without sense-making and additional exploration of the data, it is unclear whether advertising influenced sales (e.g., both could be influenced by a third factor, like seasonality). The point here is that organizations need to be cautious in interpreting data trends and rather rely on deeper analysis during the sense-making phase.

A second, related, issue is AI hallucination, where AI systems generate false or misleading information. These hallucinations are often the result of poor training data (or lack of context) and can lead to costly errors. For instance, in research and academic contexts, AI has been known to generate fake citations or scientific references that don't actually exist. Instead of producing authentic citations, AI generates a statistically likely combination of academic-sounding elements based on patterns in its training data. In fact, one study found that 18 percent of the GPT4 citations are fabricated.[35] To reduce risks associated with such hallucinations, businesses can provide human oversight, improve data quality, ensure AI-generated content is labeled, and use governance frameworks. Just like any data source on customers, sense-making via cross-functional collaboration is critical. With thoughtful strategies, organizations can manage hallucinations and responsibly leverage AI for decision-making and customer engagement. While such threats are likely to be addressed as AI systems become better trained, this is a good cautionary tale for leaders to be thoughtful and systematic when deploying AI.[36]

To make matters worse, information quality is being threatened with the broader issue of misinformation and disinformation, particularly within social media. Unfortunately, the sheer velocity and volume of information online (which is often unchecked or deliberately manipulated) can distort customer intelligence. As we know, social media amplifies unverified content, which can mislead both consumers and organizations. For example, studies show that false information spreads significantly faster than truthful content on platforms like X (formerly known as Twitter).[37] Additionally, AI systems trained on polluted data sources risk perpetuating or even exacerbating these inaccuracies.[38] All of this increases the risk of surfacing information that may be less-than-reliable; thereby making it harder for organizations to discern "truth from noise"—particularly regarding information that is based on unverified data. We are not saying that all data accessible to organizations via social media is bad, but leadership needs to carefully review and verify online information (prior to dissemination and use) and ideally adopt a "buyer beware" mentality. Without appropriate guardrails it is likely that some sources of customer intelligence may reflect more noise than signal.

Finally, when collecting, sense-making, and using customer intelligence, it is critical to keep humans in the process. While technology undoubtedly will play an important role in this process, human judgment is essential to ensuring the accuracy, context, and relevance of the information. Do not get us wrong, we acknowledge the important role of computers, AI, and advanced methods to the intelligence process. Such systems can process large volumes of information quickly, but on the flipside such systems often lack the ability to understand nuance, question assumptions, or recognize when data is incomplete or misleading. Humans (at least until AI becomes sentient) bring expertise, critical thought, and ethical awareness, and such skills allow us to interpret information, identify possible bias, and sense-make in order to align intelligence with strategic goals. Ultimately, the ideal combination is that of human insight *and* technological capability—a pairing that leads to better, more informed decisions and strategy.

Conclusion

Customer intelligence is not a luxury for today's companies—it is a necessity. As detailed in this chapter, customer intelligence is more than data collection; instead it is about transforming such data into meaningful, actionable insights to drive an organization's customer-centric strategy. Successful organizations not only generate high-quality customer intelligence but also engage in rigorous sense-making, ensure effective dissemination, and, most importantly, use that intelligence to drive decision-making. As Drucker wisely asserted, information must lead to action, a situation that will continue to evolve in the future where customer intelligence gathering, dissemination, and use will be increasingly influenced by AI and other technologies.

10

Innovation and Abandonment

"If you want something new, you have to stop doing something old."

—Peter Drucker

Introduction

In order to become more customer driven, organizations need to innovate for tomorrow and abandon yesterday. Drucker viewed innovation as everyone's responsibility. Too often organizations limit their thinking of innovation to products, services, and solutions. However, as industry and business environments fundamentally change, so too should every part of the organization. This applies to its structure, ways of working, brands, financial model, alliances, and so on. We view this as an organization-wide activity to adjust to the changing needs of the marketplace and customers.

Interestingly, since Drucker's early writing on planned organizational abandonment, there has been very little written on the topic. Quite simply, this is a twin concept with innovation. Unless the organization can "let go" of products, services, processes, or structures that are no longer viable, it cannot effectively innovate. Here we define abandonment as a conscious decision by any member(s) of an organization to completely stop the allocation of resources to a particular activity. However, we have learned over time that this principle is rarely practiced by contemporary organizations. Hence, we expect that the majority of this chapter section will be novel for readers. You may be tempted to conclude that new players in industry (e.g., Tesla, Fisker, Lucid) may have a leg up on the incumbents (e.g., Ford, GM); however, Drucker's view is that incumbents must manage both continuity and change. Over time new players will become established players and the only way to get to the future is to practice systematic abandonment—no matter who you are.

Drucker framed the challenge as follows "society, community, and family are all conserving institutions. They try to maintain stability and to prevent, or at least to slow, change. But the modern organization is a destabilizer. It must be organized for innovation, as the great Austro-American economist Joseph Schumpeter said, it is 'creative destruction.' And it must be organized for the systematic abandonment of whatever is established, customary, familiar, and comfortable, whether that is a product, service, or process; a set of skills; human and social relationships; or the organization itself. In short, it must be organized for constant change. The organization's function is to put knowledge to work—on tools, products, and processes; on the design of work; on knowledge itself. It is the nature of knowledge that it changes fast, and that today's certainties always become tomorrow's absurdities."[1]

We have organized the chapter into two major sections. In the first section, we focus on Drucker's seven sources of innovation. Here our aim is not to discuss types of innovation (e.g., innovate revenue models or new brands); rather, we are looking for a source of "inspiration" that triggers innovation (e.g., the evolution of demographics in a country). In the second part of the chapter, we focus on abandonment. Since very little is written on the topic, we begin with a discussion of why abandonment is so difficult to achieve. Next, we profile two case studies—Amazon and Microsoft—and make the argument that they are not only industry leaders on innovation, but are also enlightening case studies of abandonment. Finally, we offer a framework for organizations to apply as they think through their abandonment strategy.

Innovation

In 1985, Drucker published *Innovation and Entrepreneurship*. His aim was to "represent innovation and entrepreneurship as purposeful tasks that can be organized—are in need of being organized—and as systematic work."[2] He defined *systematic innovation* as "the purposeful and organized search for changes, and in the systematic analysis of opportunities such changes might offer for economic and social innovation."[3] Importantly, "everything" that an organization does creates a potential opportunity for innovation—it is not simply the products or offerings of the organization. And, as such, it is everyone's responsibility. We begin this section with a brief discussion of Drucker's core philosophy on innovation, including the following five principles:

- **Improved through practice.** Innovation can be learned through practice. Similar to Drucker's view on the practice of management, he believed that individuals with "normal endowments" should be able to practice and improve their innovation capabilities.
- **Behavior-based.** Drucker focused his discussion on the behaviors, actions, and resource allocation of people. He downplayed beliefs, traits, or attitudes in his work since he believed that behavior was the most direct indicator of innovation.
- **Can be organized.** An organization can put in place a system to innovate. It is not magic, but a learned discipline for organizations. Certainly, there can be some "Eureka" moments in the lab, but Drucker was fundamentally concerned about the organization's ability to continually innovate across all of its activities.
- **Not just for the R&D group.** It is part of everyone's job. Indeed, the best run organizations require that every person identify areas for improvement in their role. How can each person innovate to improve the functioning of the organization?
- **Means to an end.** Success is determined by the market—not the innovation. It is not an innovation unless the market accepts the innovation and improves the performance of the organization.

Seven Sources of Innovation

This section focuses on Drucker's seven sources of innovation. We consider the source of "inspiration" that triggers these innovations (e.g., the evolution of demographics in a country).

Source 1: Unexpected Success or Failure Consider the following scenario, which we have observed many times in organizations. An organization launches a new product with very high expectations. However, the product fails to meet expectations. As a result, the organization spends considerable time, resources, and effort to "right the ship" and get the product back on course. In the meantime, a less well-regarded product in the organization's product line continues to sell well—in spite of very little marketing and sales effort allocated to the product. What typically happens? The organization tends to keep resourcing with the expectation that the new product will take off and at the same time continues to largely ignore the existing product that is doing well.

In 2013, Google Glass was launched with considerable fanfare and high expectations. It was intended to revolutionize how people used technology to enhance their interactions with their environments. It failed to meet expectations and was discontinued for the consumer market in 2015.[4] There were a number of factors that led to its failure, including its $1,500 price point, its awkwardness as "headgear," and the actual limited functionality.[5] Despite these setbacks, Google continued to invest in Google Glass, releasing a second enterprise edition in 2019 aimed at businesses. They persisted with the product, even in the face of unexpected failure, attributing the failure to the wrong strategy, insufficient resources, and strong competition. Ultimately, in 2023, Google stopped production of the enterprise glass edition.[6]

In contrast to the struggles of Google Glass, Gmail, launched in 2004, emerged as an unexpected success for Google. Initially met with skepticism within the company and concerns about privacy due to its ad-based model, Gmail quickly gained traction with users, attracting a massive user base of 425 million by 2012. A number of factors led to its success, including significantly more storage space than competitors, search functionality, and free access supported by less obtrusive text ads.[7]

For both unexpected success and failure, organizations typically are very slow to act. For unexpected success, organizations are slow to recognize the success and, as a result, are often unprepared from a resource perspective—with both budget and people—to accelerate the success. For unexpected failures, organizations typically attribute the failure to the wrong strategy, insufficient level of resource allocation, or strong competition. Thus, this internal attribution—we did not do the right things—means that they continually resource the failure with the expectation it will ultimately be successful. Both of these pitfalls could have been avoided with a stronger focus on the customer, who is the ultimate arbiter on how products and services are received in the marketplace.

Source 2: Incongruities Between Assumptions and Realities
Executives with industries often have a "groupthink" set of assumptions that are strongly held. Indeed, they are so strongly held that they are not even considered for reexamination. In the late 1980s, every semiconductor company had their own "Fab" manufacturing facility producing their own wafer chips. This was simply the business norm. In 1987, TSMC revolutionized the semiconductor industry by pioneering the "pure-play foundry" model, focusing solely on manufacturing chips designed by other companies. This separated chip design from manufacturing, allowing companies to specialize in their core competencies of chip design. TSMC has consistently advanced the process of manufacturing leading the industry to produce smaller, more powerful, and energy-efficient chips. As of January 2025, TSMC had a market cap of $997 billion, making it the world's 10th most valuable company.

One steel company that has challenged strongly held assumptions of the industry is Nucor Steel. In particular, they "reversed" three key assumptions of the industry. First, they pioneered the use of electric arc furnaces for steel production. These "mini-mills" are smaller, more flexible, and more energy-efficient than traditional integrated steel mills. This challenged the long-held assumption that large, integrated mills were the only way to produce steel competitively. Second, they focused on particular applications in niche markets. So, instead of competing directly with large steel producers in commodity markets,

Nucor focused on niche markets like steel for construction and other specialized applications. This allowed them to command higher prices and improve profitability. Third, Nucor has a strong emphasis on employee ownership through its Employee Stock Ownership Plan, fostering a strong company culture that aligns employee interests with those of the company.[8]

Our recommendation for firms is to constantly test the strongly held assumptions of your industry. We often run a "flip it" exercise in our executive education sessions where we ask executives to identify the 5–7 major assumptions of the industry. Consider, for example, the classic "big three" of automobile rental (i.e., Hertz, Avis, Budget), all offer airport locations, high levels of personalized service, many cars to choose from, and daily rentals. What if we "flipped" these assumptions—no airport locations, no service personnel, few models to select from, and hourly rental? One would identify Zip Rental Car in the United States. Indeed, to go one step further, does one need to rent and drive? Relax these assumptions and you discover Uber. Our key point is that these assumptions are so strongly held that they are rarely challenged by incumbents. One does not need to relax all assumptions—often relaxing one or two provides momentum to change the rules of the game in the industry.

Source 3: Process Needs   Think of process needs as either increasing the efficiency of a current process or replacing the existing process with a new process. Indeed, in Chapter 2 we noted that the operational efficiency era of strategy was largely focused on this form of innovation. Elon Musk has frequently emphasized the importance of efficient manufacturing and automation in Tesla's success (and recently attempted to be applied to the U.S. government!). He has stated that Tesla's primary competition lies in optimizing its production processes—as such, they "win" on the factory floor. The products themselves are simply an "output" of the revolutionary manufacturing process. Tesla's network of large-scale manufacturing plants is designed for high-volume, efficient production of vehicles and batteries. Even though Musk has heavily invested in robotics and automation to streamline production lines and reduce reliance on manual labor, he will "swap out" automation with people if the automation does not improve the output. Finally, Tesla aims to control key aspects of its supply chain, such as battery production, to improve efficiency and reduce costs.

Match.com and other dating app pioneers changed the traditional data process with an online process that increased the breadth and depth of data options. Hinge took a different approach. They reimagined the traditional matchmaking process by combining technology and algorithms to suggest potential matches within a user's social network. Rather than relying solely on personal connections or personal "input," Hinge utilizes Facebook connections and user data to facilitate introductions. The app is built on the belief that "loose connections work best" for fostering meaningful relationships. In contrast to apps like Tinder, Hinge is designed to offer an upscale and sophisticated user experience. It also relies on caption-based profiles, with prompts like "Two truths and a lie" and "Together we could" rather than just photos and suggests a "most compatible" person for each user.[9]

The reengineering era in the 1990s—led by Michael Hammer and James Champy—focused on process improvement. *Reengineering the Corporation* argued that many companies were relying on outdated processes built for a different era and that incremental improvements were no longer enough.[10] Hammer and Champy advocate for business process reengineering—a radical redesign of core business processes to achieve dramatic improvements in cost, quality, service, and speed. Instead of tweaking existing workflows, companies should rethink how work is done from the ground up, often using information technology as a key enabler. Similar to challenging assumptions, the aim is to challenge the fundamental operational assumption of the firm—recall Musk's view that he is competing on the factory floor. What core processes that we take for granted can be fundamentally streamlined to improve the customer experience?

Source 4: Changes in Industry or Market Structure There are numerous examples, including the music industry, the technology sector (e.g., Nokia or Blackberry), and retail stores (e.g., Sears, Kmart), where changes to a market can drive innovation—and also end an organization. One recent example is Circuit City. Circuit City was not only a dominant player in the retail electronics sector, but it was also featured in the best-selling book *Built to Last*. Yet it did not; Circuit City went out of business in 2009. Indeed, in Chapter 4 we discuss the shaping of markets as one of four key evidence-based decisions. Here the firm actually accelerates changes in industry structure.

There are numerous reasons for Circuit City's failure to adapt to changing industry structure. Most important perhaps was its failure to recognize and shift its offerings to match to changing customer preferences, compared to its competitor Best Buy. They were very slow to recognize and respond to the shift in online shopping. While they eventually established an online retail presence, it was not as easy to use and well designed as Amazon. By this point, Amazon was the dominant online brand in the consumer retail electronics sector. Second, there were a series of strategic decisions made, including supply chain and inventory management. They also outsourced customer service, which impacted their customer satisfaction scores. Finally, other brick and mortar competitors—like Best Buy—continued to innovate to consumer tastes and took share from Circuit City.[11]

As noted in earlier chapters, Clayton Christensen famously labeled this type of challenge as the innovator's dilemma. Namely, it is hard for the incumbent organization to recognize and adapt to fundamental shifts in the marketplace—with a specific focus on shifts in the underlying technology of the industry (e.g., shift from mobile phones to smartphones). Beyond Christensen's work, there are several reasons why organizations do not recognize market shifts. This is often due to factors such as the incentive structure for senior executives (focused on short-term financial returns vs. longer-term), the ease of serving the existing target market versus the unknown of future segments, and the desire not to "rock the boat" on uncertain market changes.

Source 5: Changes in Demographics   Drucker argues and we agree that innovation opportunities made possible by changes in the numbers of people—and in their age distribution, education, occupations, and geographic location—are among the most rewarding and least risky of pursuits.[12] The demographic shifts are often accompanied by shifts in customer preferences—namely, generational shifts in consumption preferences. Just think how much we all rely on, discuss, and consider differences between baby boomers, millennials, Gen Z, and others.

Regarding aging populations, Japan has one of the oldest populations globally. The proportion of people aged 65 and over is rapidly increasing, while the working-age population is shrinking. This aging population poses numerous challenges ranging from the social security system to the economy. This situation is compounded by a declining birth rate. Couples are choosing to have fewer or no children due to various factors, including economic pressures, changing social norms, and the rising cost of raising children. These demographic changes present significant challenges for Japan and many other countries. A shrinking workforce and an aging population can negatively impact economic growth and productivity. The increasing number of elderly people raises concerns about the sustainability of pensions and healthcare. Declining birth rates can lead to labor shortages in various sectors of the economy. Recognized by the Japanese government, these issues can be viewed as opportunity for the country. While Japan has struggled with its lack of acceptance of immigrant and foreign labor, it is trying to promote immigration. The government is also providing financial incentives for childbirth and developing generous policies for childcare support. They are also reforming their social security system. That said, the effectiveness of these policies remains to be seen.

Demographic shifts also trigger changes in customer behavior. In recent years, wine consumption has declined, particularly with the 20–30-year-olds. These younger consumers have decreased their wine consumption in favor of already-mixed alcohol drinks, non-alcoholic beverages, and marijuana.[13] Similarly, as noted earlier, Nespresso missed the evolution of the coffee drinking habits of the youth market. In sharp contrast to their parents, the youth market is not purchasing Nespresso machines and capsules for a variety of reasons, including their perception of its lack of sustainability, their desire to consume drinks outside of the home, and their perception that it is high priced.[14]

And it is not just purchase behavior—younger consumers vary in pre-purchase behavior as well. For example, travel baby boomers tend to favor traditional package tours and established destinations. Millennials prioritize unique experiences, cultural immersion, and affordability. Gen Z values authenticity, sustainability, and social media-worthy experiences. Gen Z travelers also prefer booking trips via chat platforms and utilizing virtual tours before making decisions. They also show lower enrollment in airline frequent flyer programs than older generations, suggesting a shift in loyalty dynamics.[15]

Our advocating here is to take your core business and ask a simple question: "Do 20-25-year-old consumers care about and purchase the same way as your current core customers purchase?" If they do—you are fine. If they do not, then someone is going to enter your market (or has already) to take share from your core business. While you may be thinking this only applies in the world of B2C, we have observed these transformative changes in behavior in the world of B2B.

Source 6: Change in Customer Perceptions   Changes in customer perceptions and preferences also provide opportunities for organizations that can identify these shifts. The plant-based meat industry, initially seen as an unstoppable force with products like Impossible and Beyond Burgers, has reached a saturation point. Sales have stalled, with a decline in U.S. sales since 2022. Despite the environmental and ethical appeal, the hype around the product has not lived up to expectations, as most plant-based burger buyers also consume animal protein. Their products also fall into the category of "ultra-processed" food, and the meat industry succeeded in its efforts to make people think plant-based meat is not healthy.[16]

Youthful customers are no longer just concerned with price and quality; they are increasingly demanding that the companies they support align with their values and contribute to a better world (a topic we dive into next). This is evidenced in the hockey stick growth in vintage clothing, carbon-neutral travel, and reusable drink containers. One interesting trend in this regard is the shift regarding car ownership. While the high costs associated with car ownership (purchase price, insurance, maintenance, fuel, parking) are a major deterrent, growing awareness of climate change and the environmental impact of car emissions is influencing younger generations to prioritize sustainable transportation options. Moreover, with the rise of remote work and the gig economy, traditional commuting patterns are less predictable, making car ownership less essential for some.

Some have termed this shift as "mobility as a service." Young people are more open to car subscription services, which offer flexibility and convenience without the long-term commitment of ownership. Services like ride-hailing apps (Uber, Lyft) and well-developed public transportation systems are seen as viable alternatives to car ownership. Finally, particularly in urban areas, options like bikes, scooters, and e-scooters are gaining popularity as convenient and affordable ways to navigate cities. Thus, while car ownership still holds value for many young people, it's no longer the default option. The shift is toward more flexible, convenient, and sustainable transportation solutions that align with their evolving lifestyles and values.

Some brands, like Converse, Levi's, True Religion, and Champion have had multiple lives. At one time, there were seen as valuable brands, then lost their way, and finally recovered with a different set of brand perceptions. Several decades ago, Converse All-Stars were sport shoes—worn by pro basketball players in the 1960s and 1970s. The brand largely disappeared and reemerged as a fashion brand. By switching its target audience to everyday streetwear, All-Stars reemerged as an essential to youth culture. No amount of advertising campaigns could rival the sales that followed after Kurt Cobain sported a roughed-up pair of black Chuck Taylors. Converse became synonymous with the subcultures of the world.[17]

Our key message is to be curious. Curious about why customers are changing, how they think, how they behave, where they buy, and why they buy. One of our former colleagues at Monitor Group—Larry Keeley—was fond of saying that the future is here—it is just unevenly distributed. So, look for the leading-edge customers—those who signal where the future is going to be. This requires curiosity—to be open to market evolution and changes.

Source 7: New Knowledge   This is where organizations typically invest a great deal of time, effort, and money. Often this source of knowledge emerges from the R&D group in the organization. This is true of technology, chemical, and life science organizations.

One well-known story of innovation in the life science industry is the development of monoclonal antibodies by Amgen, Genentech, and IDEC. Monoclonal antibodies are designed to target specific cells or substances in the body. This precision makes them incredibly useful for treating diseases like cancer, autoimmune disorders, and infectious diseases. They have revolutionized the treatment of many diseases.

For example, they are used in drugs like Humira for rheumatoid arthritis, Herceptin for breast cancer, and Remicade for Crohn's disease. The development of monoclonal antibodies was a complex scientific breakthrough. It involved hybridoma technology, which fuses immune cells to create cells that produce large quantities of a single type of antibody. This innovation has had a profound impact on medicine, leading to the development of numerous lifesaving and life-improving therapies.

That stated, one key challenge with respect to new knowledge and R&D discoveries is the "not invented here" (NIH) phenomenon. The NIH effect refers to the tendency of organizations or people to reject ideas, technologies, or solutions that originate outside of the organization. This happens even when the innovations may offer clear benefits. This bias is driven by various factors such as organizational pride, internal politics, and mistrust, all of which can hinder innovation within the organization. This can be dangerous, particularly in technology-heavy industries, as NIH can create blind spots and reduce an organization's ability to adapt in fast-changing environments. Overcoming the NIH requires cultural change, incentives for external collaboration, and leadership that values openness and learning.[18]

In summary, our intent with the seven sources of innovation is to challenge how you think about your market. Markets are constantly changing—not just customers but technology, competitors, regulations, and other industry factors. All seven of the sources can be tied back to customers—what they desire, want, and are willing to pay for. All seven require a different mindset—to challenge the status quo and to be ruthless in your curiosity about how your industry will evolve. Or, better yet, how you can shape its evolution.

Strategic Abandonment

While everyone understands the value of innovation, most organizations do not have a process in place to abandon activities that no longer add value to customers or other stakeholders. To do so is critical to innovating. Without abandonment there would be many buggy-whip manufacturers populating the Fortune 500 list. As noted in the quote that opens this chapter, Drucker believed that every time an organization adds an activity, it simultaneously needs to abandon an activity. This profound insight often triggers an "aha moment" among the client firms we advise. In this section, we share the process that we use to help firms abandon products, services, ways of working, values, and systems that no longer add value. We begin with a definition of the term.

Concept

Systematic abandonment is the process of stopping to enact and invest in products, services, markets, processes, practices, systems, and value chain activities that no longer "fit" the current or future of the business. It is a commitment by the individual people, teams involved, and by the organization—and no less important than innovation itself—to create room for competing successfully in the future.[19]

Drucker was very precise in his description of organizational concepts. Hence, it is worthwhile to decompose key terms in this definition to understand his point of view on systematic abandonment.

- **Systematic.** The process of abandonment must be a practiced and structured in an organized fashion that is regular, repeatable, and practiced. It must be embedded in the workings of the organization. Many organizations have innovation practices, methods, and approaches. As you may know, these methods are common and widespread. The same is not true for abandonment. Organizations must commit to ways of working that embed systematic abandonment among their core set of activities.
- **Abandonment.** This is an interesting word choice. Drucker does not say "decrease activity x" rather, he notes that one should "stop altogether" the activity. This is a key insight. When organizations "decrease an activity," it typically returns to its normal homeostasis within an organization. Thus, activities must be stopped—not simply resourced less.
- **Organization-wide.** Like innovation, systematic abandonment is an organization-wide activity. It is not left to the product group or the innovation hub, rather every employee and function must be held accountable and responsible for abandonment. A good litmus test here is whether this is part of every individual's annual performance review and conversation. Typically, people are asked to list their accomplishments—often identified as "innovations" within their sphere of influence. However, the same is not true of abandonment.

- **Any activity—not just products.** Also, like innovation, abandonment is not just about products, services, solutions, or bundles. Rather, everything an organization does must be evaluated based on its contribution. This could be HR practices, IT platforms, supplier relationships, alliances, and ways of working—all are fair game to free up resources to innovate.
- **Criteria for abandonment.** Here Drucker had four criteria in mind. First, the activity no longer contributes to performance or results. Second, the activity has outlived its usefulness or relevance. Third, it is consuming resources that could be better used elsewhere. And fourth, activities hinder the growth of new and promising areas.

Why Is Systematic Abandonment Necessary?

For any change leader, the starting point for change is abandonment. For most "change management" frameworks, the first step is visioning the future and creating the motivation to change. This is not the first step for Drucker. The first step for Drucker is to create the time, resources, and budget space for the change effort. Too often our client will say, I cannot make any space for the organizational transformation that is being driven by our CEO. We do not have the budget or the resources to drive the fundamental aim (e.g., a transformation effort that focuses on shifting the firm from being product driven to customer driven). When we hear this message, our recommendation is to get the team to eliminate 20–30 percent of activities,

> *The first policy—and the foundation for all the others—is to abandon yesterday. The first need is to free resources from being committed to maintaining what no longer contributes to performance, and no longer produces results. In fact, it is not possible to create tomorrow unless one first sloughs off yesterday. To maintain yesterday is always difficult and extremely time-consuming. To maintain yesterday therefore always commits the institution's scarcest and most valuable resources—and above all, its ablest people—to nonresults. Yet to do anything different—let alone to innovate—always runs into unexpected difficulties. It therefore always demands leadership by people of high and proven ability. And if these people are committed to maintaining yesterday, they are simply not available to create tomorrow.*[20]
>
> —Peter Drucker

processes, or products to create room for innovation. How is this accomplished? This is the focus of this section of the chapter.

Why Is Systematic Abandonment Challenging?

While systematic abandonment may be obvious to some readers, there are a number of reasons why abandonment is even more challenging than innovation. These forces can be related to individual motivations or organizational dynamics. This section describes four barriers to abandonment.

- **Organizations thrive on stability and resist change.** It is much easier to go to work each day and simply "execute" the same way. Abandonment is change. Stopping an activity means saying "no" to existing activities, ways of working, or product investments. It is much easier to ignore the forces outside the organization that are reshaping industries than it is to continue the same pathways.
- **Firms do not invest in "processes and methods" to abandon.** We have yet to encounter a firm with an abandonment unit, function, or group. Every firm has an innovation group—indeed, it is often titled the "R&D" group with a VP or SVP in charge. Life science firms must have R&D groups to accelerate their therapy pipelines. With no function or unit to lead the way, it is hard for firms to develop the tradecraft and "know-how" for how to systematically abandon activities and practices.
- **You can always find people who make the case to keep "as is."** Beyond simply loss aversion (ala prospect theory of Kahneman and Tversky), employees have a vested interest in activities that should be abandoned. If I am the product manager in charge of a product category and the firm decides to abandon the category, I am either out of a job or need to be reassigned to another role. Oftentimes, those in charge actively resist abandonment since it is in their self-interest to keep the activity going.
- **Innovation is more highly valued for careers than abandonment.** Resumes are often filled with "lists" of innovative, "shiny new objects" that the employee created or led. It is rare to see a resume with a long list of things that have been abandoned. It is simply a fact that organizations reward innovation more than abandonment. Hence, careers are built on innovating, not abandoning.

Case Studies of Abandonment

Amazon. While Amazon is exceptionally well known for its innovations (see Figure 10.1), it has also been a "best of class" example of a firm that abandons activities, practices, and behaviors. In this section, we describe a few examples of the products, services, and businesses that Amazon had discontinued.

Amazon's Fire phone and Kindle Fire tablets were both abandoned. Amazon's own smartphone was designed to compete with the iPhone and Android devices. It failed to gain traction due to poor reviews, lack of apps, and failure to differentiate itself significantly in a crowded market. It was abandoned in 2015. Although Amazon still sells tablets under the "Fire" brand, its original tablet line (like the Kindle Fire HDX) has been discontinued in favor of more basic, budget-friendly tablets. The Kindle Fire name itself was phased out in 2019.

Amazon has been very aggressive in stopping business services that have not found a market, including:

- Amazon Webstore (2010–2016) was a service that allowed small businesses to build and host online stores using Amazon's infrastructure. The service was phased out as Amazon focused more on its core e-commerce platform and cloud offerings like AWS.
- Amazon Wallet (2012–2014) was a mobile payment service that allowed users to store credit and debit card information to make purchases. It was replaced by more popular mobile payment systems, such as Apple Pay and Google Wallet, and lacked significant adoption.
- Amazon Music Unlimited—Free (2016–2019) was a free version of Amazon Music Unlimited (before it was bundled into Amazon Prime). The free version was discontinued in favor of paid tiers and the growing integration with Amazon Prime services, making the free tier redundant.
- Amazon Local (2011–2015) was a daily deals service, similar to Groupon, where users could buy discounts for local services and experiences. The service faced intense competition from other daily deal platforms and failed to generate enough interest.

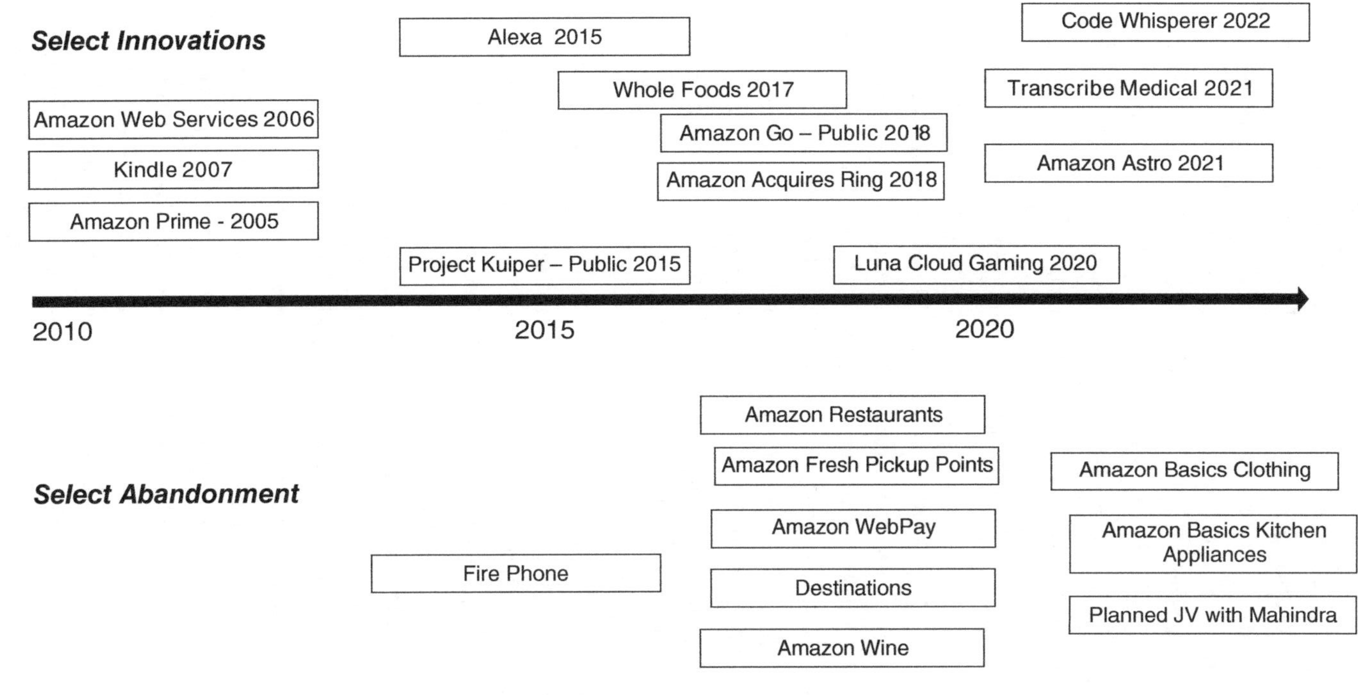

Figure 10.1   Amazon innovation and abandonment.

- Amazon restaurants (2015–2019) was their attempt to enter into the restaurant delivery business, similar to services like Grubhub and Uber Eats. It couldn't compete with established players in the food delivery space, and Amazon pivoted to focus on Whole Foods and other initiatives.
- Amazon Home Services (2015–2020) was a service where customers could book home repairs and services like cleaning, plumbing, and furniture assembly. Amazon focused more on its core retail business and other tech initiatives.

Amazon tends to rapidly adapt, pivoting its focus to services and products that align better with its overarching goals, such as cloud computing, logistics, and e-commerce. The company's ability to discard nonessential services allows it to streamline its operations and focus on areas with high growth potential. More important to the context of this book is that such approaches allow for the firm to better meet the needs of the market and customers.

Finally, it is important to point out that in several cases, Amazon did not simply abandon the business, they repeatedly tested and modified the offering. As this book goes to press, Amazon is still refining its Amazon grocery stores. Its first iteration focused on cashier-less physical stores—called Amazon Go. It refined the concept over the past several years—and the jury is still out on whether it will ultimately be a success as what they now call the variate as Amazon Fresh.

Microsoft. Similar to Amazon, Microsoft is an excellent practitioner of innovation and abandonment (see Figure 10.2). This section describes examples of products and services, strategy, leadership behaviors, solutions, and systems that were abandoned since Satya Nadella took the reigns as CEO in 2014. As such, in this case study we focus not only on products and services, but also on leadership and culture.

In the product services area, Microsoft's attempt to compete in the smartphone market was ended in 2017. Windows Phone struggled to gain market share and was eventually discontinued after the company shifted focus toward mobile apps and services. After being a dominant browser for many years, Microsoft officially ended support for Internet Explorer in 2022, pushing users toward Microsoft Edge. Microsoft Band was a fitness tracking device launched in 2014 that was

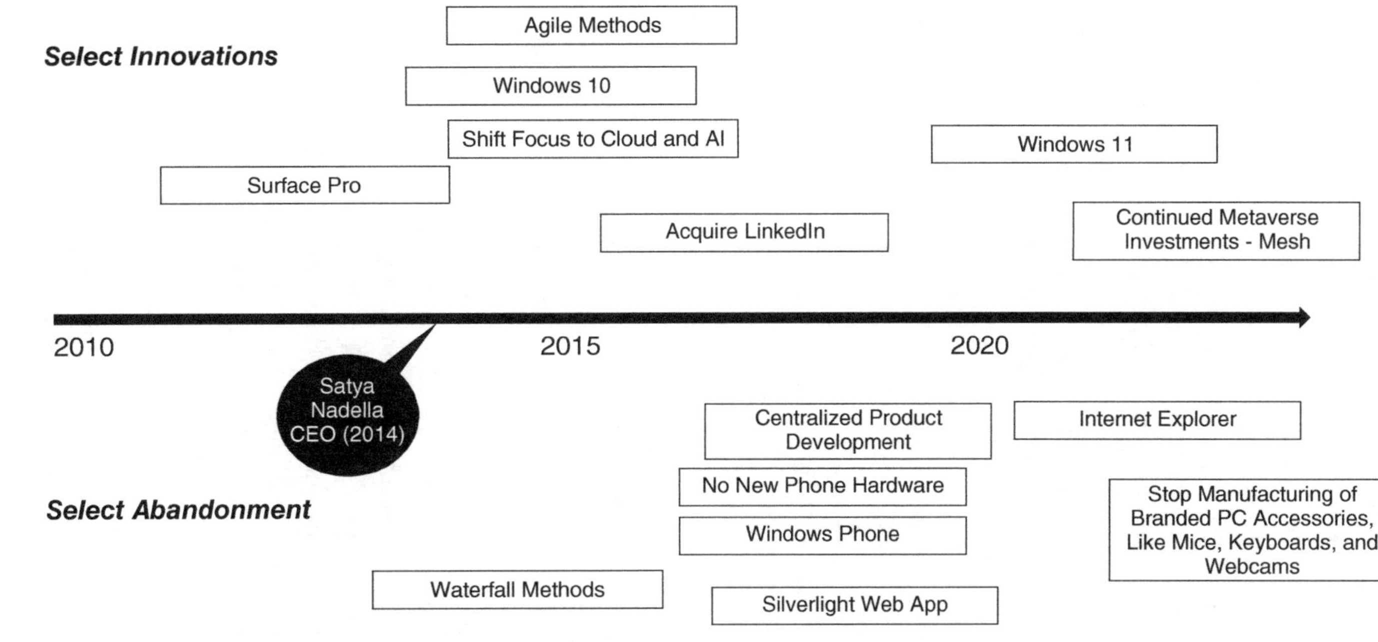

Figure 10.2   Microsoft innovation and abandonment.

discontinued in 2016. It was part of Microsoft's brief foray into the wearable tech market. Microsoft's enterprise version of Skype was phased out and replaced with Microsoft Teams, as Microsoft embraced cloud collaboration and unified communication solutions. Microsoft made some attempts with products like HoloLens, but its virtual reality and augmented reality strategy hasn't seen the same level of commitment compared to rivals like Meta. In 2019, they shifted focus from VR to more AR-like solutions that integrate with their broader cloud and productivity tools.

Microsoft has also adapted its strategy. Microsoft's approach to hardware has shifted over time. While the company initially focused on developing products like the Surface, the focus has now moved more toward cloud computing and services. Some of its hardware projects, such as the Surface Mini, were ultimately abandoned after poor reception or market demand. Microsoft transitioned away from a purely proprietary software model to embrace more open-source contributions, especially with the acquisition of GitHub and the adoption of open-source frameworks. It also shifted from traditional Windows versions (like Windows 7, Windows 8) to Windows 10 as a "service," with regular updates. This led to the abandonment of traditional "boxed" operating system versions.

Leadership styles and behaviors also changed under Nadella's leadership. Under previous leadership (like Steve Ballmer), Microsoft was known for a more hierarchical, competitive, and top-down management approach. Satya Nadella's leadership has been marked by a shift toward a more inclusive, growth-oriented, and collaborative culture with an emphasis on empathy and innovation. In the past, Microsoft was often criticized for its competitive tactics, such as aggressive bundling of products (e.g., Internet Explorer with Windows) and leveraging its dominance in the operating system market to push other products. Under Nadella, the company has taken a more cooperative approach, especially in cloud computing, partnering with companies like Salesforce and Oracle.

In general, Microsoft has increasingly focused on cloud computing (Azure), enterprise software (Office 365, Teams, Dynamics 365), and AI as primary business drivers, abandoning or refocusing on other ventures that did not fit into this ecosystem or that faced stiff competition.

This shift is reflective of Nadella's vision for the company, which centers on empowering people and organizations through cloud and artificial intelligence technologies.

Process Steps for Systematic Abandonment

In this section, we identify the process steps that can be used to practice systematic abandonment. These are relatively straightforward. As you consider these steps, keep in mind the rate of innovation you are planning for the next few years. The level of abandonment must "match" the level of innovation (i.e., for every new activity an organization must stop an activity). So, if you plan to be innovating at 20 percent, you need to identify candidates for abandonment that match this level of innovation.

Step 1: Identify Candidates   The first step is to ask the Drucker question: "If you were going to start the business all over again today knowing what you now know, what would you do?" This question typically leads to a long list of candidates—not just products, but everything an organization does is "on the table." Organizations often have a bias to work on easy things to abandon (e.g., we have seven versions of Salesforce so let's drop one or more of those). The aim is to push yourself to work on both "low hanging fruit" as well as the difficult-to-abandon activities that can free up significant resources (e.g., GM's decision to stop the Pontiac, Oldsmobile, and Saturn brands).

Step 2: Screen by Criteria   Once the list is identified, the next step is to screen each of the activities by three criteria. First, is the activity, resource, or product outdated? Does it represent an "older" or previous generation way of doing the activity? Is there a faster, better, and/or cheaper way to do the activity? Second, is there evidence that the activity is no longer necessary or important? It is often surprising to organizations that there are a host of activities that are being completed and limited evidence that they create value in the marketplace. Third, are there more effective activities, ways, or products to create a better outcome?

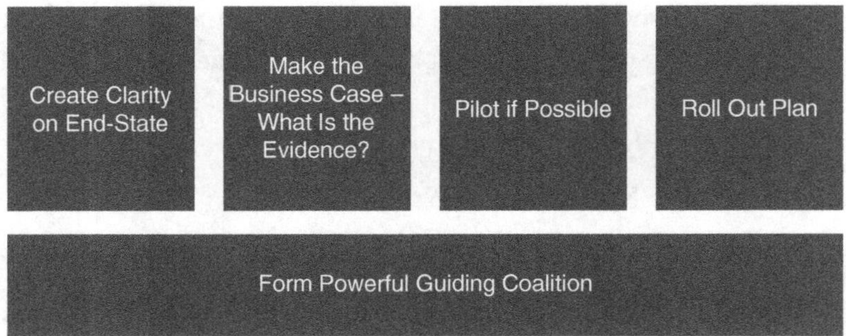

Figure 10.3   A structured approach for significant abandonment initiatives.

Step 3: Rank Order   The third step entails ranking ordered candidates for abandonment. A first step is simply to screen into three categories—high, medium, and low. Keep in mind that you want to balance the low-hanging fruit (easy to abandon, high impact on organization) and the difficult to achieve (high impact if you abandon but not easy to do).

Step 4: Abandon   As implied in Step 3, there are easy and difficult activities to be abandoned. Our experience is that it is often useful to structure the difficult to abandon activities as a change management process. In Figure 10.3, we provide a simple change management process that can be deployed. It begins with the business case for change and the "vision" of the endgame if we are successful. Next, it is often useful to have a few pilot examples, rather than simply go "all in." However the process is managed, it must have a strong guiding coalition of key stakeholders that have "skin in the game" on the activity to be abandoned.

Conclusion

We began this chapter with a simple message—companies cannot innovate effectively without creating space for change. The more aggressive the abandonment, the more time, energy, and resources are freed up for innovation. This is not done for its own sake—it is done in response to the evolution of the marketplace and customer needs, behaviors, and wants. As markets evolve, so too should the organization. It is what Drucker termed the "theory of the business." Namely, the strongly held assumptions about the industry, markets, and strategy of the organization. If the theory of the business changes, the organization must take bold moves to adjust its strategy to fit the environment and, often to change the environment in which they compete.

PART

IV

The Purpose-Led Organization

WE CLOSE OUR book with the fourth section and a final important chapter on the critical role of purpose, particularly through the lens of the customer. Customers and employees both increasingly expect companies to consider broader societal issues (anything from the environment to diversity). We argue that companies that align profit with purpose are better positioned for long-term success. Building on Drucker's core philosophy of a functioning society, we assert that organizations must function as responsible contributors to society, not just economic actors. Through examples like Salesforce, Microsoft, and TOMS, we illustrate how purpose can energize employees, strengthen customer trust, and enhance performance.

Yet, we also acknowledge the challenges facing organizations, including competing pressure from stakeholders, market complexities, purpose-washing by competitors, and the ever-shifting expectations of customers. To help fight against these forces, organizational purpose must be: authentic; embedded across strategy, operations, and culture; and clearly communicated. To navigate this kind of terrain, organizations must deeply understand their customers and be explicit about what they stand for. Done well, purpose becomes a powerful differentiator—driving innovation, loyalty, and societal value in tandem with business performance.

11

The Purpose of Organizations

"We believe our core business strategy, to make great ice cream, is entirely compatible with our belief in doing good in the world. In fact, they go hand in hand."

—Ben Cohen & Jerry Greenfield[1]

Introduction

All types of companies (e.g., Unilever, IKEA, Patagonia, Salesforce, and Microsoft) have made purpose central to their organization's respective strategies. Salesforce, for example, has integrated purpose throughout its organization, as well stated in its stakeholder impact report (2024): "We believe we have a broad responsibility to society, and we aspire to create a framework for the ethical and humane use of technology that not only drives the success of our customers, but also upholds the basic human rights of every individual."[2] By embedding purpose into their core strategy and operations, companies like Salesforce demonstrate that doing good and doing well in business are not mutually exclusive.

The need for organizations to consider the broader society is real. As our world faces significant challenges (regarding prosperity, equity, and environmental sustainability), societal demands are increasing on organizations to respond. For example, concerns have been raised regarding the effects of computer processing required to support emerging technologies, such as machine learning and generative AI. We used AI to support our development of this book and it makes you wonder how many "trees were killed" so that you could read our thoughts, produced in a more efficient manner.

The large-scale data centers required to fuel AI tools are creating significant environmental concerns from many in society. Data centers consume huge amounts of electricity and require ample water for cooling. The need for this water and energy is already great within society and using these resources for emerging technologies has raised questions about the sustainability, infrastructure, and need for more efficient computing solutions.[3] This situation is of concern across the tech industry, with Microsoft committing to becoming carbon negative by 2030—a decision aligned with its long-term positioning in the market.[4]

While a strong case can be made for organizations to consider how they impact society, the reality is that for-profit companies are strongly encouraged to pay attention to financial matters. Pressure to do so comes from a variety of internal (e.g., executive compensation, board governance) and external (investors, competition, capital markets) factors. Such a focus is imbedded in decades of economic thinking that emphasizes profit maximization and shareholder returns. Growing interest in purpose and stakeholder capitalism, however, is changing thinking in business. Returning to Salesforce, Marc Benioff (its CEO) last year in Davos said: "Capitalism as we have known it is dead . . . This obsession that we have with maximizing profits for shareholders alone has led to incredible inequality and a planetary emergency."[5]

Consumers are a significant driving force as organizations shift from a near-singular focus on shareholder returns to a focus aimed at broader societal responsibility. This situation is being propelled by increased consumer awareness of various societal and environmental issues, as reflected in the UNSDGs (the United Nations' Sustainable Development Goals). Organizations that respond are rewarded with stronger brand preference and a greater willingness to pay a premium for products.[6] In the luxury watch market, for example, IWC Schaffhausen has integrated sustainability into its core operations via the use of renewable energy, recycled materials, and sustainable manufacturing. The brand's luxury craftsmanship has thereby aligned with growing demand for environmentally conscious products.[7] Of course, as our experience tells us, other pressures also exist for organizations to be responsible. For example, when organizations fail to adopt responsible practices, consumers let them know, via boycotts, advocacy, social media, and other forms of activism. Ultimately, an organization's purpose, when viewed through the lens of the customer, becomes not just a strategic differentiator but a necessity.

We contend that for today's businesses, purpose is no longer an option or aspiration, but rather it is a competitive imperative. Customers (and employees!) now expect organizations to take clear stands on social and environmental issues. For those organizations shifting toward a greater purpose, McKinsey suggests that organizations need to move from the "why" to the "how" when doing so. Of course, the level of attention paid to the why and how of purpose varies considerably across countries—the EU for example is far ahead of the U.S. in terms of the how of sustainability. Businesses need to embed purpose into strategy, operations, and culture.[8] When all are aligned, organizations are likely to see improvements regarding innovation, trust, and market position. Thus, when done right, purpose can be a win-win-win for not only the organization, but also for its customers and broader society.

In this chapter, we focus on purpose from the lens of the customer—a critical consideration when establishing the purpose of an organization. In today's world, we do not expect that consumers are likely to sit idly by while firms maintain a focus on shareholder profit maximization to the detriment of broader society. As consumer expectations continue to (de)evolve (at a dizzying pace in early 2025), firms must recognize that long-term success increasingly depends on aligning profit motives alongside societal values. Indeed, the concept of performance and purpose is key—a core view of Peter Drucker.

Why For-Profit Firms?

Throughout this book, we balanced our discussion on various forms of organizations as the ideas contained in these chapters apply to all. While purpose is undeniably important across all types of organizations, many of them—nonprofits, public sector institutions, NGOs, and religious groups—have long operated with societal missions at their core. In many ways, these entities exist primarily to serve social, environmental, or spiritual goals. In this chapter we focus primarily on for-profit firms for a simple but significant reason: We believe that for-profit organizations have not historically been structured nor incentivized to prioritize societal good. And yet, these companies wield tremendous influence over economic systems, cultural trends, and environmental outcomes.

Unlike nonprofits or religious organizations, for-profit firms are often bound by market logic that prioritizes shareholder returns, efficiency, and competitive positioning. As a result, we believe it makes the integration of societal purpose both more complex and, arguably, more urgent. Businesses account for the vast majority of economic output, innovation investment, and employment worldwide. Their decisions shape not only customer experiences but also supply chains, labor practices, human health and safety, and environmental impact on a global scale. As such, the stakes are high when these firms shift toward or steer away from a broader conception of purpose. To reiterate Drucker's view of the responsibilities of management, organizations must take on social responsibility. With the emergence of an organization-based society, he noted, "There is no one else around in the society of organizations to take care of society itself. Yet they must do so responsibly, within the limits of their competence, and without endangering their performance capacity."[9]

What Is Purpose?

Our view of purpose aligns with that of Henderson and Van den Steen (2015) who defined it as "a concrete goal or objective for the organization that reaches beyond profit maximization."[10] Put differently, purpose emphasizes a company's broader role in society beyond profit. A firm's purpose is often expressed in a purpose statement that is part of its strategic plan. Here are some examples: "Refresh the world. Make a difference." (Coca-Cola); "Our purpose is to move the world forward through the power of sport. Worldwide, we're leveling the playing field, doing our part to protect our collective playground, and expanding access to sport for everyone." (Nike); "Build a better working world." (EY); "We're in relentless pursuit of breakthroughs that change patients' lives. We innovate every day to make the world a healthier place. It was Charles Pfizer's vision at the beginning and it holds true today." (Pfizer).[11] While varying in length and focus, these purpose statements share a common emphasis on contributing positively to society (e.g., by improving lives, advancing equity, promoting well-being). We return to what makes a good purpose statement in a moment.

Numerous terms have been used in various circles (both academic and practitioner) to describe purpose and include phrases such as: values-driven business, stakeholder capitalism, and conscious capitalism. Others use the terms ESG (Environmental, Social, Governance) or CSR (Corporate Social Responsibility) to describe specifically how companies integrate social and environmental goals within the organization.

> *We contend that for today's businesses, purpose is no longer an option or aspiration, but rather it is a competitive imperative.*

No matter the terminology, the core idea is that businesses need to create value for all stakeholders (e.g., customers, employees, communities, the planet) and not just shareholders.

The concept of an organization's purpose was relevant to the philosophy of Peter Drucker, who framed the idea around that of a functioning society. Drucker's formative years were spent in Europe where he observed the rise of fascist governments and saw how nonfunctioning society can negatively impact the world. Drucker argued that all types of institutions (government, businesses, and nonprofits) are critical to how society functions. He even goes so far as to argue that there is no one else in society other than organizations to take care of society itself. Drucker therefore maintained that for-profit companies, being economic actors, have responsibilities beyond profit generation and also must contribute to society (e.g., by providing meaningful employment, driving innovation, addressing societal issues). While he argues that firms must act responsibly (within the limits of their competence), they cannot endanger their performance capacity.

To be clear, Drucker holds that businesses have social responsibilities, but to achieve such goals organizations must remain viable. As he noted, "The enterprise can fulfill its human and social functions only if it prospers as a business." Thus, he argues that firms should focus on purpose *and* performance, not one to the detriment of the other. Aligned with the concept of stakeholder theory, we have seen such a view as being more widely adopted by many in industry. A great example of this comes from Indra Nooyi (former CEO of PepsiCo), who noted, "Make no mistake about it: Performance is absolutely key for a growth company like ours and for driven perfectionists like each of us. But the fact is that all of us come to work every day looking for meaning . . . as well as money. We want to construct a life . . . as well as make a living. I believe that's true of individuals, and it goes for companies as well."

Drucker was strongly known for his role in the field of management, even being noted the "Father of Modern Management" on the cover of *BusinessWeek*. So you may be asking yourself: How does a management thinker like him end up focusing on purpose and the idea of a functioning society? The answer is quite simple: Organizations are composed of people and the management of them is core to organizational performance. As he noted, he was more interested in people than businesses. Drucker's core view was that organizations must be built from within in terms of social responsibility. Management is the one function that can help achieve such a goal. As he wrote, "No society can function as a society, unless it gives the individual member social status and function, and unless the decisive social power is legitimate." Thus, management was a means to an end for Drucker, with the end being a better world.

Why Purpose?

There are a variety of answers to the question of "why purpose"—answers that will vary across organizations, industries, geographies, and countries. While McKinsey suggested the better question is "how," we focus here on the "why" of purpose to ensure clarity on why organizations should consider broader stakeholders when setting strategy—particularly consumer-centric ones. As we see it, there are at least four reasons why a company should consider a clear purpose in terms of impacting society, including:

- It's the right thing to do and the world needs it.
- Employees and customers care—a lot.
- Organizations benefit from pursuing a purposeful agenda.
- There are significant costs for not doing so.

First, there is a strong argument that for-profit firms should consider broader stakeholders simply because it is the right thing to do, not only for the larger world, but also for the company itself. Forever chemicals, microplastics, lead in the drinking water—history is replete with examples where for-profit firms did not adequately consider (or at times, ignored or hidden) their impact on the world around them. For example, cigarette manufacturers for decades ignored the health risks of smoking cigarettes and went so far as to encourage greater consumption via the addictive nature of nicotine and heavy marketing communications.

While the bad behavior of organizations can damage the environment and people, it is important to remember that negative effects can also amass to the firm as well. For example, in Libby, Montana in the western United States, the W. R. Grace and company mined vermiculite for nearly 70 years. The mined product included asbestos, with its contaminated dust causing significant health issues (including lung cancer) among workers and town residents. In addition to the firm going bankrupt, several executives from this company were indicted on outcomes of this crisis.[12] Risks from the operation of for-profit business have not gone away—nearly everyone reading this book today has microplastics and forever chemicals in their bodies. A clear example of how unbridled, non-socially responsible, and unthoughtful business practices can impact us all.

The United Nations reflects the impact of consumption on world development in goal 12 of its Sustainable Development Goals, which aims to: "Ensure sustainable consumption and production patterns."[13] Estimates vary widely in terms of how much population the planet can handle, but many estimates are that it is no more than eight billion people—the size of Earth's current population. Of course, estimates range greatly, differences that are driven by assumptions and factors used by researchers ranging from levels of consumption across the globe to the impact of current and future technologies. That said, if all people on the planet consumed as much as Western countries, the Earth's current population would clearly be too large. Some estimates suggest that the Earth could only handle a population of 1–2 billion if we all consumed like those in the United States.[14]

Second, customers and employees alike care about an organization's purpose and expect companies to operate in a manner that goes beyond profits, particularly among younger segments. For employees, their organization's purpose can be a source of engagement with the organization and pride. When people see their work contributing to something larger than financial gain, they tend to be more productive, committed, and satisfied. Further, purpose-driven organizations have employees with higher levels of job satisfaction and psychological well-being.[15] When a company's purpose aligns with employees' personal values, it fosters a stronger sense of identity and belonging, enhancing loyalty and reducing turnover.[16] From the customer's perspective, purpose drives trust, emotional connection, and engagement and loyalty with the organization, among other positive outcomes. It is our experience that today's consumers expect more from companies than just quality products and services; rather, they want brands to reflect their values regarding sustainability, equity, and social responsibility.

Third, numerous benefits accrue to organizations that consider the impact of what they do on broader society. For example, accounting research has shown that companies investing in material sustainability issues significantly outperformed peers on stock returns and accounting performance.[17] As noted earlier, benefits of a purpose-centered strategy accrue to organizations via engagement of an organization's employees and customers. But the story does not end there; the impact of purpose can also be seen on the firm's overall performance. For example, academic research has shown that firms adopting stakeholder-focused practices (e.g., ESG and CSR) achieve superior financial performance over time. For-profit firms can also learn about the value of focusing on society from other types of organizations. The Nature Conservancy (TNC) illustrates how stakeholder engagement works in the practice of NGOs. TNC's approach connects to Drucker's argument about organizational legitimacy and shows that conservation organizations, just like businesses, must ground their legitimacy in performance as well as good intentions. Such stakeholder-centered approaches generate tangible benefits for firms, including reduced costs of capital, improved operational efficiencies, and enhanced investor confidence.

Finally, organizations that have not adopted a purpose-led strategy cannot expect to accrue the benefits just outlined. But the reality is that negative reactions from customers, employees, and other stakeholders can be quite damaging. Organizations that do not adopt a clear purpose run the risk of being weaker in the market, having a hard time retaining employees, and difficulty in building a loyal customer base. Boycotts are becoming more common as there is greater political polarization in western economies. Customers from both sides of the political spectrum will often punish firms that wade in to corporate political activities—an extension of today's cancel culture. For example, in 2025, Yeti (the thermal drink container maker) faced backlash after canceling an order from a conservative women's group; the decision led to accusations of political bias and sparked consumer boycotts of the brand.[18]

Purpose and the Customer

As detailed in the preceding sections, customers care that organizations pursue (or fail to pursue) a purpose-centered strategy. For organizations that take the path that considers the impact on a range of stakeholders, they are rewarded by customers. The growing trend toward corporate purpose is heavily influenced by shifting expectations among customers and the broader public. As noted earlier, customers in today's marketplace expect more than quality products or services, but also expect organizations to act ethically, demonstrate social responsibility, and have a commitment to addressing broader societal issues.

Modern customers, especially younger generations like Millennials and Gen Z, often base purchase decisions on a company's stance on a range of societal issues ranging from environmental sustainability to social justice. A recent customer study by IBM illustrates this point quite well. Results found that purpose-driven consumers constitute the largest market segment (45 percent of consumers select products that align with their own values). Importantly for firms, the vast majority (73 percent) of these consumers are willing to pay more for such products.[19] While the rewards are potentially significant, pressure from

> *Today's customers increasingly expect companies to do more than deliver quality products or services. Rather, they want organizations to act ethically, demonstrate social responsibility, and have a commitment to addressing broader societal issues.*

customers is ever present, with expectations that companies will behave in a manner consistent with their values. To make matters more difficult, today's digital era has empowered the public to scrutinize company actions in real time, with reactions posted nearly instantaneously via social media, online reviews, and watchdog platforms (as explicated in more detail in Chapter 3). Pressure from such transparency urges organizations to act with integrity and consistency across their operations.

Unfortunately, views of societal issues are shifting at a rapid pace in many societies, leaving organizations with a difficult situation to diagnose and respond to in terms of strategy. Nothing in recent memory illustrates the pendular nature of a social issue more than the swings around DEI (diversity, equity, and inclusion). Recently, several companies (ranging from Lowe's to Harley Davidson) have scaled back or altered their approach to DEI, as driven by shifting political views of DEI. These actions prompted significant backlash from not only customers, but also employees and advocacy groups. Not long ago, DEI was a well-accepted part of society and doing business, but that is no longer the case. Such a situation highlights the precarious balance companies must navigate in addressing social responsibility while also managing stakeholder expectations. A recent example of this balance is Ford's decision to withdraw from an equality index that assesses workplace inclusivity for LGBTQ+ employees. The move got mixed reactions from stakeholders, with some supporting it and others responding with backlash.[20]

While there are clear benefits accruing to organizations that are purpose driven, getting it right can be difficult with the ever-shifting sands of broader society. So, what is an organization to do? Our primary advice (not surprising given the topic of our book) is to know your customer. You must understand the people buying your product or service in terms of their wants and needs, particularly as it relates to what they expect in terms of society. What works for Lowes, for example, will not likely work for Home Depot. Active monitoring of these customer trends is a good first step, but once the data is in, it will be critical for a cross-functional team to make sense of the data within the macro context of broader society.

But there is an incredibly important caveat: Organizations must know what they stand for and make that clear to customers. Equivocation on core societal issues, whether it be diversity or the environment, has proven a less-than-successful approach in the market (think of our earlier example regarding Target and its recent attempt to find a balanced approach to DEI, compared to that of Costco).

The Organization's Purpose

Not too long ago, it was rare to find organizations that took the time and effort to define a purpose statement. While there are no formal statistics on purpose statements, it has been suggested that about 25 percent of Fortune 500 organizations now have a purpose statement or a statement that closely resembles one.[21] Organizations have increasingly become more societally focused—attempting to articulate a reason for being that is not simply about shareholder value. Certainly, one significant trend in this direction is work on the circular economy and sustainability. However, purpose is broader—it is about how society functions more effectively, or simply better off, as a result of the organization's activities.

Four Key Criteria for Purpose Statements

A purpose statement should be simple, clear, and energizing for the workforce. Here we focus on four key characteristics of a great purpose statement: (1) specifies how the organization's activities or products help society (locally or globally) function more efficiently and/or effectively, (2) triggers positive emotions and touches the heart and mind, (3) answers the simple question of why every employee should love to come to work each day, and (4) connects the dots from the organization's products/offers to the societal outcomes.[22]

Characteristic 1: Helps Society   We believe that purpose statements must make it eminently clear to employees, customers, and other stakeholders how they intend to improve society. Ben & Jerry's (the ice cream company) is known for its strong commitment to social justice, environmental sustainability, and ethical business practices.

The company is dedicated to making the best possible ice cream while using its platform to advocate for various social causes. They focus on environmental sustainability, climate change awareness, racial justice, and fair trade practices, striving to make a positive impact on both society and the planet. As Ben & Jerry's CEO, Matthew McCarthy, noted, "We are committed to using our business to make the world a better place."[23] Again, to be very clear, like Drucker, we believe the first responsibility of management is to deliver economic performance. Full stop. But it doesn't end there. At the same time, organizations must play a role in helping society function.

Characteristic 2: Touches the Heart and Mind   We also believe that a good purpose statement is emotional—it triggers positive associations for the employees and the customers. Salesforce's purpose statement is "We believe business is the greatest platform for change."[24] Similar to Ben & Jerry's, Salesforce's purpose is to empower its employees to make a positive impact in the world through business. It emphasizes the idea of equality, community, and giving back, which deeply connects with employees' aspirations to do meaningful work.

Characteristic 3: Energizes the Workforce   Third, we have observed that purpose statements can energize and motivate the workforce. An excellent example of a purpose-driven company is TOMS shoes. TOMS has built its brand around its "One for One" model, where the company donates a pair of shoes to a person in need for every pair sold, and later expanded to other initiatives like providing clean water and supporting mental health. As such, the company focuses on creating social change and giving back to communities through its products. Their mission is to improve lives by creating a positive impact in underserved communities around the world, making purpose central to their business strategy and a key differentiator in developing a customer advantage.

TOMS CEO, Blake Mycoskie, notes, "I think that's really the job of a manager or an executive, is not just to lead the vision of the business, but to really serve those that are working for them so that they feel empowered to really serve the customer." [25] This quote highlights how TOMS' purpose of giving back has a direct effect on energizing the workforce. When employees are aligned with the company's mission and see the real-world impact of their work, it inspires and motivates them to give their best.

Characteristic 4: Connects the Dots to Societal Impact   Finally, it is often the case that organizations need to explicitly connect their purpose to a functioning society. Often, we have seen organizations drop the ball on this key connection. The most obvious way to connect the dots to social impact is a B Corp. A B Corp is a certification given to companies that meet high standards of social and environmental performance, accountability, and transparency. Unlike traditional for-profit companies, B Corps (e.g., Patagonia, Ben & Jerry's) are legally required to consider the impact of their decisions on various stakeholders, such as employees, customers, the environment, and the community—not just shareholders.

That stated, a number of firms have had a long-term commitment that extends beyond shareholders. In 1943, Robert Wood Johnson crafted a company credo for Johnson & Johnson company. The credo, which has dictated the course of action for the company for decades, included five key responsibilities:

- To the doctors, nurses, hospitals, and mothers who use our products
- To the company's employees
- To the company's management
- To the communities in which the company operated
- And to the stockholders.[26]

Today, the credo is still a foundation for everything that J&J does as an organization.[27] Importantly, this is a very balanced stakeholder perspective—where value is created for all stakeholders. Consistent with a Drucker view, profit is essential for the firm to survive and thrive. This is the very first responsibility of leaders. That said, it is done in a way that enables the firm to invest in its people—to give them status and function. And, as a result of serving their customers well (those who use J&J products), they are able to successfully compete in the present and transform into the future.

Why Purpose Is Tough

There are distinct headwinds associated with companies that decide to include broader societal issues in corporate strategy. Within the organization, challenges to implement a purpose-driven strategy range from a lack of clarity about what purpose means to difficulties in implementation. Indeed, implementing such a strategy requires alignment between the strategy and business practice. Companies face scrutiny if actions are perceived as misaligned with the overall purpose.[28] For example, in 2020, BP committed to the strong climate goal of cutting oil and gas production by 40 percent in 10 years. Due to market realities and political pressures, the company pulled back with a goal to reduce production by 25 percent. The move raised concerns and kindled criticism from environmental groups. This example illustrates an important point; namely that it is difficult for firms to balance purpose and performance.[29] There are three other types of headwinds to discuss including those related to the marketplace, competitors, and customers.

Marketplace Headwinds

A counterforce to a purpose-centered strategy is the pervasive (or is invasive a better word?) stakeholder view of for-profit firm performance, which was introduced by Milton Friedman. In contrast to a Druckerian view (where purpose *and* performance are the focus), Friedman argued that the primary responsibility of any firm is to maximize shareholder profits (assuming it does so in a legal and ethical manner).[30] This approach has been the dominant framework for decades, shaping corporate governance, CEO (over) compensation, and regulation of markets. In contrast to a stakeholder approach, this view has driven a collective mindset of profit primacy—a situation that encourages firms to prioritize short-term financial gains, often at the expense of broader stakeholder interests. While Friedman's view is widely taught in business schools, critics have challenged this approach, noting that it has contributed to income inequality, environmental degradation, and public distrust of corporations.[31] Even with the presence of such criticism, we expect that the views outlined by Friedman will continue to drive market behavior and society for quite some time—there are simply too many financial incentives aligned with maintaining this view.

Competitor Issues

At times, at the competitor level, firms may project a socially responsible image without being committed to it. Sometimes called *purpose-washing,* such behaviors can have significant effects on firms truly committed to making positive impacts on stakeholders and the planet. Unfortunately, such actions are not uncommon and witnessed with firms such as H&M, Volkswagen, and L'Oreal. A great example of this is VW's "diesel gate" involving software that cheated emissions tests worldwide on millions of diesel vehicles.[32] Often framed around green-washing, customers are more than willing to call out firms that are acting in ways misaligned with stated values. For organizations that are truly committed to a broader purpose, potential negative outcomes may occur, including erosion of trust, reputational contagion, market confusion, consumer cynicism, regulatory backlash, and dilution of industry standards. Thus, purpose-washing does not just harm the guilty companies, but it also likely undermines the credibility, effectiveness, and competitiveness of all firms in a particular industry. For firms that genuinely adopt a purpose-driven strategy, it is important to clearly communicate their goals and actions that support broader society and to ensure that actions and practices are aligned.[33]

Customer Desires

At the core of a customer-centric strategy is meeting the needs and wants of customers. Just like balancing purpose with financial performance, organizations also need to balance customers' true desires with the impact of those desires on society. Take, for example, issues related to sustainability. While customers often expect convenience, quality, and inclusivity in their purchases, to meet such expectations often conflicts with what is required to offer an eco-friendly product (e.g., due to higher costs, supply

> *At the core of a customer-centric strategy is meeting the needs and wants of customers.*

chain complexity, material constraints). Many companies have struggled with this issue, including industry leaders like Coca-Cola, which has grappled with the introduction of eco-friendly packaging.[34] The balancing act between what is desired and what is best for society also puts pressure on consumers. Prosocial consumption is unique, in that supporting broader societal goals may take up additional resources, time, and effort of the consumers to help the world.[35]

Conclusion

While the journey toward developing a truly purpose-driven organization has its difficulties, the alternative (i.e., lacking a clear purpose) presents even greater risks to an organization's relevance and success in today's and future markets. The push and pull over serving shareholders versus stakeholders will not likely go away anytime soon, at least as long as the market is focused on earnings per share and quarterly performance. The right place to be, in our view and Peter Drucker's, is where purpose *and* performance are the firm's primary focus, all while addressing the needs, wants, and desires of its customers.

Epilogue

In this book, we have argued that the "soul" of any strategy is not the competition, external forces, core competencies, nor clever market positioning (while each is valuable in its own way for the organization). Rather, strategy must be centered on the only entity capable of sustaining a business over time: the customer. As noted earlier, we are not saying that the competition nor organization resources are unimportant, but we are arguing that such things are less important to setting organizational strategy compared to unique, actionable customer insights. To reiterate an earlier point—the starting point of all strategy must begin with customers.

While the basic idea of a customer focus may not be hard to sell within your organization, leaders need to be prepared to assess whether the organization is ready and willing to make the structural, behavioral, and cultural shifts needed to fully live a customer-centric strategy. Customer needs are evolving more quickly than ever before, driven by digital transformation, global complexity, and societal change. Companies that thrive will be those that embrace this pace—not by

> *We contend that organizational strategists must have a nuanced understanding of customers as a starting point to setting strategy, rather than as a consequence of doing so.*

chasing trends, but by shaping their organizations around a deeper understanding of customer experience and aspiration.

As we close this book, we want to leave with you some of our final thoughts on the pathway to embracing a customer-centric strategy. We have had the good fortune of being part of several such transformations, either as advisors or researchers studying the customer-centric transformational journey. As you contemplate the book (and hopefully reread portions), we encourage you to keep in mind four key themes:

- **First, this journey often takes several years.** For large global organizations, the shift from product-centered to customer-centered takes years to complete.[1] If the starting point is an organization that is siloed within divisions and within functions—and the aim is to be "one firm"—this campaign is to going to take several years. On the other hand, if we are focused on a startup that is launching with a product or offering, the shift can occur in a much shorter timeframe. Our message, however, is the journey may never be complete. The cycle of intelligence—get, reach conclusions, and exploit—needs to be done on a continual basis. Think of the journey more as a practice than an end state.[2]

- **Second, the roadmap for the journey needs to be updated periodically.** Organizations begin their journey with a particular destination in mind. After a few years of work and innovation, there is a realization that a great deal of progress has been made. However, there is also a realization that the progress was not linear—new competition may have entered the market, regulations have changed, and expected product successes were actually failures. The result is that a new roadmap for change needs to be drafted to reflect the new realities—and it will likely require the discipline to abandon.

- **Third, strategy, at its most effective and enduring, is not a static plan nor a once-a-year slide deck.** Strategy must be a commitment and an organizational mindset; however, there are forces at work to slow down or impede the journey. One force at work is simply the length of time in the role. Key senior executives who started the initiative may have been promoted, moved to new responsibilities, or left the organization. Thus, the champions and "coalitions" are no longer present. The new executives may have ideas for a different set of priorities or journey, and, as a result, the customer-centered journey stalls. Also, fluctuations in the business may require cutbacks in resources. It is difficult to sustain these initiatives for several years. There is the natural burnout, lack of focus, or emergence of new priorities.

- **Fourth, it takes committed C-level leadership teams.** This cannot be the leadership of a single, powerful leader. This takes a senior team who are all committed, tell the story the same way, and are "all in" on the vision. Any guiding coalition to drive an organization to be more customer-centric must have a few key members of the C-level team. They must represent powerful units within the firm (not just marketing). They must be widely respected up and down the organization.

The journey to be customer-centric is not for the fainthearted. It is not easy to understand the outcomes that customers are looking for when they purchase your product. It is much easier simply to ask about new features than it is to understand the motivation behind the purchases. However, the rewards of being a truly customer-centered firm—happier customers, happier employees, and outsized financial returns—truly merit the journey.

As Peter Drucker reminded us, "The purpose of a business is to create a customer." To do so, we must create organizations worthy of that customer's loyalty, trust, and admiration. Thus, the future of strategy is when the customer is at the center and the soul of the firm is aligned accordingly.

About the Authors

At the time of writing this book, Bernie Jaworski and Dave Sprott are both professors at the Peter F. Drucker and Masatoshi Ito Graduate School of Management (aka the Drucker School) at Claremont Graduate University. The namesake of their school was Peter F. Drucker, often referred to as the "Father of Modern Management." Peter worked and taught in Claremont for more than three decades, where he wrote two-thirds of his books, taught many students, and consulted firms ranging from the Girl Scouts to General Electric, and cemented his place as "The Man Who Invented Modern Management." The authors are proud to animate Drucker's ideas in this book and wish Peter could see how his core ideas are alive and well today. In many ways, we hope that this book would be one Peter had wished he wrote.

Bernie Jaworski is the Drucker Chair in Management and the Liberal Arts, which is named in honor of Peter Drucker. Jaworski is an ISBM and American Marketing Association Fellow. He is recipient of the three major *Journal of Marketing* awards—the Alpha Kappa Psi award (received twice), the Maynard award, and the Sheth award. He also received the Converse award and the Vijay Mahajan lifetime achievement award for contributions to marketing. His 2020 book on

Organic Growth (with Bob Lurie) received the Leonard Berry AMA book of the year award. His work is highly cited (more than 57,000 citations as of May 2025). He has been voted MBA teacher of the year (both at USC and Drucker).

Jaworski came to the Drucker School from the Switzerland-based IMD, a highly regarded international business school. Prior to working at IMD, Jaworski spent a decade as a senior partner of the Monitor Group, a global management consulting firm. During his Monitor career, he co-founded and co-led two of the global practice areas, the e-commerce practice and the executive education unit. Among other activities, he was a senior team member of a number of significant multiyear corporate transformations for multinational clients in a variety of sectors, notably pharmaceuticals, biotech, and medical devices.

From 1996 to 1999, Jaworski served as the Jeanne and David Tappan Marketing Fellow and a tenured full professor of marketing at the University of Southern California. He has also served on the faculty at the University of Arizona and as a visiting professor at Harvard Business School as well as on the review boards of the *Journal of Marketing*, *Journal of the Academy of Marketing Science*, and the *Journal of Marketing Research*. He is the co-author of four textbooks on e-commerce and two management-focused books (the most recent *Creating the Organization of the Future* with Virginia Cheung) and has taught topics including leadership, corporate strategy, and marketing strategy.

Dave Sprott is the Henry Y. Hwang Dean and professor of marketing at the Drucker School; he is also on faculty at the University of St. Gallen in Switzerland. Sprott is a lifelong academic who asked one of his freshman professors how he could be an academic. The funny guy said, "Pass my class Mr. Sprott." Fast forward, he has served as professor at three universities and has taught students around the world. Beyond passion for his research and teaching, he has an abiding love of the international dimensions of business (a unifying force in the world, in his view) and graduate education.

Sprott joined the Drucker School in May 2021. Immediately prior to this, he served as dean and professor at the University of Wyoming in Laramie. Fun fact: He is one of the few people who moved from

Wyoming to California during the COVID-19 pandemic (normally the direction of movement was opposite, much to the chagrin of Wyomingites!). Before that, he served in various associate dean roles at Washington State University, where he was part of the leadership team in WSU's Carson College of Business from 2007 until 2018. Sprott's accomplishments at CGU, UW, and WSU all reflect his leadership style that focuses on developing and maintaining relationships, working in an interdisciplinary fashion across various academic and support units, and enabling qualified team members to succeed.

As a faculty member, Sprott's research surrounds topics on consumer behavior, retailing, branding, social influence, and marketing public policy. His driving interest is understanding why customers do what they do, in various settings. While customers are messy to study, their cognitions and behaviors hold a fascination for him. His work is well cited (more than 11,000 citations as of May 2025). His research has been published in the field's top journals such as *Journal of Applied Psychology*, *Journal of Consumer Research*, *Journal of Marketing*, *Journal of Marketing Research*, and *Journal of Retailing*. Sprott's teaching reflects similar interests, including retail management, leadership, brand management, consumer behavior, sales management, and research methods. He happily teaches at the undergraduate, masters, and PhD levels. Sprott is the co-editor of the *Handbook of Research on Customer Engagement* (Edward Elgar, 2019). He is a member of several marketing and consumer organizations, including the American Marketing Association, the Association for Consumer Research, and the Society for Consumer Psychology.

Acknowledgments

We want to acknowledge our colleagues at the Drucker School and Claremont Graduate University. As Dean of the college, Dave has led the school for the past five years and has the full support of the staff, faculty, and CGU administration in driving fundamental changes at the school. Bernie has held the Peter F. Drucker Chair in Management and the Liberal Arts. Similarly, he has appreciated the support and colleagueship of the faculty.

It may go without saying, but we want to acknowledge the enduring ideas of Peter F. Drucker, who often described himself as an observer in this world. During his lifetime, Peter (co-)authored 39 books, the majority of which he wrote in Claremont when he worked at the Drucker School. The core ideas of this book relate well to Peter's ideas, particularly regarding the importance of customers to any organization. Peter considered that customers are the heart of any business—a view that we could not agree with more. While his ideas were generated in the 20th century, his core ideas related to human centricity and a functioning society have never been more important than today. As we like to say, "the world needs more Drucker," and we are hopeful this book helps to achieve that goal.

We also want to acknowledge our friends and colleagues at SMA. Ajay Patel and Liz Stillman have been strong supporters of the school and us—in many different capacities. As a yearly "Drucker partner," SMA has provided financial support for the school and has been involved in a host of engagements with the school (e.g., the Drucker Virtual Museum). Ajay made the initial connection with Wiley. Without Ajay, this book would not have been possible. Indeed, Ajay is the author of Chapter 2 of the book on the evolution of strategy. More generally, both Ajay and Liz have been unwavering supporters and friends of the school, and we deeply appreciate their commitment.

Without our incredible research assistant—Teresa Contino, a CGU graduate student—this book would not have been possible. She has been involved since the start and has played numerous roles, including basic research on the topic, finding examples of customer-centric firms, providing chapter-by-chapter commentary, checking references, and providing feedback. We would have been lost without her. Thank you Teresa!

The Editorial team at Wiley provided invaluable support. In particular, we want to thank four team members. Kezia Endsley was our development editor providing exceptionally detailed commentary and guidance on each chapter of the book. Sangeetha Suresh in her role as managing editor and overall project management lead for the book kept us on track for a 2025 publication date. Amanda Pyne, editorial assistant, provided invaluable advice on the commercialization plan for the book. Finally, we would like to thank Zach Schisgal for finding us, signing us up, and providing overall guidance to the project. Thank you all.

Bernie

There are three individuals I would like to thank. First, is my wife Maria Jaworski. A lion's share of the book was written while on sabbatical in Europe. Maria was incredibly supportive of the time and effort it took to craft the manuscript. Each day I would wake up and start to write. The challenge, of course, was right outside our door was Paris, Florence, Madrid, and several other destinations. Somehow she managed to fully support me when the temptation to experience

Europe was a step away. I am forever grateful that she not only let me "do my thing," but did so without any hesitation and with good cheer. Thank you Maria for being such a great wife, friend, and journey-mate!

Second, I would like to thank Ajay Kohli. For more than 40 years we have been great friends and co-authors on some important papers in the marketing discipline. This book has many of Ajay's ideas expressed in the volume. Chapter 4 in particular is based on our decades of research on what it takes to build a market-driven firm. We also worked on the concept of driving and shaping markets—so not just taking the market as a given. I am forever grateful for our friendship and colleagueship. My career would have taken a very different turn if not for Ajay.

Third, I have been blessed with the friendship and co-authorship of Jeffrey Rayport. Jeffrey and I have crafted several books and the idea of putting the customer first has been at the core of our work. In *Best Face Forward*, we explored the changing role of how firms interacted with customers in a world supported by technological interfaces. It was a very early perspective on what is now termed "digital transformation." Jeffrey opened my eyes to a world where technology could fundamentally change the customer experience.

Dave

I am thankful for various people in my life whom I wish to formally acknowledge. First and foremost is my wife Constance, whom I call Betty. Her unwavering love and support for my life and career goals is humbling and unbelievably important to my success. In addition to putting me through doctoral school, she has supported me in every dimension of my academic and personal life for more than three decades. Without you Betty, I would have been unable to achieve what I have achieved. I also thank my three amazing daughters (Chapin, Arden, and Piper) who have taught me so much about being a better person. Thank you all!

In my professorial life, I have been blessed to be surrounded by incredible role models and peers. First is Terry Shimp, my advisor, coauthor, and friend, who introduced me to the world of academics and how studying consumers could be fascinating, exciting, and rewarding.

When you hear the phrase "a gentleman and a scholar," Terry immediately comes to mind. Next is my friend, co-author, and mentor, Eric Spangenberg. He was my big brother in the academy and a partner in so many ways. His leadership, values, passion, and humor remain inspirations for me to this day. Finally, my three compatriots, Mike Barone, Ken Manning, and Anthony Miyazaki, in the South Carolina PhD program have been and remain a constant source of motivation and friendship for me. Thank you all for being part of my academic family and such important anchors in life.

Finally, I want to thank my dad, uncle, and grandfathers, who showed me the worth and dignity in work and provided me insights into customers from an early age. All of them were entrepreneurs and role models in my life. I was blessed to grow up in Sprott and Sons General Store in Ravenna, Ohio, where I learned from a young age that organizations (even a country store) can create community via their customers. The store was more than selling goods, but rather a place for people to meet, convene, and catch up after a long day at work. My interest in customers is firmly grounded in what I observed as a little boy standing behind the counter with my dad and uncle.

We hope that you enjoy the book as much as we have enjoyed writing it.

—Bernie Jaworski, Sicily, IT

—David Sprott, Claremont, CA

Notes

Chapter 1

1. Drucker, P.F. (1954). *The Practice of Management*, 37. Harper Business.
2. Drucker, P.F. (2008). *Management (Revised Edition)*, 101. Harper Collins.
3. Merriam-Webster. (n.d.). Soul. Merriam-Webster.com Dictionary. Retrieved May 9, 2025. https://www.merriam-webster.com/dictionary/soul.
4. Westphal, Jonathan, "Descartes and the Discovery of the Mind-Body Problem." https://thereader.mitpress.mit.edu/discovery-mind-body-problem/.
5. https://www.emarketer.com/content/how-trader-joe-s-erewhon-h-e-b-have-cultivated-cult-following.
6. https://www.cnn.com/travel/trader-joes-tourist-attraction-cult-products/index.html.
7. https://www.forbes.com/sites/daviddisalvo/2015/02/19/what-trader-joes-knows-about-making-your-brain-happy/.
8. Drucker, P.F. (2004, February 27). Defining business purpose and mission. In: *The Daily Drucker: 366 Days of Insight and Motivation for Getting the Right Things Done*. HarperBusiness.

9. In a review article of empirical studies of the resource based view of the firm—the customer is rarely mentioned Armstrong, C.E. and Shimizu, K. (2007). A review of approaches to empirical research on the resource-based view of the firm. *Journal of Management* 33 (6): 959–986. https://doi.org/10.1177/0149206307307645.
10. https://www.amazon.com/Five-Important-Questions-About-Organization/dp/0470227567.

Chapter 2

1. Drucker, P. (2012). *Managing for results*. Routledge.
2. Chandler, A.D. Jr. (1962). *Strategy and Structure: Chapters in the History of the American Industrial Enterprise*. MIT Press. Learned, E.P., Christensen, C.R., Andrews, K.R., and Guth, W.D. (1965). *Business Policy: Text and Cases*. R.D. Irwin.
3. Chandler, A.D. Jr. (1962). *Strategy and Structure: Chapters in the History of the Industrial Enterprise*. MIT Press.
4. Learned, E.P., Christensen, C.R., Andrews, K.R., and Guth, W.D. (1965). *Business Policy: Text and Cases*. Homewood/IL: Irwin.
5. Andrews, K.J. (1971). *The Concept of Corporate Strategy*. Irwin.
6. Porter, M.E. (1980). *Competitive Strategy: Techniques for Analyzing Industries and Competitors*. Free Press.
7. Penrose, E. (1959). *The Theory of the Growth of the Firm*. Oxford: Basil Blackwell.
8. Wernerfelt, B. (1984). A resource-based view of the firm. *Strategic Management Journal* 5 (2): 171–180. https://doi.org/10.1002/smj.4250050207.
9. Barney, J.B. (1991). *Firm resources and sustained competitive advantage*. *Journal of Management* 17 (1): 99. SAGE Publishing. https://doi.org/10.1177/014920639101700108.
10. Teece, D.J., Pisano, G.P., and Shuen, A. (1997). Dynamic capabilities and strategic management. *Strategic Management Journal* 18 (7): 509. Wiley. https://doi.org/10.1002/(sici)1097-0266(199708)18:7<509::aid-smj882>3.0.co;2-z.
11. Mintzberg, H. (1978). Patterns in strategy formation. *Management Science* 24 (9): 934. Institute for Operations Research and the Management Sciences. https://doi.org/10.1287/mnsc.24.9.934.
12. Prahalad, C.K. and Hamel, G. (1990). The core competence of the corporation. *Harvard Business Review* 68: 79.

13. Porter, M.E. (1996). What is strategy? *Harvard Business Review* 74 (6): 61–78.

14. Ghemawat, P. (1991). *Commitment: The Dynamic of Strategy*. Free Press.

15. Mainardi, C. and Kleiner, A. (2010). "The Right to Win." https://www.strategy-business.com/article/10407.

16. The interested reader can learn more about how strategy theories have evolved over time from two sources. The first is *Competition and Business Strategy in Historical Perspective* by Ghemawat (2002); it offers a valuable historical context for understanding the evolution of competitive strategy frameworks. The second is *The Lords of Strategy* by Kiechel (2010). This work focuses on the historical development of strategic thinking as a field, tracing its evolution through key figures, ideas, and organizations.

17. It is important to stress that the four schools of thought we note here are based on the foundation provided by Kiechel (2010) and *Right to Win* by Cesare Mainardi and Art Kleiner. We differ from the four schools in the Right to Win in a couple of respects. They focused on four schools: (1) positioning, (2) execution, (3) concentration, and (4) adaptation. The two that are not often talked about as a "school" are operational excellence and the dynamic capability. . . In our view they have been very significant and continue on. Also, we subjugated the environmental based view as a part of MBV. The RBV in itself seems very "pure" in that it's largely singularly focused.

18. Porter, M.E. (1980). *Competitive Strategy: Techniques for Analyzing Industries and Competitors*. Free Press. Porter, M.E. (2008). The five competitive forces that shape strategy. *Harvard Business Review*. In *PubMed* 86 (1): 78. National Institutes of Health. https://pubmed.ncbi.nlm.nih.gov/18271320.

19. Kim, W.C. and Mauborgne, R. (2004). Blue ocean strategy. *Harvard Business Review* 82 (10): 76. National Institutes of Health.

20. Porter, M.E. (1980). *Competitive Strategy: Techniques for Analyzing Industries and Competitors*. Free Press.

21. Porter, M.E. (1985). *Competitive Advantage: Creating and Sustaining Superior Performance*. http://ci.nii.ac.jp/ncid/BA00852365.

22. Henderson, B. (1970). *The Product Portfolio*. The Boston Consulting Group.

23. Henderson, B. (1973). *The Experience Curve - Reviewed II: History*. The Boston Consulting Group.

24. Kim, W.C. and Mauborgne, R. (2004). Blue Ocean strategy. *Harvard Business Review* 82 (10): 76. National Institutes of Health.

25. Wernerfelt, B. (1984). A resource-based view of the firm. *Strategic Management Journal* 5 (2): 171–180. https://doi.org/10.1002/smj.4250050207.

26. Penrose, E. (1959). *The Theory of the Growth of the Firm*. Oxford: Basil Blackwell.

27. Wernerfelt, B. (1985). Resource based view of the firm. *Strategic Management Journal* 5: 171–180.

28. Barney, J.B. (1991). *Firm resources and sustained competitive advantage. Journal of Management* 17 (1): 99. SAGE Publishing. https://doi.org/10.1177/014920639101700108.

29. Prahalad, C.K. and Hamel, G. (1990). The core competence of the corporation. *Harvard Business Review* 68: 79.

30. Deming, W.E. (1982). *Out of the Crisis*. MIT Press.

31. Hammer, M. and Champy, J. (1993). *Reengineering the Corporation: A Manifesto for Business Revolution*. Harper Business.

32. Womack, J.P., Jones, D.T., and Roos, D. (1990). *The Machine that Changed the World: The Story of Lean Production—Toyota's Secret Weapon in the Global Car Wars That Is Now Revolutionizing World Industry*. Free Press.

33. Peters, T.J. and Waterman, R.H. (1982). *In Search of Excellence: Lessons from America's Best-Run Companies*. Harper & Row.

34. Mintzberg, H. (1994). *The Rise and Fall of Strategic Planning*. Free Press.

35. Teece, D.J. (2009). *Dynamic Capabilities and Strategic Management: Organizing for Innovation and Growth*. Oxford University Press.

36. Hamel, G. and Prahalad, C.K. (1994). *Competing for the Future*. Harvard Business School Press.

37. Drucker, P.F. (1954). *The Practice of Management*. New York: Harper & Row.

38. Friedman, M. (1970). *A Friedman Doctrine - The Social Responsibility of Business is to Increase its Profits* (p. 17).

39. Dooley, B. (2024, December 18). How 7-Eleven Japan became the envy of the retail world. *The New York Times*. https://www.nytimes.com/2024/12/18/business/7-eleven-japan-corporate-culture.html.

40. Treacy, M.E. and Wiersema, F. (1995). *The Discipline of Market Leaders*. https://en.wikipedia.org/wiki/The_Discipline_of_Market_Leaders.

41. Kohli, A.K. and Jaworski, B.J. (1990). Market orientation. *Journal of Marketing* 54 (2): 1–18.

42. Pine, B.J. II and Gilmore, J.H. (1999). *The Experience Economy*. Boston: Harvard Business School Press.

43. Thor Olavsrud. *"Feeding America Turns to Data to Feed the Hungry."* CIO, July 18, 2022. https://www.cio.com/article/403152/feeding-america-turns-to-data-to-feed-the-hungry.html.
44. St. Jude Children's Research Hospital. *"Unique Operating Model."* Accessed July 15, 2025. https://www.stjude.org/about-st-jude/unique-operating-model.html.
45. Crisis Text Line. *"Crisis Trends."* Accessed July 15, 2025. https://www .crisistextline.org/crisistrends/.

Chapter 3

1. Ford, H. and Crowther, S. (1922). *My Life and Work*. Garden City, NY: Doubleday, Page & Company.
2. Low, G.S. and Fullerton, R.A. (1994). Brands, brand management, and the brand manager system: a critical-historical evaluation. *Journal of Marketing Research* 31 (2): 173–190.
3. U.S. Bank. (2024, October 11). *How does consumer spending impact the health of the economy?* U.S. Bank. https://www.usbank.com/investing/ financial-perspectives/market-news/consumer-spending.html#:~:text= Consumer%20spending%20is%20by%20far,economy%20is%20grow ing%20or%20shrinking.
4. Samuelson, P.A. (1970). *Economics*, 8e. McGraw-Hill.
5. Ford, H. and Crowther, S. (1922). *My Life and Work*. Garden City, NY: Doubleday, Page & Company.
6. Mica, R. (2010). *And the ugliest car in the world award goes to Paris Hilton's pink Bentley*, August 20, TFLCar, https://tflcar.com/2010/08/ and-the-ugliest-car-in-the-world-award-goes-to-paris-hiltons-pink-bentley/.
7. Hofstede, G. (2001). *Culture's Consequences: Comparing Values, Behaviors, Institutions, and Organizations Across Nations*. Thousand Oaks, CA: Sage Publications.
8. Drucker, P.F. (1973). *Management: Tasks, Responsibilities, Practices*. Harper & Row.
9. Dooley, R. (2020). "H-E-B: The Smartest Supermarket You've Just Heard Of," Forbes, January 10. https://www.forbes.com/sites/rogerdooley/2020/ 01/10/heb-smartest/. Gonzales, G. (2023). "The Culture of H-E-B: Why Employees (and Customers) Are So Devoted." https://www.fromday one.co/stories/2023/7/19/the-culture-of-heb-why-employees-and-cus tomers-are-so-devoted?utm.

10. McCorvey, J.J. (2024, March 10). *'Buy now, pay later' goes from niche to normal as young people use it for daily essentials.* NBC News. https://www.nbcnews.com/business/personal-finance/buy-now-pay-later-daily-essentials-groceries-young-adults-rcna141718.

11. *How Spotify Delivers a Unique Customer Experience (CX) with Personalized Music Recommendations,* Renascence, September 4, 2024, https://www.renascence.io/journal/how-spotify-delivers-a-unique-customer-experience-cx-with-personalized-music-recommendations.

12. Boehm, C. (1999). *Hierarchy in the Forest: The Evolution of Egalitarian Behavior.* Harvard University Press. Sapolsky, R.M. (2017). *Behave: The Biology of Humans at Our Best and Worst.* Penguin Press. Wilson, E.O. (1975). *Sociobiology: The New Synthesis.* Harvard University Press.

13. Ohanian, S. (1990). Construction and validation of a scale to measure celebrity endorser's perceived expertise, trustworthiness, and attractiveness. *Journal of Advertising* 19 (3): 39–52.

14. Kuzminov, M. *How Influencers Can Drive Consumer Purchasing Behavior,* Forbes, August 24, 2024, https://www.forbes.com/councils/forbesagency council/2024/08/14/how-influencers-can-drive-consumer-purchasing-behavior/.

15. Townsend, A. *Influencer Spotlight: Danielle Bernstein | We Wore What,* Medium, June 13, 2020, https://medium.com/@ash8320/influencer-spot light-danielle-bernstein-we-wore-what-e6584ca1eb83.

16. TikTok for Business, *Success Stories: Chipotle,* accessed May 14, 2025, https://ads.tiktok.com/business/en-US/inspiration/chipotle-80.

17. Allport, G.W. (1954). *The Nature of Prejudice.* Addison-Wesley.

18. Hill, L.W. *Why Customers Waited 8 Hours for In-N-Out Burger, The Takeout,* December 21, 2023, https://www.thetakeout.com/in-n-out-burger-1st-idaho-location-8-hr-drive-thru-line-1851116523/.

19. Swanson, S. *12 Top Brands on TikTok Who Are Killing It (+ What You Can Learn from Them),* WebFX, 2023, https://www.webfx.com/blog/social-media/top-brands-on-tiktok/.

20. Wisner, R. (2023). "Cat's New VisionLink Consolidates Fleet Management – Regardless of Brand," Equipment World. https://www.equipmentworld.com/technology/article/15448149/caterpillar-helps-customers-manage-fleets-with-visionlink-App.

21. Azzi, M. "*Philosophy.*" Accessed July 15, 2025. https://michelle-azzi-3gkk.squarespace.com/philosophy.

22. Klee, M. (2023). Conservatives Heartbroken that Kid Rock Gave Up Bud Light Boycott," *Rolling Stone,* December 15. https://www.

rollingstone.com/culture/culture-news/kid-rock-bud-light-conserva tives-heartbroken-1234930200/.

23. Dudkin, I. (2024). "Predictive Analytics in Salesforce: Enhancing Decision-Making with AI," Data Groomr, October 31. https://datag roomr.com/predictive-analytics-in-salesforce/.

24. Sinclair, U. (1906). *The Jungle.* Project Gutenberg.

25. Reuters, *EU Privacy Regulator Fines LinkedIn 310 million Euros,* October 25, 2024, https://www.reuters.com/technology/eu-privacy-regulator-fines-linkedin-310-mln-euro-2024-10-24/.

26. Google Cloud. (n.d.). *What is big data?* Google. https://cloud.google.com/learn/what-is-big-data.

27. https://www.fashionnetwork.com/news/Inditex-to-establish-a-logistics-center-in-zaragoza-generating-1500-job-opportunities,1614469.html.

28. BBC News. (2011, August 18). *Mexico's drug war: 55,000 killed in five years.* https://www.bbc.com/news/world-latin-america-14570564; Galeana, E. (2024, April 16). *H&M, Zara face scrutiny amid supply chain allegations.* Mexico Business News. https://mexicobusiness.news/ecom merce/news/hm-zara-face-scrutiny-amid-supply-chain-allegations.

29. *Firms That Withdrew from Russia Following Ukraine Invasion Earn Higher Consumer Sentiment, University of Notre Dame,* September 23, 2024, https://news.nd.edu/news/firms-that-withdrew-from-russia-following-ukraine-invasion-earn-higher-consumer-sentiment/.

30. Ihle, J. *Swoop Founder Won't Take Fintech Success for Granted, The Sunday Times,* February 9, 2025, https://www.thetimes.com/world/ireland-world/article/swoop-founder-wont-take-fintech-success-for-granted-zc576cjlj.

31. Eun-jin, K. *Samsung's SmartThings Platform Hits 20 million Users in South Korea, Business Korea,* December 30, 2024, https://www.busi nesskorea.co.kr/news/articleView.html?idxno=232785.

32. Schwaar, C. (2022, September 30). *Is 3D printing the sustainable manufac- turing solution?* Forbes. https://www.forbes.com/sites/carolynschwaar/2022/09/30/is-3d-printing-the-sustainable-manufacturing-solution/.

33. Palvel, S. *How Airbnb Uses AI for Dynamic Pricing: A Deep Dive into Smart Revenue Optimization, Medium,* December 6, 2024, https://subash palvel.medium.com/how-airbnb-uses-ai-for-dynamic-pricing-a-deep-dive-into-smart-revenue-optimization-66b17c532080.

Chapter 4

1. Thompson, T.W., Berry, L.L., and Davidson, P.H. (1978). *Banking Tomorrow: Managing Markets Through Planning.* New York, NY: Van Nostrand Reinhold Company.

2. Drucker, P.F. (1954). *The Practice of Management*. New York: Harper Business.

3. From Merck's corporate website. Merck, *Culture and Values*, accessed May 14, 2025, https://www.merck.com/company-overview/culture-and-values/.

4. From the USAA corporate website. USAA, *About USAA*, accessed May 14, 2025, https://www.usaa.com/about/.

5. From Intel's corporate website. Intel, *Our Values*, accessed May 14, 2025, https://www.intel.com/content/www/us/en/corporate-responsibility/our-values.html.

6. Palmatier, R.W., Moorman, C., and Lee, J.-Y. (2019). *Handbook on Customer Centricity: Strategies for Building a Customer Centric Organization*. Northampton, MA: Edward Elger Publishing.

7. Ascarza, E., Fader, P.S., and Hardie, B.G.S. (2017). Marketing models for the customer-centric firm. In: *Handbook of Marketing Decision Models*, 297–329. Cham: Springer. Lee, J.-Y., Sridhar, S., Henderson, C.M., and Palmatier, R.W. (2015). Effect of customer-centric structure on long-term financial performance. *Marketing Science* 34 (2): 250–268.

8. Fader, P. (2011). *Customer Centricity: Focus on the Right Customers for Strategic Advantage*. University of Pennsylvania Press.

9. Palmatier, R.W., Moorman, C., and Lee, J.-Y. (2019). *Handbook on Customer Centricity: Strategies for Building a Customer Centric Organization*. Northampton, MA: Edward Elger Publishing.

10. Drucker, P.F. (1954). *The Practice of Management*. New York: Harper Business.

11. Another word on vocabulary. This three phase intelligence process was identified in an article by Kohli, A. and Jaworski, B. (1990). Market orientation: the construct, research propositions, and managerial implications. *Journal of Marketing* 54 (April): 1–18. In related work, other authors have identified customer orientation and competitor orientation as part of the market oriented concept. Thus, one could have chosen the term "customer orientation" to refer to this three-phase process. To keep things simple, we have chosen to use the term "phases of customer centricity" rather than customer orientation.

12. MacInnis, D., Hoyer, W., and Pieters, R. (2023). *Consumer Behavior*, 8e. Cengage Learning.

13. Fahey, L. (2020). *The Insight Discipline: Crafting New Marketplace Understanding That Makes a Difference*. Emerald Publishing.

14. See Kim, W.C. and Mauborgne, R. (2005). *Blue Ocean Strategy: How to Create Uncontested Market Space and Make the Competition Irrelevant.* Harvard Business School Press.

15. Charity: Water. "Our Work." Accessed July 15, 2025. https://www.charitywater.org/our-work.

16. Drucker, P.F. (1964). *Managing for Results.* New York: Harper & Row.

Chapter 5

1. Lafley, A.G. and Martin, R.L. (2013). *Playing to Win: How Strategy Really Works.* Harvard Business Review Press.

2. Porter, M.E. (1996). What Is Strategy? *Harvard Business Review* 74 (6) November–December: 61–78.

3. It is often the case that we begin our conversations with clients with their company's purpose, mission, vision, and associated goals and aspirations. This enables us to move away from the typical starting point of strategy focused on existing products, markets, and technology. Our aim here is to open the lens to a very broad outside-in view.

4. Kotler, P. and Keller, K.L. (2021). *Marketing Management*, 16e. Pearson.

5. See, for example, Dib, S. (2010). "New millennium, new segments: moving to a segment of one," *Journal of Strategic Marketing* 9 (3): 193–213. https://doi.org/10.1080/713775742.

6. Grace Snelling, "These Ikea Essential Boxes Make Moving into Your College Dorm Instant-Ramen-Level Easy," *Fast Company*, May 29, 2024. https://www.fastcompany.com/91132085/ikea-college-essentials-boxes.

7. See Fader, P.S. (2012). *Customer Centricity: Focus on the Right Customers for Strategic Advantage.* Wharton Digital Press.

8. See Christensen, C.M. (1997). *The Innovator's Dilemma: When New Technologies Cause Great Firms to Fail.* Harvard Business School Press.

9. See, for example, Day, G.S., Shocker, A.D., and Srivastava, R.K. (1979). Customer-oriented approaches to identifying product-markets. *Journal of Marketing* 43 (4): 8–19. https://doi.org/10.2307/1250252.

10. Porter, M. (1996). *What is Strategy.* Harvard Business Review.

11. Porter, M.E. (1996). What is strategy? *Harvard Business Review* 74 (6): 61–78.

12. Our critique of the resource-based view of the organization is that this "line of sight" of linking capabilities to customer needs is rarely done. For example, in a review of 125 empirical studies in RBV where apparently only one measured anything related to the customer. Indeed, in the Armstrong, C. and Shimizu, K. (2007). A Review of Approaches to

Empirical Research on the Resource-Based View of the Firm. *Journal of Management* 33 (6): 959–986, the customer is only mentioned three times.

13. Wittwer, J., *"World Central Kitchen: How Chef José Andrés Uses Culture to Address Rapid Food Response,"* Success Across Cultures, July 8, 2022. https://successacrosscultures.com/2022/07/08/world-central-kitchen-how-chef-jose-andres-uses-culture-to-address-rapid-food-response/.

14. Ira Kalb, *How to Compete Against the Big Guys*, CBS News, accessed May 14, 2025, https://www.cbsnews.com/news/how-to-compete-against-the-big-guys/#.

15. Jeannet, J.-P., Collins, R. S., and Schüpbach, L. M. (2003). *Real Madrid Club de Fútbol* (Case No. IMD-3-1321). International Institute for Management Development.

16. Abbas Haleem, *Costco Ecommerce Sales Growth in Q2 Reaches Three-Year High*, Digital Commerce 360, March 7, 2025, https://www.digitalcommerce360.com/article/costco-ecommerce-sales/.

17. Habitat for Humanity. *"What Is Sweat Equity?"* Accessed July 15, 2025. https://www.habitat.org/stories/what-is-sweat-equity.

18. Slywotsky, A. (1999). *Profit Patterns: 30 Ways to Anticipate and Profit from Strategic Changes Reshaping Your Business.* New York: Random House.

19. Christensen, C.M. (1997). *The Innovator's Dilemma: When New Technologies Cause Great Firms to Fail.* Harvard Business School Press.

20. Nina Sheridan, *"Nespresso Marketing Strategy 2025: A Case Study,"* Latterly. Accessed July 15, 2025. https://www.latterly.org/nespresso-marketing-strategy/.

21. Jaworski, B.J. (2021). Netflix: reinvention across multiple time periods. *Academy of Marketing Science Review* 11: 180–193. https://doi.org/10.1007/s13162-021-00195.

Chapter 6

1. Kennedy, J.F. (1962). *Special Message to the Congress on Protecting the Consumer Interest.* The American Presidency Project. https://www.presidency.ucsb.edu/node/237009.

2. U.S. Environmental Protection Agency, *National Overview: Facts and Figures on Materials, Waste and Recycling,* last modified November 8, 2024, https://www.epa.gov/facts-and-figures-about-materials-waste-and-recycling/national-overview-facts-and-figures-materials.

3. James, W. (1890). *The Principles of Psychology.*

4. Lockley, L.C. (1950). Notes on the history of marketing research. *Journal of Marketing* 14 (5 April): 733–736.

5. Gordon, R.A. and Howell, J.E. (1959). *Higher Education for Business.* New York: Ford Foundation. Pierson, F.C. (1959). *The Education of American Businessmen: A Study of University-College Programs in Business Administration.* New York: McGraw-Hill.

6. Malter, M.S., Holbrook, M.B., Kahn, B.E. et al. (2020). The past, present, and future of consumer research. *Marketing Letters* 31 (2/3) (September): 137–149.

7. *Journal of Consumer Research, Policy Board,* n.d., https://consumerresearcher.com/policy-board.

8. Future Market Insights (2025), "Rising Health Consciousness Fuels Non-Alcoholic Beer Industry Growth: Projected to Reach USD 43,926.9 million by 2034", January 10, 2025 08:00 ET, Future Market Insights Global and Consulting Pvt. Ltd. https://www.globenewswire.com/news-release/2025/01/10/3007653/0/en/Rising-Health-Consciousness-Fuels-Non-Alcoholic-Beer-Industry-Growth-Projected-to-Reach-USD-43-926-9-Million-by-2034-Future-Market-Insights-Inc.html.

9. Malter, M.S., Holbrook, M.B., Kahn, B.E. et al. (2020). The Past, Present, and Future of Consumer Research. *Marketing Letters* 31 (2/3) (September): 137–149.

10. Google, *How News Works,* n.d., https://www.google.com/intl/en_us/search/howsearchworks/how-news-works/.

11. *Google AI Tools for News, Google AI Tools,* n.d., https://newsinitiative.withgoogle.com/resources/trainings/google-ai-tools/.

12. Edell, J.A. and Burke, M.C. (1987). The power of feelings in understanding advertising effects. *Journal of Consumer Research* 14 (3): 421, 433. Poels, K. and Dewitte, S. (2006). How to capture the heart? Reviewing 20 years of emotion measurement in advertising. *Journal of Advertising Research* 46 (1): 18–37.

13. LeClair, C. *How Brands Are Breaking into Animal Crossing to Launch Products and Create In-Game Experiences, Business Insider,* October 12, 2020, https://www.businessinsider.com/brands-are-hiring-pro-animal-crossing-players-advertise-in-game-2020-9.

14. Noble, E., Wodehouse, A., and Robertson, D.J. (2023). Face pareidolia in products: the effect of emotional content on attentional capture, eagerness to explore, and likelihood to purchase. *Applied Cognitive Psychology* 37 (5): 1071–1084.

15. Krishna, A. and Schwarz, N. (2014). Sensory Marketing, Embodiment, and Grounded Cognition: A Review and Introduction. *Journal of Consumer Psychology* 24 (2): 159–168.

16. Spangenberg, E.R., Sprott, D.E., Grohmann, B., and Tracy, D. (2006). Gender-congruent ambient scent influences on approach and avoidance behaviors in a retail store. *Journal of Business Research* 9 (November): 1281–1287.

17. Society for Neuroscience, *Oxytocin Increases Advertising's Influence: Hormone Heightened Sensitivity to Public Service Announcements*, ScienceDaily, November 16, 2010, https://www.sciencedaily.com/releases/2010/11/101115160404.htm.

18. Clatworthy, B. *Ferrari Considers Ban on Zany Customisation from Ultra-Rich Buyers*, The Times, February 5, 2025, https://www.thetimes.com/uk/transport/article/ferrari-considers-ban-on-zany-customisation-from-ultra-rich-buyers-m26rs80dt?region=global.

19. Park, C.W., Jaworski, B.J., and MacInnis, D.J. (1986). Strategic brand concept-image management. *Journal of Marketing* 50 (4): 135–145.

20. Allport, F.H. (1954). The structuring of events: outline of a general theory with applications to psychology. *Psychological Review* 61 (5): 281.

21. Kassin, S., Fein, S., and Markus, H.R. (2020). *Social Psychology*, 11e. Boston: Cengage Learning.

22. Festinger, L. (1957). *A Theory of Cognitive Dissonance*. Stanford, CA: Stanford University Press.

23. Mishra, H., Shiv, B., and Nayakankuppam, D. (2008). The blissful ignorance effect: pre- versus post-action effects on outcome expectancies arising from precise and vague information. *Journal of Consumer Research* 35 (4): 573–585.

24. *Shorty Awards, Ariana Madix x Duracell: I Buy My Own Batteries*, n.d., https://shortyawards.com/16th/ariana-madx-x-duracell-i-buy-my-own-batteries.

25. Brady, J. *Home Generator Sales Are Booming with Mass Outages, Climate Change and COVID*, NPR, January 31, 2022, https://www.npr.org/2022/01/31/1076375363/home-generator-sales-boom-power-outages-climate-change.

26. https://www.reddit.com/r/preppers/comments/vjs3j5/whole_home_generator_worth_it/u/PreppersAnonymous, *Whole Home Generator Worth It?, Reddit*, June 24, 2022, https://www.reddit.com/r/preppers/comments/vjs3j5/whole_home_generator_worth_it/.

27. Cialdini, R.B., Reno, R.R., and Kallgren, C.A. (1990). A focus theory of normative conduct: recycling the concept of norms to reduce littering in public places. *Journal of Personality and Social Psychology* 58 (6): 1015–1026.

28. Danziger, P.N. *Costco Is Caught in the Crosshairs of the DEI Controversy*, *Forbes*, January 1, 2025, https://www.forbes.com/sites/pamdanziger/2025/01/01/costco-is-caught-in-the-crosshairs-of-the-dei-controversy/.

29. Meyersohn, N. (2025). A 40-Day Target Boycott Starts Today. It Couldn't Come at a Worse Time for the Company. *CNN.* https://www.cnn.com/2025/03/05/business/target-boycott-jamal-bryant.

30. Dye, T.R. (2016). *Understanding Public Policy*, 15e. Boston: Pearson.

31. Moorman, C., Ferraro, R., and Huber, J. (2012). Unintended nutrition consequences: firm responses to the nutrition labeling and education act. *Marketing Science* 31 (5): 717–737.

32. Rogers, K. *FDA Bans Red Dye No. 3 from Food, Drinks and Ingested Drugs in the US*, CNN, January 15, 2025, https://www.cnn.com/2025/01/15/health/red-dye-no-3-ban-fda-wellness/index.html.

33. O'Henry (1906). *The gift of the magi.* In: *The Four Million.* New York: Doubleday, Page & Company.

34. Drucker, P.F. (1954). *The Practice of Management*, 37. New York: Harper & Row.

35. Reichheld, F.F. and Earl Sasser, W. (1990). Zero defections: quality comes to services. *Harvard Business Review* 68 (5): 105–111.

36. Renascence, *How The Ritz-Carlton Enhances Customer Experience (CX) through Personalized Service and Luxury*, September 4, 2024, https://www.renascence.io/journal/how-the-ritz-carlton-enhances-customer-experience-cx-through-personalized-service-and-luxury.

37. Arnold, T.J., Fang, E.E., and Palmatier, R.W. (2010). The effects of customer acquisition and retention orientations on a firm's radical and incremental innovation performance. *Journal of the Academy of Marketing Science* 38 (2): 193–210.

38. Horymski, C. (2024, July 24). *State of retail cards and buy now, pay later in 2024.* Experian. https://www.experian.com/blogs/ask-experian/retail-credit-card-study/.

39. Selyukh, A. (2024, April 3). *No more 'Just Walk Out' at Amazon grocery stores. The new bet is smart shopping carts.* NPR. https://www.npr.org/2024/04/03/1242508931/no-more-just-walk-out-at-Amazon-grocery-stores-the-new-bet-is-smart-shopping-car.

40. Knowledge at Wharton. (2018, January 25). *Brand Crisis Management: Responding to the Tide Pod Challenge* [Audio podcast episode]. In *Knowledge at Wharton*. Wharton School, University of Pennsylvania. https://knowledge.wharton.upenn.edu/podcast/knowledge-at-wharton-podcast/fallout-tide-pod-challenge/.

41. Mackintosh, J. (2024, April 25). *How Taylor Swift fans broke economics*. *The Wall Street Journal*. https://www.wsj.com/finance/taylor-swift-tickets-fans-economics-e04f0395.

42. O'Brien, D. (2024, November 25). *Fading to black: The last of the television repairmen*. Business Journal Daily. https://businessjournaldaily.com/fading-to-black-the-last-of-the-television-repairmen/.

43. Edmonds, A. (n.d.). *Recrafting*. AllenEdmonds.com. https://www.allenedmonds.com/recrafting/?utm.

44. Pulvirent, S. (2021). *Rewind: How Patek Philippe Changed Watch Advertising Forever by Appealing to Moms & Dads*. Hodinkee. https://www.hodinkee.com/articles/patek-philippe-generations-ad-campaign-fathers-day.

45. Renascence. (2024, September 7). *How Rolls-Royce delivers exceptional customer experience (CX) with bespoke luxury services*. https://www.renascence.io/journal/how-rolls-royce-delivers-exceptional-customer-experience-cx-with-bespoke-luxury-services.

46. Hardcastle, K. (2022). *Generation Z are the Driving Force of the Recommerce Marketplace*. Forbes. https://www.forbes.com/sites/katehardcastle/2022/04/25/generation-z-are-the-driving-force-of-the-recommerce-marketplace/.

47. Sturrock, T. (2019, July 27). *In Philippine slums, meat scavenged from dumpsters feeds those short of meals and hope*. South China Morning Post. https://www.scmp.com/week-asia/society/article/3020306/philippine-slums-meat-scavenged-dumpsters-feeds-those-short-meals.

48. Tari, A. and Trudel, R. (2023). *Good for the environment and good for business: How circular take-back programs enhance consumer valuation*. American Marketing Association. https://www.ama.org/2023/10/31/good-for-the-environment-and-good-for-business-how-circular-take-back-programs-enhance-consumer-valuation/.

49. Amperage Marketing. (2016, April). *What can Disney teach us about journey mapping?* https://www.amperagemarketing.com/2016/04/what-can-disney-teach-us-about-journey-mapping/.

50. Hendrickson, J. (2025, February 9). *What is Hims actually selling?* The Atlantic. https://www.theatlantic.com/ideas/archive/2025/02/hims-super-bowl-ad/681626/.

51. Jenkins, S. (2021, February 2). *Customer journey mapping and its essential place for today's modern marketer*. Forbes. https://www.forbes.com/councils/forbesagencycouncil/2021/02/02/customer-journey-mapping-and-its-essential-place-for-todays-modern-marketer/.

52. Renascence. (2024, September 4). *How Disney creates magical customer experience (CX) through immersive storytelling.* https://www.renascence.io/journal/how-disney-creates-magical-customer-experience-cx-through-immersive-storytelling.

53. Hollander, J. (2022, October 28). *Disney's MagicBand: Breaking down one of hospitality's greatest innovations.* Hotel Tech Report. https://hoteltechreport.com/news/disneys-magicband.

Chapter 7

1. Drucker, P.F. (1973). *Management: Tasks, Responsibilities, Practices,* 621. New York: Harper & Row.

2. See Jaworski, B. and Cheung, V. (2023). *Creating the Organization of the Future: Building on Drucker and Confucius Foundations.* Emerald Publishing Limited.

3. Relihan, T. *How Costco's Obsession with Culture Drove Success, MIT Sloan Management Review,* May 11, 2018, https://mitsloan.mit.edu/ideas-made-to-matter/how-costcos-obsession-culture-drove-success.

4. Cisco, *What Makes Cisco's Culture Unique?,* accessed May 14, 2025, https://www.cisco.com/c/en/us/about/careers/we-are-cisco.conscious-culture.html.

5. *How Cisco Helps Its Employees Make an Impact Beyond Company Walls, Fortune Brand Studio,* accessed May 14, 2025, https://brand-studio.fortune.com/cisco/how-cisco-helps-its-employees-make-an-impact-beyond-company-walls/?prx_t=AXUHAAAAAATB8RA.

6. Ibarra, H. and Rattan, A. (2018). Microsoft: instilling a growth mindset. *London Business School Review* 29 (3): 50–53.

7. Catholic Relief Services, *Guiding Principles: Subsidiarity,* accessed July 15, 2025, https://www.crs.org/about-us/guiding-principles#section-subsidiarity.

8. Jaworski, B.J., Kohli, A.K., and Sahay, A. (2000). Market-driven versus driving markets. *Journal of the Academy of Marketing Science* 28 (1): 45–54. https://doi.org/10.1177/0092070300281005.

9. Roi, R. and Piskorski, M. *Developing Ambidextrous Leaders: A Solution to Strategic Talent Deficit, IMD – I by IMD,* December 17, 2021, https://www.imd.org/ibyimd/human-resources/developing-ambidextrous-leaders-a-solution-to-strategic-talent-deficit/.

10. Underhill, P. (2000). *Why We Buy: The Science of Shopping.* Touchstone.

11. Christensen, C.M. (1997). *The Innovator's Dilemma: When New Technologies Cause Great Firms to Fail*. Harvard Business School Press.

12. Peterson, C. and Seligman, M.E.P. (2004). *Character Strengths and Virtues: A Handbook and Classification*, 29. New York: Oxford University Press; Washington, DC: American Psychological Association.

13. Peterson, C. and Seligman, M.E. (2004). *Character Strengths and Virtues: A Handbook and Classification*, vol. 1, 127. Oxford University Press.

14. Loewenstein, G., Litman, J.A., and Silvia, P.J. (2018). Epistemic curiosity and enjoyment of problem-solving. In: *Advances in Motivation Science*, vol. 5, 47–88.

15. Immelt, J. (2010, May 24). *Driving Change can be Unpopular ("View from the Top" speech, Stanford Graduate School of Business)*. Stanford University.

16. Piskorski, M. and Roi, R., *The Five Dimensions of Ambidextrous Leadership, IMD – I by IMD*, January 27, 2022, https://www.imd.org/ibyimd/brain-circuits/the-five-dimensions-of-ambidextrous-leadership/.

Chapter 8

1. Chandler, A.D. (1962). *Strategy and Structure*. Cambridge: MIT Press.

2. This citation is a classic overview of various designs.Clegg's, S.A. (1990). *Modern Organizations*. Sage traces the evolution from traditional to contemporary organization designs.

3. Customer-Centric Org Charts Aren't Right for Every Company by Lee, J.-Y., Sridhar, S., and Palmatier, R.W. July-August 2015, *Harvard Business Review*.

4. For the reader who is interested in more details. Please refer to the following sources: Burton, R.M., Obel, B., and Håkonsson, D.D. (2020). *Organizational Design: A Step-by-Step Approach*, 4e. Cambridge University Press. Goold, M. and Campbell, A. (2002). *Designing Effective Organizations: How to Create Structured Networks*. John Wiley & Sons. Galbraith, J.R. (2002). *Designing Organizations: An Executive Briefing on Strategy, Structure, and Process*. Jossey-Bass. McDowell, T. (2023). *Strategies for Organization Design: Using the Peopletecture Model to Improve Collaboration and Performance*. Wiley.

5. Drucker, P.F. (1954). *The Practice of Management*, 119. Harper Business.

6. McKinsey & Company, *Organization Design*, accessed May 14, 2025, https://www.mckinsey.com/capabilities/people-and-organizational-performance/how-we-help-clients/organization-design.

7. *tED Magazine*, "Siemens Announces New Company Structure," accessed May 14, 2025, https://tedmag.com/siemens-announces-new-company-structure/.

8. Nike, Inc., *Company Overview*, accessed May 14, 2025, https://about.nike.com/en/company

9. "The Matrix Master: Philips Redraws the Lines," *The Economist*, January 21, 2006, https://www.economist.com/special-report/2006/01/21/the-matrix-master.

10. The Coca-Cola Company, *About*, accessed May 14, 2025, https://investors.coca-colacompany.com/about.

11. This set of data on P&G comes directly from their website. Source Procter & Gamble, *Corporate Structure*, accessed May 14, 2025, https://us.pg.com/structure-and-governance/corporate-structure/.

12. See Jaworski, B. and Lurie, R. (2018). *The Organic Growth Playbook.* Emerald Publishing.

13. Taylor, F.W. (1911). *The Principles of Scientific Management.* Harper & Brothers.

14. BRAC (2020). *Social Business Initiative 2020: Annual Report.* Dhaka: BRAC. https://www.brac.net/downloads/ar2020/SBI2020.pdf.

Chapter 9

1. Fiorina, C. "Information: The Currency of the Digital Age," speech, Oracle OpenWorld, San Francisco, December 6, 2004, HP, https://www.hp.com/hpinfo/execteam/speeches/fiorina/04openworld.html.

2. Drucker, P.F. (2001). *The Essential Drucker: The Best of Sixty Years of Peter Drucker's Essential Writings on Management.* New York: Harper Business.

3. Moore, K. and Reid, S. (2008). The birth of brand: 4000 years of branding. *Business History* 50 (4): 419–432.

4. Hollander, S.C., Rassuli, K.M., Brian Jones, D.G., and Dix, L.F. (2005). Periodization in marketing history. *Journal of Macromarketing* 25 (1): 32–41.

5. Greif, A. (2006). *Institutions and the Path to the Modern Economy: Lessons from Medieval Trade.* Cambridge: Cambridge University Press.

6. Fullerton, R.A. (1988). How modern is modern marketing? Marketing's evolution and the myth of the 'production era'. *Journal of Marketing* 52 (1): 108–125.

7. Snowflake, *Gaming Analytics: Leveling Up with Data-Driven Insights*, accessed May 14, 2025, https://www.snowflake.com/trending/gaming-analytics-leveling-data-driven-insights/.

8. Bousquette, I. "How Tech Helped Levi's Ride the 'Baggy Jeans' Trend," *Wall Street Journal*, January 27, 2025, https://www.wsj.com/articles/how-tech-helped-levis-ride-the-baggy-jeans-trend-f290721d.

9. There are many articles and books providing insights into marketing research and related methods. We based our section here on Malhotra, N.K. (2019). *Marketing Research: An Applied Orientation*, 7e. Upper Saddle River, NJ: Pearson Education.

10. Malhotra, N.K. (2019). *Marketing Research: An Applied Orientation*, 7e. Upper Saddle River, NJ: Pearson Education.

11. Worley, C.G. and Lawler, E.E. (2009). Building a change capability at Capital One Financial. *Organizational Dynamics* 38 (4): 245–251. https://ceo.usc.edu/wp-content/uploads/2018/03/12_Building_a_Chg_Capability.pdf.

12. Drenik, G. (2024, June 13). *Next-gen tech turns customer experience into a competitive advantage*. Forbes. https://www.forbes.com/sites/garydrenik/2024/06/13/next-gen-tech-turns-customer-experience-into-a-competitive-advantage/.

13. Jaekel, B. "Sephora's Virtual Artist Brings Augmented Reality to Larger Beauty Audience," *Mobile Commerce Daily*, January 25, 2016, https://www.retaildive.com/ex/mobilecommercedaily/sephoras-virtual-artist-brings-augmented-reality-to-larger-beauty-audience.

14. Google Cloud, "Domino's: Increasing Monthly Revenue by 6% with Google Analytics Premium, Google Tag Manager, and Google BigQuery," accessed May 14, 2025, https://cloud.google.com/customers/dominos.

15. Mathews, A. "How Nike Is Using AI to Transform Product Design, Customer Experience, and Operational Efficiency," *AIM Research*, July 3, 2024, https://aimresearch.co/market-industry/how-nike-is-using-ai-to-transform-product-design-customer-experience-and-operational-efficiencyhttps://aimresearch.co/market-industry/how-nike-is-using-ai-to-transform-product-design-customer-experience-and-operational-efficiency.

16. Reuters, "23andMe's Journey from DNA Testing Pioneer to Bankruptcy," *Reuters*, March 24, 2025, https://www.reuters.com/business/healthcare-pharmaceuticals/23andmes-journey-dna-testing-pioneer-bankruptcy-2025-03-24/.

17. Hawkins, A.J. "GM Banned from Selling Your Driving Data for Five Years," *The Verge*, January 16, 2025, https://www.theverge.com/2025/1/16/24345470/gm-banned-selling-driving-data-insurance-ftc.

18. Malhotra, N.K. (2019). *Marketing Research: An Applied Orientation*, 7e. Upper Saddle River, NJ: Pearson Education.

19. Drucker, P.F. "The Next Information Revolution," *Forbes ASAP*, October 5, 1998.

20. Jaworski, B. (2024). 2024 Drucker Institute Practice of Management Award to Parker Aerospace.

21. Parker Aerospace, *Moving Ahead*, accessed May 14, 2025, https://www.parker.com/content/dam/Parker-com/Literature/Aerospace-Group/Aerospace-Static-Files/Moving.Ahead.pdf.

22. Government Technology Agency. "Your Sentiments Matter in the Design of Government Digital Services." GovTech Singapore. Accessed July 15, 2025. https://www.tech.gov.sg/technews/your-sentiments-matter-in-the-design-of-government-digital-services.

23. Government Technology Agency. "FormSG." Products and Services. GovTech Singapore. Accessed July 15, 2025. https://www.tech.gov.sg/products-and-services/for-government-agencies/productivity-and-marketing/formsg.

24. Nemeth, C.J. (1987). Dissent, group process, and creativity. *Advances in Group Processes* 4: 57–75.

25. Deci, E.L. and Ryan, R.M. (1985). *Intrinsic Motivation and Self-Determination in Human Behavior*. New York: Plenum.

26. Federal Aviation Administration. "Pilot's Handbook of Aeronautical Knowledge," FAA-H-8083-25B. Washington, DC: U.S. Department of Transportation, 2016.

27. Schein, E.H. (2010). *Organizational Culture and Leadership*, 4e. San Francisco: Jossey-Bass.

28. SSI Staff, "Panda Express Adds Business Intelligence to Security Menu," *Security Sales & Integration*, July 17, 2018, https://www.securitysales.com/news/panda-express-3xlogics-bi-software/79033/.

29. Nisen, M. "The CEO of Caterpillar Once Gave a Brutally Honest Answer About What He Looks for in Workers," *Business Insider*, May 3, 2013, https://www.businessinsider.com/caterpillar-ceo-quote-on-workers-2013-5.

30. Neammanee, P. "Workers Blame Workplace Conditions after a Father Fell into a Vat of Molten Iron and Died," *Business Insider*, November 3, 2022, https://www.businessinsider.com/workers-blame-workplace-conditions-after-a-father-fell-molten-iron-2022-11.

31. Schein, E.H. (2010). *Organizational Culture and Leadership*, 4e. San Francisco: Jossey-Bass.

32. Kahneman, D. and Tversky, A. (1979). Prospect theory: an analysis of decision under risk. *Econometrica* 47 (2): 263–291. https://doi.org/10.2307/1914185.

33. Segal, E. "How 4 Well-Known Companies Recovered from Their Crisis Situations," *Forbes*, December 26, 2024, https://www.forbes.com/sites/edwardsegal/2024/12/26/how-4-well-known-companies-recovered-from-their-crisis-situations/.

34. Drucker, P.F. (1999). Knowledge-worker productivity: the biggest challenge. *California Management Review* 41 (2): 79.

35. Walters, W.H. and Wilder, E.I. (2023). Fabrication and errors in the bibliographic citations generated by ChatGPT. *Scientific Reports* 13: 14045. https://doi.org/10.1038/s41598-023-41032-5.

36. Denning, S. "Peter Drucker's Virtuous Firm vs. the World's Dumbest Idea," *Forbes*, May 30, 2018, https://www.forbes.com/sites/stevedenning/2018/05/30/peter-druckers-virtuous-firm-vs-the-worlds-dumbest-idea/.

37. Vosoughi, S., Roy, D., and Aral, S. (2018). The Spread of True and False News Online. *Science* 359 (6380): 1146–1151. https://www.science.org/doi/10.1126/science.aap9559.

38. Chui, M. and Malhotra, S. 2023. "Tackling the Risks of Generative AI." Harvard Business Review, August 22, 2023. https://hbr.org/2023/08/tackling-the-risks-of-generative-ai.

Chapter 10

1. Drucker, P.F. (1993). *Post-Capitalist Society*, 57. HarperBusiness.

2. Drucker, P. (1985). *Innovation and Entrepreneurship*, vii. Harper Business.

3. Drucker, P. (1985). *Innovation and Entrepreneurship*, 35. Harper Business.

4. Heater, B. "Goodbye, Google Glass, We Knew You Well," *TechCrunch*, March 16, 2023, https://techcrunch.com/2023/03/16/goodbye-google-glass-we-knew-you-well/.

5. Hollister, S. "Ready or Not, the Glassholes Are Coming Back: Is the World Finally Prepared for Hands-Free Cameras?" *The Verge*, July 25, 2022, https://www.theverge.com/2022/7/25/23054367/google-ar-glasses-glassholes-coming-back.

6. Montecinos-Deppe, M. "Year of Glass: Google Glass," *Cooper Hewitt, Smithsonian Design Museum*, August 31, 2022, https://www.cooperhewitt.org/2022/08/31/year-of-glass-google-glass/.

7. McCracken, H. "How Gmail Happened: The Inside Story of Its Launch 10 Years Ago," *Time*, April 1, 2014, https://time.com/43263/gmail-10th-anniversary/.

8. Great Speculations, "A Quality Exec Comp Plan Lowers the Risk of Investing in Nucor," *Forbes*, August 12, 2024, https://www.forbes.com/

sites/greatspeculations/2024/08/12/a-quality-exec-comp-plan-lowers-the-risk-of-investing-in-nucor/.

9. Casey, T. "Hinge Matchmaker App Extends Online Dating to Non-Singles," *Forbes*, September 22, 2017, https://www.forbes.com/sites/theodorecasey/2017/09/22/hinge-matchmaker-app-extends-online-dating-to-non-singles/.

10. Hammer, M. and Champy, J. (1993). *Reengineering the Corporation: A Manifesto for Business Revolution. Harper Business.* HarperBusiness.

11. Tellis, G. and Golder, P. "When Innovation Disappears: Five Lessons from Circuit City," *Forbes India*, April 7, 2010, https://www.forbesindia.com/article/thunderbird/when-innovation-disappears-five-lessons-from-circuit-city/21392/1.

12. Drucker, P.F. (1985). *Innovation and Entrepreneurship: Practice and Principles.* Harper & Row.

13. Reynolds, A. "Wine Sales Drying Up as Americans Turn Elsewhere," NBC News, January 19, 2025, https://www.nbcnews.com/data-graphics/data-shows-wine-decline-consumers-spending-less-drinking-less-rcna187628.

14. Challagalla, G. and Court, D.L. (2024). Nespresso: Strategy reset for growth: The youth market (Abridged) (IMD-7-2574). IMD. https://www.imd.org/research-knowledge/marketing/case-studies/nespresso-strategy-reset-for-growth-the-youth-market-abridged/.

15. Sources: (1) Schroeder, B. "Baby Boomers, Millennials and Gen Z Are All Changing the $8 Trillion Dollar Travel Industry in the Same Way—Major Opportunities for Entrepreneurs and Marketers," Forbes, November 13, 2019, https://www.forbes.com/sites/bernhardschroeder/2019/11/13/baby-boomers-millennials-and-gen-z-are-all-changing-the-8-trillion-dollar-travel-industry-in-the-same-way-major-opportunities-for-entrepreneurs-and-marketers/. (2) Whitmore, G. "How Generation Z Is Changing Travel for Older Generations," Forbes, September 13, 2019, https://www.forbes.com/sites/geoffwhitmore/2019/09/13/how-generation-z-is-changing-travel-for-older-generations/. (3) Reed, T. "Report Says Young Travelers Don't Value Airline Loyalty; Airlines: That's News to Us," Forbes, June 4, 2024, https://www.forbes.com/sites/tedreed/2024/06/04/report-says-young-travelers-dont-value-airline-loyalty-airlines-thats-news-to-us/.

16. Graham, M. "Plant-Based Meat Once Seemed Unstoppable. What Went Wrong?" Canary Media, September 5, 2023, https://www.canarymedia.com/articles/food-and-farms/plant-based-meat-once-seemed-unstoppable-what-went-wrong.

17. Lyons, K. "A Conversation about Converse's Timeless Shoe," The Badger Herald, March 4, 2021, https://badgerherald.com/fashion/2021/03/04/a-conversation-about-converses-timeless-shoe/.

18. Katz, R. and Allen, T.J. (1982). Investigating the Not-Invented-Here (NIH) syndrome: a look at the performance, tenure, and communication patterns of 50 R&D project groups. *R&D Management* 12 (1): 7–20. Lichtenthaler, U. and Ernst, H. (2006). Attitudes to externally organizing knowledge: a review of the literature. *Journal of Engineering and Technology Management* 23 (4): 231–255.

19. Drucker, P.F. (1985). *Innovation and Entrepreneurship*. Harper Business.

20. Drucker (1999). Management for the 21st century. Chapter 3. In: *The Change Leader*, 71.

Chapter 11

1. https://www.benjerry.com/values.

2. Salesforce. *Salesforce FY24 Stakeholder Impact Report*. San Francisco: Salesforce, 2024. https://a.sfdcstatic.com/a.sets/prod/documents/white-papers/salesforce-fy24-stakeholder-impact-report.pdf.

3. Forbes Technology Council. "The Silent Burden of AI: Unveiling the Hidden Environmental Costs of Data Centers by 2030." *Forbes*, August 16, 2024. https://www.forbes.com/councils/forbestechcouncil/2024/08/16/the-silent-burden-of-ai-unveiling-the-hidden-environmental-costs-of-data-centers-by-2030/; Moore, E. "Data Centres and AI: The Environment Is Already Paying the Price." *Financial Times*, April 17, 2024. https://www.ft.com/content/65fff689-bd47-4c15-bdb8-083e5ccd84dc.

4. myHerb. "Carbon Negative by 2030: Microsoft's Bold Commitment and Progress." *Microsoft Tech Community*, December 17, 2024. https://techcommunity.microsoft.com/discussions/greentech/carbon-negative-by-2030-microsoft's-bold-commitment-and-progress/4358191.

5. Salesforce. "Salesforce at Davos: The Most Memorable Quotes." *Salesforce Newsroom*, January 24, 2020. https://www.salesforce.com/news/stories/salesforce-at-davos-the-most-memorable-quotes/.

6. Mohr, L.A., Webb, D.J., and Harris, K.E. (2001). Do consumers expect companies to be socially responsible? The impact of corporate social responsibility on buying behavior. *Journal of Consumer Affairs* 35 (1): 45–72.

7. Small, D. "How Sustainable Are Luxury Watches?" *Eluxe Magazine*, March 4, 2025. https://eluxemagazine.com/fashion/how-sustainable-are-luxury-watches/.

8. Gast, A., Illanes, P., Probst, N., Schaninger, B., and Simpson, B. "Purpose: Shifting from Why to How," *McKinsey & Company*, April 22, 2020. https://www.mckinsey.com/capabilities/people-and-organizational-performance/our-insights/purpose-shifting-from-why-to-how.

9. Drucker, P.F. (1993). *Post-Capitalist Society*, 97. Harper Business.

10. Henderson, R. and Van den Steen, E. (2015). Why do firms have 'purpose'? The firm's role as a carrier of identity and reputation. *American Economic Review* 105 (5): 2.

11. The Coca-Cola Company, "Purpose and Vision," accessed May 18, 2025, https://www.coca-colacompany.com/about-us/purpose-and-vision; Nike, Inc., "Impact," accessed May 18, 2025, https://about.nike.com/en/impact; Ernst & Young Global Limited, "Purpose," EY, accessed May 18, 2025, https://www.ey.com/en_gl/insights/purpose.; Pfizer Inc., "About," accessed May 18, 2025, https://www.pfizer.com/about.

12. Schneider, A. and McCumber, D. (2004). *An Air That Kills: How the Asbestos Poisoning of Libby, Montana, Uncovered a National Scandal.* New York: G.P. Putnam's Sons.

13. United Nations, "Goal 12: Ensure Sustainable Consumption and Production Patterns," *United Nations Sustainable Development*, accessed May 18, 2025, https://www.un.org/sustainabledevelopment/sustainable-consumption-production/.

14. Australian Academy of Science, "How Many People Can Earth Actually Support?" *Curious*, reviewed by Professor Stephen Dovers (Australian National University) and Professor Colin Butler (University of Canberra), accessed May 18, 2025, https://www.science.org.au/curious/earth-environment/how-many-people-can-earth-actually-support.

15. Zhang, K., Jie, H., and Zhang, W. (2020). The role of meaningful work in employees' work engagement: a longitudinal study. *Frontiers in Psychology* 11: 572343.

16. Henderson, R. and Van den Steen, E. (2015). Why do firms have 'purpose'? The firm's role as a carrier of identity and reputation. *American Economic Review* 105 (5): 326–330.

17. Khan, M., Serafeim, G., and Yoon, A. (2016). Corporate sustainability: first evidence on materiality. *The Accounting Review* 91 (6): 1697–1724.

18. Maracina, C. "Abominable Move: 'Spineless' Cup Brand Hit by Boycott as Shoppers Vow to 'Never Purchase' Them Again over Controversial Cancelation," *The U.S. Sun*, March 27, 2025, https://www.the-sun.com/news/13883050/yeti-clare-booth-luce-center-for-conservative-women/.

19. Forbes Technology Council, "Are We Living in a Generation of Purpose-Driven Consumers?" *Forbes*, December 5, 2024, https://www.forbes.com/

councils/forbestechcouncil/2024/12/05/are-we-living-in-a-generation-of-purpose-driven-consumers/.

20. *Industrial Equipment News*, "Ford Joins Growing List of Companies Changing DEI Policies," August 28, 2024, https://www.ien.com/opera tions/news/22919038/ford-joins-growing-list-of-companies-changing-dei-policies.

21. This section draws heavily from Jaworski, B. and Chung, V. (2023). *Creating the Organization of the Future: Building on Confucian and Drucker Foundations*. Emerald Publishing.

22. See Jaworski and Cheung (2003), Chapter 3. Purpose Statements.

23. McCarthy, M. "To Move Forward, We Must be Honest About Our Past," *Ben & Jerry's*, February 17, 2021, https://www.benjerry.com/whats-new/2021/02/ceo-message-hr40-reparations.

24. Salesforce. *Our Story*. Accessed May 18, 2025. https://www.sales force.com/company/our-story/.

25. Kotik, S. (2024, February 15). *TOMS founder Blake Mycoskie on leading with authenticity*. Haas Newsroom, University of California, Berkeley. https://newsroom.haas.berkeley.edu/toms-founder-blake-mycoskie-on-leading-with-authenticity/.

26. Bergeron, T. "Why Johnson & Johnson's Famous Credo, Written 80 Years Ago, Is as Impactful Now as Ever: As Company Celebrates Splitting in Two, Values That Have Guided It Show the Way," *ROI-NJ* (New Brunswick), December 18, 2023, https://www.roi-nj.com/2023/12/18/healthcare/why-johnson-johnsons-famous-credo-written-80-years-ago-is-as-impactful-now-as-ever/.

27. Johnson & Johnson, "Our Credo," accessed May 18, 2025, https://www.jnj.com/our-credo.

28. Patnaik, D. "Why Being Purpose-Driven Can Be Painful—And Why the Alternative Is Even Worse," *Forbes*, September 24, 2023, https://www.forbes.com/sites/devpatnaik/2023/09/24/why-being-purpose-driven-can-be-painfuland-why-the-alternative-is-even-worse/.

29. Topham, G. "'Very Concerning': BP Dilutes Net Zero Targets as Global Retreat from Green Standards Gathers Pace." The Guardian, October 13, 2024.

30. Friedman, M. (1970). A Friedman doctrine—The Social Responsibility of Business is to Increase its Profits (p. 17).

31. Henderson, R. "Reimagining Capitalism." Harvard Business Review, January–February 2021.

32. Hotten, R. "Volkswagen: The Scandal Explained," *BBC News*, December 10, 2015, https://www.bbc.com/news/business-34324772.

33. AlSalim, F. and Etter, M. (2023). *Purpose-Washing: What It Is, and How to Avoid It.* King's College London.

34. Charlotte, A. "How Coca-Cola Consolidated Is Driving Sustainability in Charlotte," March 28, 2025, https://www.axios.com/local/charlotte/sponsored/how-coca-cola-consolidated-is-driving-sustainability-in-charlotte.

35. White, K., Habib, R., and Hardisty, D.J. (2019). How to SHIFT consumer behaviors to be more sustainable: a literature review and guiding framework. *Journal of Marketing* 83 (3): 22–49.

Epilogue

1. In recent years there have been a number of excellent articles on the topic of a customer-centric journey. Here are some specific articles we recommend. De Keyser, A. and Van Vaerenbergh, Y. (2024). Beyond the snafu: research directions in customer experience-led business transformation. *AMS Review* 14 (1–2): 144–157. https://doi.org/10.1007/s13162-024-00210.1.
Jaworski, B. (2024). The customer-centered transformational journey. *AMS Review*, 14(1–2), 143. https://doi.org/10.1007/s13162-024-00209-8
Kohli, Ajay K. Bernard J. Jaworski, and Nabil Shabshab (2019). Customer centricity: a multi-year journey. *Handbook on Customer Centricity: Strategies for Building a Customer-Centric Organization* edited by Robert Palmatier, Christine Moorman, and Ju-Yeon Lee. Edward Elgar Publishing.
Meehan, S. (2024). Transforming customer experience: a story of ambition, values, beliefs, and digital capabilities. *AMS Review*, 14(1–2), 158–167. https://doi.org/10.1007/s13162-024-00211-0.
Urbany, J. E. and Dapena-Baron, M. (2024). The pursuit of customer centricity. *AMS Review*, 14(3–4), 298–307. https://doi.org/10.1007/s13162-024-00288-4.
Urbany, J. E. (2024). The customer-centered transformational journey. *AMS Review*, 14(1–2), 143. https://doi.org/10.1007/s13162-024-00209-8.

2. Challagalla, G., Jaworski, B. J. and Gray, D. (2019). *Becton Dickinson: Creating the customer-centric organization* (A)(IMD Case No. IMD-7-1967). IMD International.
Challagalla, G., Jaworski, B. J. and Gray, D. (2019). *Becton Dickinson: Creating the customer-centric organization* (B)(IMD Case No. IMD-7-1968). IMD International.

Index